APPLICATIONS of INTERACTIONIST PSYCHOLOGY:

Essays in Honor of Saul B. Sells

APPLICATIONS of INTERACTIONIST PSYCHOLOGY:

Essays in Honor of Saul B. Sells

Edited by
Steven G. Cole
Robert G. Demaree
Texas Christian University

Advisory Editor
William Curtis
*Microelectronics
and Computer
Technology Corp.*

 LAWRENCE ERLBAUM ASSOCIATES, PUBLISHERS
1988   Hillsdale, New Jersey   Hove and London

Lawrence Erlbaum Associates, Inc., Publishers
365 Broadway
Hillsdale, New Jersey 07642

Library of Congress Cataloging in Publication Data

Applications of interactionist psychology: essays in honor of Saul B.
Sells / edited by Steven G. Cole and Robert G. Demaree; advisory
editor, Bill Curtis.

p.   cm.

Includes index.

ISBN 0-8058-0188-X

1. Social psychology—Congresses. 2. Social interaction—Congresses.
3. Personality and situation—Congresses. 4. Sells, Saul B., 1913-
1988—Congresses. I. Sells, Saul B., 1913-1988. II. Cole, Steven G.
III. Demaree, Robert G. IV. Curtis, Bill.

302—dc19
87-27115
CIP

Printed in the United States of America
10 9 8 7 6 5 4 3 2 1

This volume is dedicated
to the memory of
Saul B. Sells (1913-1988)

Contents

Preface

The purpose of this book is to honor Dr. S. B. Sells, while at the same time adding to the understanding of the science of psychology and the application of that knowledge to meaningful human endeavors. In Part I, Paul Nelson begins the process by apprising the reader of the contributions to understanding human behavior made by Dr. Sells during his professional career, and the application of that knowledge to social and business settings. The interview with Dr. Sells enlightens the reader about the importance of science in his career and points out the need to understand psychology's place in science. Moreover, the interview reveals the symbiotic relationship between basic and applied science that dominated Dr. Sells' career. Lois Chatham's chapter emphasizes that relationship through the revelation of one person's view of the impact that Dr. Sells had on the appropriate use of psychological knowledge in the administration of public policy. The fact that Part I ends with a chapter by J. W. Mann, who uses knowledge gathered by Dr. Sells 50 years ago as he prepared his doctoral dissertation, emphasizes the demand Dr. Sells had for thoroughness and accuracy in his research, and that when he decided that the results were ready to be communicated to the appropriate audience, they were results that were not transitory. That is, they were building blocks on which other researchers could rely.

The last four parts of the book deal with varying areas of theory and research that are representative of the research into which Dr. Sells had immersed himself. The chapters by J. McVicker Hunt and Donald Fiske represent specific models of the more general interactionist strategy that had been central to Dr. Sells' research. They also remind the reader of the ever present need to overcome the problems associated with accuracy of measurement if one is to move ahead toward the understanding of human behavior. Chapters by David Magnusson, Raymond Cattell, and Desmond Cartwright point out the necessity of understanding personality characteristics in order to more clearly understand how they affect and are affected by the environment. They also emphasize the interactionist approach and the importance of multivariate design. Lawrence James and Robert Houston lead us into the more applied interests of Dr. Sells with chapters on the relationship between the organizational and psychological climate of the workplace, and on personnel selection in aviation respectively.

Finally, Dwayne Simpson and Barry Brown tell of the contribution of the Drug Abuse Reporting Program, which was one of the major efforts of the Institute of Behavioral Research established by Dr. Sells. The discussants—Goldine Gleser, Susan Embretson (Whitely), Norman Endler, Richard Gorsuch, Maurice Lorr, Allan Jones, and Jack Greener—have provided interpretations to the chapters that broaden the perspective on each topic while giving the reader valuable evaluative insights. It is noteworthy that the use of discussants for each chapter is an example of the collegial interaction and criticism that is what I believe to have been central to Dr. Sells' approach to science.

Although, in their introductory remarks, each of the authors pays respect to the contributions made by Dr. Sells, it is likely that the reader will not need those words to understand the significance of his contributions to psychology. As Paul Nelson states in his chapter, "Saul Sells epitomizes the scientist-practitioner." He had a positive impact on psychology, government, business, his colleagues, his associates, and his students.

Steven G. Cole

Acknowledgments

The editors wish to acknowledge the assistance of Nancy Bruce, Jan Fox, Mary Louise Long, and Brad Olson who were central to the running of the symposium on which this volume was based. They also thank Johnmarshall Reeve for videotaping the festschrift, Carolyn Smith and Nancy Karbach for typing the manuscript, Stephanie Smith for agreeing to do all of the figures, Brent Jones for editorial assistance, and the other people who have helped without much notice from us. Finally, we would like to thank Dr. Saul B. Sells for having been a psychologist worth honoring.

Acknowledgments

Foreword

J. M. Moudy
Chancellor Emeritus
Texas Christian University

Inside Saul B. Sells there must have been a dynamo. Such a word describes what always impressed me most about this remarkable person.

Saul Sells was not the only intelligent person in the universe. Not a few could match his mental energy. Poise and verbal virtuosity were not his possession exclusively. And perserverance? Well, even drones have perserverance.

But Saul somehow combined intelligence, energy, poise, and a flowing oral and written articulation, and perserverance in ways that produced a truly notable career.

Saul's 60-year career prompted his friends, associates, former students, professional colleagues, and other admirers to put forth this festschrift.

A 2-day symposium in his honor near the date of his retirement was held April 21-22, 1983 and drew a distinguished cast of participants. Their papers and addresses constitute the body of this volume. Its publication now is intended to convey the warm and continuing esteem in which our mentor and friend, S. B. Sells, PhD., was held.

The "dynamo" metaphor can be expanded a little. A dynamo consists of a moving part and a stationary part. The moving part cuts through lines of magnetic force and thereby converts one form of energy into a more desired form of energy, as in generators and motors. In the dynamo, both parts are necessary, but it is the moving part that makes things happen. Saul was the moving part.

Saul made things happen. As the moving force of the Institute of Behavioral Research (IBR) at Texas Christian University (TCU), his creative leadership brought scholarly ideas, manpower, and money together to produce useful and acclaimed studies, projects, conferences, and numerous publications.

His research and teaching career began in the mid-1930s, coincident with his university preparation. During wartime he served in the nation's price stability effort. For the next 10 years, he served as professor and chairman of medical psychology at the U.S.A.F. School of Aviation Medicine, Randolph Field,

Texas. Then he was invited to become professor of psychology at TCU, where his service spanned from 1958 to 1983, and where he received TCU's first appointment as research professor.

Along with his colleagues across the nation, I was always impressed by the breadth and diversity of Saul's interests and his continued attention to them over time. These are apparent in his extensive bibliography and were well represented in the program of his Institute. Briefly, they spanned theory, policy, and empirical research. His seminal contributions emphasized the necessity to understand the interaction of the individual and the environment if one wished to understand behavior. His efforts to develop taxonomies of situational-environmental variables to support such understanding, and his skepticism concerning the laboratory as a surrogate for the real world, led him to prefer large-scale field over laboratory research in the areas of his interest. His concern with multivariate methods in order to properly support field research, and his development of the concept and models of the organization as a social system stand out as examples of his contributions to understanding human behavior.

In relation to research policy, he used the Institute as an instrument to train competent investigators. Every project of the IBR included graduate students as apprentices to senior staff members and, in most cases, advanced students (doctoral candidates) as responsible staff. This accounted for over 40 dissertations in psychology by IBR students during its existence and for the high collective achievement of this group in their subsequent careers. The fields of psychology in which the IBR programs made significant contributions included mental health and medical problems, effects of isolation in long-duration space missions, selection of pilots and other airline personnel, peer relations and personality development, organizational climate, personality factor structure, epidemiology of drug abuse, and evaluation of treatment for drug abuse.

My dealings with Saul were in academic and financial administration. He would present his ideas and budgets for those ideas. Always, they involved risk for the university as well as for him and for his staff. But because he seemed prudent as well as ambitious, and because the results always proved him much more right than wrong, I was usually inclined to go along. The success of his Institute is history. TCU shared in its success. In gratitude, TCU paid him a rare tribute, conferring upon one of its own family the honorary degree, Doctor of Science.

And for me, I was also pleased to find in him and in his late, dear wife and working partner, Helen, real friendship.

I AN OVERVIEW

1 An Overview of Sells' Contribution to the Science of Psychology and Its Applications

Paul D. Nelson
American Psychological Association

In presenting a paper a few years ago, on some historical developments in Navy clinical psychology and psychiatry, I commented on the significance for American psychology as well as for the Navy of the work done in training commands and hospitals by Bill Hunt, Walter Wilkins, Arthur Benton, and a few others during the early days of World War II. Inasmuch as I had not personally participated in that work, although one or two in the audience had, I was reminded of a letter received some years earlier from another distinguished mentor and friend of many years. In lamenting how often lessons of the past are lost or ignored, he wrote what I presumed at the time was an accidental, yet has become on occasion an altogether fitting, variation of the well-known adage: "Those who are ignorant of history are destined to *report* it." Thus, it is my calling again to report the history experienced firsthand by most of you, some for longer periods than others to be sure, as scholarly peers, as students, or otherwise as professional and scientific colleagues of the person whose illustrious career we celebrate in this volume--Saul B. Sells.

My familiarity with Sells' work, however, is not entirely limited to secondhand accounts. For more than the past 2 decades I have been privileged to associate, at times quite closely, with Sells and his staff. Nevertheless, I find it an awesome task to summarize his contributions to the science of psychology and its applications. For, how many psychologists, over a period of nearly 50 years have contributed through systematic research to a better understanding of human personality, the dynamics of groups, and behavior in large organizations? And how many at the same time have applied that knowledge and the methods of psychology to a range of problems as varied as those of personal selection and training, leadership and team development, human factors design of manned systems, physiologic adaptation to unusual environments, mental health and illness, adjustments and achievements of school children, and the abuse of drugs in society? Sells' writings of those endeavors and their implications for the science and profession of psychology appear in nearly 90 journal articles, some 80 books (on one fourth of which he was an author or editor--a few with his wife and colleague, Helen), and 170 technical reports and monographs.

Truly, to present an overview of Sells' contributions to the science of psychology and its applications requires a multivariate perspective, a multitrait-multimethod assessment (of which the very structure and substance of this symposium is an exciting analog), and an appropriate taxonomic system to account for half a century of interactions between our colleague and his environments. Short of that, albeit at risk of missing the mark, I have opted for a simpler analysis--an ecological adaptation of my own, if I may.

Foremost, Sells epitomizes the scientist-practitioner model that so explicitly has characterized professional education in psychology for the past 35 years. The history of American psychology is replete with illustration of schisms: academic versus applied; "tender-minded" versus "tough-minded"; experimental versus clinical; phenomenological versus empirical; science versus practice; and so on. By striking contrast, Sells' career is testimony to the potential of psychology as a unified discipline, however many subsets of interest there may be. Recognized by his colleagues as a Fellow of 10 divisions of the American Psychological Association (APA), representing the history and philosophy of the discipline, its methods of science and practice, a number of substantive areas, and its professional applications, Sells exemplifies a balance of scientist-practitioner psychologist achieved by few.

The objective of that model was perhaps stated as well as at any time since in a report of 1942 issued by what was then (APA) Subcommittee on Survey and Planning for Psychology. Chaired by Robert Yerkes, with E. G. Boring, Alice Bryan, Edgar Doll, Richard Elliott, Ernest Hilgard, and Calvin Stone as the other members, that Subcommittee stated its conviction "that the development of psychology as a science and practice should proceed in close relation; and that the scientists of the profession should welcome technological developments and generously aid and encourage them" (Boring et al., 1942, p. 624). What a blueprint that was for Sells' career, and his contributions to psychology and society!

Sells' contribution to the science of psychology is both conceptual and methodological. The two cannot be separated. Concepts and methods are not regarded by Sells, however, as ends in themselves. Rather they are in his thinking the logical means for achieving better classification, measurement, prediction, understanding, and control of human behavior--ultimately to benefit society. Subject always to modification from experience, concepts are crucial in science; and their linkage into theoretical statements of relationship is as essential to the scientist as is a chart to the navigator. Sells knows this implicitly, for such a premise is a natural part of his thinking in virtually all of his work. In the sense that for Sells theory is a guide, one is reminded of Kurt Lewin's dictum that "there is nothing as practical as a good theory" (Marrow, 1969, p. ix).

This of course, is not to say that either Sells' writing or Lewin's field theory statements are necessarily "practical" in the common understanding of that word. Rather, for both, theory is useful, and therefore practical, for directing questions, organizing facts, formulating hypotheses, interpreting observations, and for stimulating further research, not to mention graduate students.

The concept of person-environment interactions is central to Sells' thinking, writing, and research. It has shaped his perspective since the days of his first publication in 1936, that of his doctoral work that (as an unusual honor for a young psychologist) was referenced 3 years later by Gordon Allport in his American Psychological Association Presidential Address entitled "The Psychologist's Frame of Reference" (Allport, 1940). As expressed by Allport, "frame of reference has to do with any context whatever that exerts a demonstrable influence upon the individual's perceptions, judgments, feelings, or actions" (p. 24).

It is the temporal and situational context of human behavior that seems most salient in Sells' work. The interaction between person and environment over time reflects, in his opinion, an adaptive process rather than a series of random encounters (Sells, 1963a). In this sense, Sells invites our attention at a macro level of analysis to theories of evolution and species adaptation. He states, for example that "The phylogenetic perspective is intrinsic to the structure of the science of psychology" (Sells, 1966, p. 132). At a microlevel of analysis, he attends equally to the importance of personal and cultural histories as well as immediate tendencies and stimuli that influence the behavior of persons in particular settings or situations. In these respects, perhaps, his theoretical writing is more integrative than altogether original, being influenced by the likes of Dobzhansky's (1962) evolutionary perspective, Helson's (1964) adaptation-level theory, Hunt's (1961) writings on intelligence and experience, Murphy's (1947) treatise on biosocial origins of human personality, the theoretical and empirical work of Barker and his team

(1963) on ecological aspects of behavior, and the sociological essays by Parsons, Shils, Naegele, and Pitts (1961) on the nature of human society. Furthermore, I would describe Sells as a "general systems" theorist, best illustrated perhaps in his frequently cited article "Ecology and the Science of Psychology" (Sells, 1966). For Sells, simply stated, both structure and function must be considered from the perspective of the biological and psychological aspects of the organism, as must the physical and social aspects of environment, and of course the interactions over time of those elements of organism and environment, in understanding behavior. Few would disagree with Sells, I'm sure. On the other hand, few have attempted as he has to put such eclectic thinking to work in formulating strategies for research.

If Sells had no more than an inkling early in his career that such a holistic conceptual system would be necessary for psychological theory to be useful, it seems evident that after his first 25 years as a scientist-practitioner he was convinced of such. In the opening chapter of his book, *Stimulus Determinants of Behavior* (1963b), Sells wrote:

> The principle that behavior represents the interaction of the individual and the environmental situation implies that the total variance of any response can be accounted for only in part by individual differences in characteristics of the participating persons. It depends also on the stimulus characteristics of the environmental situation (both physical and social) and in part on the interactions between aspects of each. Full exploitation of this principle has not yet been achieved, largely because the methodological implications have not been systematically explored. (p. 2)

A few pages later, Sells continues stating what was to become a major part of his work for the next two decades:

The most obvious need is for the development of a
taxonomy and measurement technology of variables
describing the stimulus situation. However
unsatisfactory they may be regarded, at least some
generally accepted taxonomy and devices for
measuring individual behavior characteristics have
been produced by psychology. But no comparable
dimensions of the stimulus situation have been
systematically studied, and consequently only
piecemeal and usually inadequate account can be
taken of variance attributable to the situation.
(p. 5)

By the time of that writing, of course, Sells
had already launched his efforts to develop such a
classification system for situations. He also
maintained through his own work and with that of other
personologists, particularly Cattell, Fiske, and
Guilford, a continual quest for better definition and
measurement of human abilities and personality traits.
In so doing, Sells and others of like mind were
compelled by the complexity of their models and data to
advance the case for multivariate research strategies
and analyses of behavior, rendered possible in the
practical sense by the increasing availability at that
time of computer technology for behavioral scientists.
As one effort in that direction, Sells participated in
launching a new journal in 1966, *Multivariate
Behavioral Research*, of which he became managing
editor.

Throughout the course of his career, Sells has
demonstrated an understanding and respect, however
cautious, for the value of laboratory science in the
study of certain aspects of human behavior. On
balance, however, he is drawn by his theoretical
perspective and methodological persuasion to the field
and natural observations of behavior for most of his
data. Sells has been a distinguished leader, indeed,
among field methodologists. In virtually every
instance during the course of that research, Sells and
his colleagues were simultaneously working on real-
world problems, including those, which seemed less real

at the time, of man in outer space. In addition to NASA, in fact, airlines, banks, school systems, military planners, naval commanders, and national drug abuse treatment program policy planners and managers come to mind as examples of institutions and persons served by Sells and his staff.

It would not be entirely speculative to suggest that the earlier work environments and assignments in Sells' career were influential in shaping his commitment to large-scale-of-effort research in the field. Beginning with the New York City public school system, then with the Office of Price Administration in Washington during World War II, and subsequently to the U.S. Air Force School of Aerospace Medicine, Sells had opportunity to develop his conceptual frame of reference, and related methodological perspective, over 2 decades of large-scale institutional research and professional consultation on the everyday problems of sizable populations diverse in their nature, circumstances of life, and working/living environments.

Interestingly enough, Don Fiske, as a relatively young although already experienced psychologist, wrote in 1947, after the war and just prior to receipt of his doctoral degree at Michigan, what now seems in retrospect also to have been part of the script for Saul Sells' career. In a comment published in *The American Psychologist*, Fiske (1947) raised the question, "Must Psychologists be Experimental Isolationists?" (p.23). From that titular lead, Fiske offered some observations which are perhaps as profound today for psychology as they were in the 1940s:

> Psychologists spend too much time and energy upon research yielding only suggestive results. Work is wasted on samples that are too small for anything but pilot studies and on local studies whose significance for the field is obscured by the indeterminate effect of local conditions. There is a need for coordinated research on significant problems. The same project should be carried out at a number of different institutions

spread over the country and the separate findings pooled. Cooperative efforts are currently the exception in psychological research.(p. 23)

Fiske's plea did not go altogether unheeded, as things turned out. For at about the time Fiske wrote, and continuing into the 1950s, probably on the impetus of their respective experiences as psychologists for the War Department or national civil defense agencies during World War II, a few pioneers led the way in establishing, what has become much more commonplace today, non-governmental institutions for applied psychological research on a national scale. They were to fulfill as well, each one in a way uniquely related to its major purpose and style of operation, the challenge posed by Fiske.

Although there were a few others, I mention five that in relative ways have been recognized leaders in psychological research of significance to our society over the past quarter of a century. One was established by a Harvard graduate of the earlier 1930s, John Flanagan, who in 1946 established the American Institute for Research. The other four leaders, undoubtedly by coincidence, were doctoral graduates of Columbia between 1931 and 1936. I include Jack Dunlap who founded what became a major human factors R&D consulting firm; Rensis Likert who formed what was to become the Institute for Social Research at Michigan; Meredith Crawford who established what we know today as the Human Resources Research Organization; and a few years later, the junior colleague among the group, Saul Sells, who in 1962 founded the Institute of Behavioral Research associated with Texas Christian University.

The collective bibliographies and records of contracts and grants with national and local government agencies, private industry, and private foundations tell the rest of the story for these research institutions as public servants, for profit or not. Though no two are alike in detail of mission, organization, or staff, each has contributed in scholarly and applied fashion to the advancement of our science and the practice of our profession as psychologists. Each has served, in addition, as a resource for training psychologists in the scientist-- practitioner tradition. In the latter, Sells has been a master teacher and role model for the next generation of psychologists.

Sells' contributions to the science of psychology and its applications, in the final analysis, cannot be separated from either the context of the era in which he was trained and has served, or from the flow of influence to and from his mentors, colleagues, and even his students. To be otherwise is simply not in the nature of science or professional practice. It is also contrary to his own theoretical and operational perspective. What, then, might we conclude from his work?

Perhaps there is a clue from the published proceedings 10 years ago of the Third Banff Conference on Theoretical Psychology (Royce, 1973a), in which Sells contributed an overview of his thinking in a paper entitled *Prescriptions for a Multivariate Model in Personality Theory: Ecological Considerations.* Following the paper are comments from two distinguished discussants, Donald Fiske and Joseph Royce.

Fiske (1973) concluded that much more work is needed of the kind represented in Sells' paper. "Saul Sells has done us an important service in reminding us that the behavior of interest to personology is a function of the person and the stimuli or setting, and their interactions" (p. 121).

By contrasting critique, Royce (1973b) reflected that although he finds little of what Sells writes to be objectionable, he finds it "simply too programmatic" and comes away from it all with a "so-what" reaction. The latter he attributes to Sells not really getting "down to concepts at a substantive level." Royce then asks, to make his point, "do we get an inventory of hypotheses or generalizations as to relationships between ecological dimensions and various facts of behavior?" (p.122).

To conclude, therefore, Fiske notes very simply, but accurately, the central theme of Sells' life-long contributions, that of an interactionist looking at the environment. At least implicit in Fiske's remarks is the point that all too often such a frame of reference is not maintained in the study of human personality, and that such theoretical and empirical neglect has limited our understanding of the behavior we study. Sells' work contributes to our scientific quest, therefore, by serving as a reminder in substance of that point.

By critical question, on the other hand, Royce in fairness seeks the consequences of Sells' conceptual work for advancing the science of psychology and its applications. Now, 10 years later, perhaps the response to Royce's question is forthcoming in part. It comes, however, from the substrates of theory developed, and hypotheses tested, by those with whom Sells has closely interacted as a colleague, teacher, and consultant. Although they are but a few examples, the illustrations of theory and applied research that follow on this symposium, presented by academic colleagues, business and government executives, and former students of Saul Sells, hold the key. They respond, indeed, to the question, "So what?" They speak, as well, to Saul Sells' contributions as a scientist, practitioner, and teacher to the science and applications of psychology.

REFERENCES

Allport, G. W. (1940). The psychologists' frame of reference. *Psychological Bulletin, 37*, 1-28.

Barker, R. G.(Ed). (1963). *The stream of behavior.* New York:Appleton-Century-Crofts.

Boring, E. G., Bryan, A. I., Doll, E. A., Elliot, R. M., Hilgard, C., Stone, P., and Yerkes, M. (1942). First report of the subcommittee on survey and planning for psychology. *Psychological Bulletin, 39*, 619-630.

Dobzhansky, T. (1962). *Mankind evolving.* New Haven, CT:Yale University Press.

Fiske, D. W. (1947). Must psychologists be experimental isolationists? *American Psychologist, 2*, 23,28.

Fiske, D.W. (1973). Comments on Sell's paper. in J.R. Royce (Ed.). *Multivariate analysis and psychological theory* (pp. 119-121). New York: Academic Press.

Helson, H. (1964). *Adaptation-level theory.* New York:Harper & Row.

Hunt, J. McV. (1961). *Intelligence and experience.* New York: Ronald Press.

Marrow, A. J. (1969). *The practical theorist: The life and work of Kurt Lewin.* New York: Basic Books.

Murphy, G. (1947). *Personality: A biosocial approach to its origins and structures.* New York: Harper & Row.

Parsons, T., Shils, E., Naegele, K. D., & Pitts, J. R. (1961). *Theories of society: Foundations of modern sociology.* Glencoe, Il: The Free Press.

Royce, J. R. (Ed.). (1973a). *Multivariate analysis and psychological theory.* New York: Academic Press.

Royce, J. R. Comments on Sells' paper. (1973b). in J.R. Royce (Ed.). *Multivariate analysis and psychological theory* (p. 122). New York: Acacemic Press.

Sells, S. B. (1963a). An interactionist looks at the environment. *American Psychologist, 18*, 696-702.

Sells, S. B. (Ed.). (1963b). *Stimulus determinants of behavior.* New York: Ronald Press.

Sells, S. B. (1966). Ecology and the science of psychology. *Multivariate Behavioral Research, 1*, 131-144.

Sells, S. B. (1973). Prescriptions for a multivariate model in personality and psychological theroies: Ecological considerations. in J. R. Royce (Ed.). *Multivariate analysis and psychological theory* (pp. 103-119). New York: Academic Press.

2 An Interview of Saul B. Sells at Symposium Honoring Dr. Sells

Richard I. Evans
University of Houston

INTRODUCTION

Malcolm D. Arnoult
Professor of Psychology
Texas Christian University

Some years ago Richard I. Evans of the University of Houston undertook a very ambitious project, which was to interview on film some of the most distinguished psychologists of our time. He not only carried off the project, he carried it off extremely successfully. While doing do, he interviewed such people as B. F. Skinner, Erik Erickson, Carl Rogers, Raymond Cattell, and many more. As a consequence, he has provided for us a priceless record not only of the thinking but of the personalities of these significant individuals. We are pleased that Dr. Evans has agreed to initiate this symposium by interviewing Professor Sells.

INTERVIEW

Dr. Evans:

Before I ask Professor Sells to come forward, I would like to make a few preliminary remarks. I am reminded of many years ago when we were just learning how to get film interviews, C. G. Jung agreed to work with us to become the first to be filmed. As you probably know, historically, American anthologist Rudy Peters was doing very badly there because somehow they had misinterpreted Jung in the textbooks in respect to what he has thought about people and that there were two types of people, introverts and extroverts. Of course, this is ridiculous as he never thought that. So, arriving in Zurich, I found that he had turned down many interviews, although for some reason he did decide to grant one to this strange person from Houston, Texas. We walked into his home and before he even said hello, he said, "Why do American psychologists hate me so much?"

I would like to say at this gathering that the present interview is quite the opposite. Our subject is one of our very prolific colleagues, who is generally loved and admired among psychologists. It is a pleasure for us to interview my good friend, Saul Sells. I have always been impressed by the fact that everyone I have met who has been trained by Saul Sells has been precise, thoughtful, accurate, and imaginative.

Years ago, he was talking about social systems and a host of other things that have become very much a part of the scene today. Thinking through structurally these types of things long before many others became interested, he was anticipating life-support problems in space and a number of things that I think are truly amazing. I have not seen Saul for several years, but I see his sharpness and wit are still with him. In fact, I would say that some of his former students here would still have trouble keeping up with him. So, I would like to introduce my interviewee, Saul Sells. This will be informal; it is not rehearsed at all. I think we can give him the opportunity to tell us a little bit about Saul Sells as a particular professor of psychology. So, Saul, I want you to come up.

Well, Saul, I think that one of the things that impresses me as I look over your many contributions is that your background encompasses the whole history of the field. I have noticed, for example, that various of your publications involved issues addressed by people who were interviewed in my project. For example, I noticed your interest in anthropology resulted in two very good, timely articles. Your whole idea of multivariate epistemology sounds like evolutionary epistemology as a product of adaptation. Certainly your discussions of the environment and the nature of the containing environment are reminiscent of Skinner. A number of your ideas recall the work of Lewin. So, I hope, Saul, that you will share the way you have profited from so many of these ideas and somehow adapted them to your own system. Looking back over some of these individuals with whom you have had contact, beginning perhaps with your affiliation at Columbia, who were in fact the individuals that you feel did influence you rather directly?

Dr. Sells:

To answer your question, there are perhaps three kinds of influence that I need to mention. I majored in philosophy before I went into psychology. Indeed, I taught a course in logic. In the course of studying philosophy, I think I became impressed with the relationships among all the sciences and the place of psychology among them. I was convinced even before I went into psychology that psychology alone is not going to save the world. Subsequently, I have read extensively in other fields; I will come back to that.

In the field of philosophy, I think Montague, the epistemologist at Columbia, and Cohen and Nagel were the people who influenced me most. I had courses with them, all three of them. Then, in the field of psychology, the first psychologist I knew personally and exchanged ideas with was Joseph Jastrow. He was retired and I was an undergraduate student in New York. I used to visit him and he was kind to me. To thank him for his kindness, I used to run errands for him. From him, I developed a broad interest in personality theory and in application of psychology to human affairs. He left me all his papers when he died, which I have saved and of which I have frequently made good use. At Columbia, there were a number of people with whom I studied. R. S. Woodworth was first. He was a very kind man. He had voluminous notes which he would lend to his students. I think my first interest in Atmosphere Effect, which was the subject of my dissertation, came from reading his notes. In fact, my first publication was by Woodworth and Sells, and was on Atmosphere Effect. This was very helpful to me, since the paper was translated and appeared in four different languages and in as many anthologies. That was pretty good for a first year graduate student.

Dr. Evans:

I dare say!

Dr. Sells:

The next was Gardner Murphy, who was a dear friend of Helen's and mine. Woodworth and Murphy together taught me about interactionism. Otto Klineberg, of the psychology faculty was also an anthropologist. Through him I met Franz Boas and a number of other anthropologists, and even went on an anthropological trip at one time. As a young student, I very quickly realized that the world was not confined to the boundaries of Manhattan Island, and things were different in many other parts of the world, and not necessarily worse. In many cases we could learn a lot from other societies. So, I would say that those were the people who influenced me earliest.

Then I worked for E. L. Thorndike as a research assistant, and I interacted very closely with Irving Lorge. He was Thorndike's number 1 assistant, and I think I was about number 18 or something under him. Lorge and I worked together on many projects and were warm friends. In fact, I remember still one weekend when he and I did the intercorrelations of 18 variables on a sample of 200 cases. It took us 2 1/2 days to do the job working with two hand calculators in tandem. We called out the numbers to each other, and we developed a real good system, but it still took us 2 1/2 days to complete it. Then, when we got the job done, we took it in and showed it to Thorndike. He looked at it, that great old man, and said, "That is about what I expected".

There were many things about Thorndike that impressed me. One was the fact that he, as in the case of Woodworth and Murphy and many other of the most eminent psychologists whom I knew, would not confine his activities simply to his own major area or his own principal area of interest. Woodworth, the great experimentalist, was the author of the Woodworth-Matthews Psychoneurotic Inventory in World War I. Thorndike, the learning expert, many years later wrote a book on the effective society. In fact, one thing that I shall always remember vividly is a review of Thorndike's book on society, written by Herbert Conrad; he tore that book to shreds. Mainly he did so because he felt that Thorndike had made the same error in using his own background as the standard for everything that later American psychology was accused of in relation to the so-called institutional racism in tests. If one were to pick out an ideal place to live, then Montrose, New York, as an upper middle class academic community would be wonderful. Unfortunately, such an environment is not available to everybody. Conrad's review of Thorndike was an eye-opener to me because Thorndike was one of my early idols. When Herb tore him to bits as he did, Thorndike still came out as an important figure, but in a better perspective than I had before.

Another influential teacher that I am proud to mention is Joe Hunt, who is here today. He was one of my most helpful consultants during my tour at the Air Force School of Aviation Medicine. I was greatly impressed by his two-volume *Personality and the Behavior Disorders*, and his later contributions. I had the experience of writing a textbook under his guidance as the publisher's house editor. I am sure that I learned more from Joe while writing that book than any students learned from reading it. I still say that is a very important book, and I want to talk about that, too, if time permits. I learned from an outstanding role model how to be a good teacher, a good editor, and

a good leader, and I also got a much   broader
perspective than I had before.

Still another who has influenced me is Ray
Cattell, who unfortunately will not be with us today.
His blood pressure has already run out of bounds and
the doctors told him that if he made the trip he might
not survive. We will see him later on tape. I first
knew Ray when he came to the United States as an
associate at Thorndike's institute. He had just come
over from England. He is probably one of the most
thorough scholars I have ever known.   He has many
foibles, but if you can look at Cattell in terms of the
pluses and the minuses, you have an awful lot of plus
left over.   I think he is a giant who has not been
adequately appreciated.   There are many others whom I
should mention, but certainly those are among the top
people.

Dr. Evans:

Well, I will tell you, this is fascinating to me
because not only do you talk about contact with these
people, but your little descriptions of them   as
individuals add color with which I think we have all
got to be fascinated. Moving away a little bit from
this aspect of your background, Saul, I would like to
talk now about some of your theoretical conceptual
contributions. I think in looking over your work, one
is impressed with the kind of model and the way you
look at things in your work. You have presented your
ideas very clearly and concisely concerning factors
that determine behavior and certainly you are aware of
the impact of these formulations. You seem to feel
that you cannot separate individuals from the
environment. Of course, Lewin, in his formula that
behavior is a function of a person interacting with his
environment, articulated that and also mathematical
systems to look at it. I see in your work many ways of
modeling further kinds of trails of these elements.   I
wonder if you would like to talk a little bit about
your interactional approach and to review it?

Dr. Sells:

I really appreciate the opportunity to do this for another reason. I was thinking about this in anticipation of this session, and I realize that my interests and my programs are atypical of most of the people I know. I appear in many different contexts, as almost a different individual. For example, I have a certain position in the field of aviation and I deal with many people in that field who think of me as an applied aviation psychologist, I have a similar position in drug research and also in industrial-organizational psychology, and perhaps in personality and interaction theory. I remember a few years ago when we were dealing with the National Institute on Drug Abuse, I shocked Bob DuPont one day when I told him that drug abuse was not the entire program of our institute, nor of my own work, but rather that we were involved extensively in many other areas.

What I would like to do is to relate many of my applied side interests, so to speak, to a more integrated approach that perhaps I have never fully communicated. I gave a colloquium at Texas A&M University recently, and Ben Benjamin, who is here today and is one of our Ph.D.s introduced me at that program. I thought he expressed it very well. In fact, it might be more illuminating to have him answer your question than to answer it myself; but I am going to try to answer it.

The first thing I would mention is that when I was a student, psychology was not as specialized as it is now. In fact, the whole trend in psychology has gone from very broad characterizations, where people thought of themselves in such global terms as, for example, structuralists or functionalists, to very narrow paradigmatic positions. One of my fellow students at Columbia said once, in a rather bragging way, "I am an S.R. man." I do not know exactly what he was trying to convey, but I think that what he meant was that he was empirical and not speculative. The difference is seen most clearly in the doctoral examination. Today, a student finishing a Ph.D. works with one committee--social, personality, industrial, learning, whatever, and his area of expertise is confined. At the time I was a student, the people of that generation were supposed to know the whole field. Of course, there were not as many books in the library then as there are now, yet it was still a pretty good sized field. The emphasis was on the idea of a science. As you pointed out, this implied determinism, and it implied a number of other assumptions. As Donald Hebb wrote in his introductory textbook, "You have to have a science before you can apply it." However, at the same time, one of the strong beliefs I have acquired in the course of my own career is that the science is not an end in itself, but that its application is an important outcome that provides us justification and rationale for the scientific enterprise. We have to see both the science and its technological applications.

Throughout my own career, I have always been interested on one side in the development of science, and on the other side in showing that science was worthwhile by being able to apply it. With regard to the nature of that science, Woodworth first mentioned that we cannot think of behavior only in terms of stimulus and response, but as in his formula "W - S - O - R - W". The "W" that he put around it was the "world" and this provided an environmental context; "O" represents the "organism". Unfortunately, he never pursued that important issue, but I regarded his formulation as a major insight and have tried to embellish it. The Gestaltists--Lewin, Brunswick, and others--brought it along.

I have thought more in interactional terms, of behavior as a product of the interaction of the person and his environment. In order to design research relevant to this formulation, we have to identify not only the person variables, but also the environmental variables. It is easy to talk about this and it makes very interesting essay writing, but it is extremely difficult to implement it. The implementation question led me to a number of positions that are still unpopular in many circles, indeed among some of my colleagues here at TCU. But I still believe that they are important. These positions are outlined rather completely in several papers. Two were published in the *American Psychologist*. One was called "An Interactionist Looks at the Environment;" it was published around 1956 and was my Presidential Address to the Southwestern Psychological Association. The second, some years later, was "Ecology and the Science of Psychology." Subsequently, I developed a social system model that extended these ideas further.

In brief, I presented the following conclusions with reference to the paradigm in which behavior is the result of the interaction of person variables and environment variables. Number one, we cannot at this time specify what the environment variables are. Most of our efforts as psychologists until quite recently, and to a great extent still, have been preoccupied with the person variables. In a paper that I presented at a conference in Banff, I tried to outline how one could approach some of these environmental variables. One, for example, was taken from Barker and Gump, *Big School, Small School*. They demonstrated a kind of force that appears to be generated in the environment when the number of people available to participate in an activity is fewer than the number of people required by that activity, as with children choosing up sides to play baseball. If there are not enough people to staff the teams, forces of inclusion are generated: they will bring in a mother, a 5-year-old kid sister, or anybody, just to fill all the bases. If the number of people available to participate exceeds the number that are required, forces of exclusion are generated. They demonstrated this in their book in a wide range of circumstances.

I think this is a good example of how some factors in the environment influence behavior. It is something that you have to infer from the environmental situation, it is not a situation by itself. I think that there are many forces like that and we need to investigate them. Otherwise, we will never be able to work out a satisfactory causal model. Until we can specify what the environmental forces are to a great extent, we will be stymied. We get along pretty well with demographics and with representing effects of different policies and things like that, but there is more to a comprehensive study of the environment. That represents the first of my conclusions. The second general conclusion has gotten me in hot water many times and is one for which I have been accused of being antiexperimental. I say right now that I am not antiexperimental, I am merely skeptical! There is a difference! I feel that when you are engaged in any kind of research, the goal is obviously to generalize to some real life situations. Therefore, the structure of the research must be such that it can be generalized. In my opinion, many laboratory situations are not generalizable to the real world. They are convenient and fit academic scheduling requirements, but they tend to be artificial and have no referents in the real world. I will simply stand on that. If you want to shoot me down, you may try. This is mostly true for problems of social, environmental, industrial, clinical, and educational psychology.

It is difficult to think of a laboratory in which role playing or other kinds of simulation devices that are frequently used are really adequate. Going out into the field and trying to study behavior as it actually occurs strikes me as more important, although often very frustrating. Coming back to Barker, another example from his work involved a study of frustration. The investigators were able to generate frustrating situations very easily in a laboratory setting. However, when they went out to the school yard to study children who were frustrated in natural settings, they never saw any frustration. Apparently, the reason for this was that *Homosapiens* (as with other species) is equipped with devices that help us avoid situations that are likely to frustrate and to seek situations that put ourselves in a better light. Many of the conclusions from the laboratory studies were just not applicable. As a result, I subscribe to the principle that the laboratory should be a surrogate for the life situations to which the results are to be generalized. If this can be accomplished by simulation

or in any other way, fine; if not, I prefer to work out
in the real world, the field.

Another important conclusion that I arrived at
from this kind of examination has had a major influence
on my overall approach to research.   In brief,   I
believe   that   we   have   methods   available   in   the
field   that   enable   us   to control about as well as it
is   often   possible to control   in   a   laboratory.   I
visualize   every real life situation as a   multivariate
situation   and I am committed to multivariate   analysis
as   the   solution.   It certainly is   a   very   powerful
methodology   despite   limitations   that   we   must
acknowledge.   With   the   new   computers   and   the   new
programs   that   are   becoming   available   now   and,
hopefully,   as   we   learn   to   identify   environmental
variables,   it is becoming more powerful all the   time.
So, that is still another principle.   There is still
another one.   In fact, there are two that go   together
and   they   were   discussed   in   the   ecology   paper.   A
consequence   of   the commitment to the field   study   of
behavior,   where   it occurs, is   the   realization that
every species has its ecological niche.   It has adapted
to   a particular environment that is important   to   its
development, and therefore to the understanding of   its
behavior.   Frequently, the laboratory   environment   is
not   appropriate.   For example, a colleague of mine   in
the   Air   Force in San Antonio,   Paul   Fields,   studied
problem solving in rats, and created what was virtually
a   "university"   environment for rats.   He   gave   them
extremely   difficult   "human" problems and   they   could
solve many of them.   I wondered whether that was   going
to contribute   anything, because I see the   study   of
rat behavior as fitting into the phylogenetic   position
in the evolution of the species and requiring behaviors
appropriate to to the ecological niche of the   species.
Thus,   I recognized the importance of the   phylogenetic
perspective   as well.   When I saw that, I realized   the
importance of adaptation.   The principle of   adaptation
applies   in   evolution.   It applies   in   phylogeny.   It
applies   in ontogeny, and also in learning, and I   have
tried to   generalize   this into a very   broad   system.
Thus, what I am trying to say, and I will not enumerate

too many points, is that I believe that these have defined for me a systematic approach to the study of psychology.

I would also like to mention one additional issue that is basically methodological. That is the problem of aggregation. Today, there are a great many psychologists doing what is technically sociological work and a great many sociologists doing psychological work. The critical difference between the two disciplines lies in the unit of behavior that is studied. Psychologists are interested in the behavior of the individual and sociologists are interested in the behavior of groups or institutions. All too often, studies have been presented in both disciplines that have used aggregate data incorrectly or that have disaggregated data incorrectly.

To carry out the plan that I have described, the first issue is that of the variables in the environment. Psychology cannot do it alone. We need to have other related disciplines such as economics, anthropology, and sociology to help us map out the many problems in the environment that we need to take into account.

I have not said anything about the biological side, although this is necessary because we are also biological organisms. This just increases the complications to a much greater extent. When we have gotten all this done, I still feel I would like to see a program to advance psychology as a scientific discipline. I am terribly interested and proud when we can apply psychology usefully in society. In the course of my career, I have had opportunities to work in aviation, in drug abuse, in organizational and management studies, and a number of other fields that we cannot take time to mention, such as education, classroom work, and so forth. This was the concept that I had in mind when we started the IBR. I would like to say that the IBR was good, not because of me, but because there were people in it such as Bob Demaree, who is a genius in many ways both in his multivariate psychology and his teaching, and

Dwayne Simpson, George Joe, Larry James, Jack Greener, Allan Jones, and many others. We have had really a surplus of riches in terms of the caliber of our faculty and the students we were able to attract. Right now, if there is one regret I have, it is that at the end of next month this whole thing is going to grind to a halt. Larry is now at Georgia Tech with one program, Dwayne and George are at A&M with another, and I have retained some that I will continue to pursue. Everything is being removed and I think I am going to sit here and write some memoirs.

Dr. Evans:

Thank you. When you eventually write your memoirs, I think they will be very important. They will reflect the wisdom of your position and your enthusiasm for it. I believe that people are no longer committed to internalism and your views on interaction are timely. As we face society's challenges, I think that unless we can do work that has maximum external validity, our field may lose considerable ground. I think that your particular approach to the drug abuse problem is very interesting, and is related to the efforts to rehabilitate in alcohol, cigarette smoking, and other addictive areas. Now it seems to me that your way of looking at drug abuse has a lot of policy impact, but I am not sure that all people who look at your work fully understand it. It would be interesting to have you review the approach you used, how you moved into this drug field in which you have been so very productive.

Dr. Sells:

I agree that we had some trouble communicating. One of the unfortunate things is that our journals have so much competition for space that they require excessive compression. As a result, most papers that are published now are understood only by people who specialize in that particular paradigm and do not really need to see the assumptions that have to be made. We have preferred to write detailed technical reports and have published them in books.

Parenthetically, I would like to add a "brag" for the journal with which I am closely identified, *Multivariate Behavioral Research*, because at MBR we encourage people to report at greater length and in a more meaningful way. Another problem has derived from pressure from the granting agency to write technical reports in language and formats that would be more intelligible to the medics and clinicians. Dwayne Simpson, Bob Demaree, George Joe, and I, along with others, have for years been squabbling within our office about how to focus our reports. I think most of us agree now that we did the right thing by insisting on complete scientific reports. Of course, it is one thing to write a complete scientific report, and another one to get people to read it. I think that some of the people who criticized our work earlier have even now admitted that they have not read our reports. Many administrators and clinicians have not been sophisticated in relation to analytic statistics and the complex problems that are involved in this type of field research. In every study we have found it necessary to use devices that insured accurate analysis of the data, but at the same time were virtually incomprehensible to the naive reader. This has probably been at the root of the communication problem. But there are some others.

There is in the treatment of drug abuse, as in other fields, a basic reality that "You get what you pay for." Many people think of drug abuse as some kind of fixed procedure, and it really is not. The outcomes that are expected in treatment are also rarely clearly stated. In fact, the only way we could find out the goals of the Federal treatment program (and this was program-wide and not representative of all treatment clinics) was to read the Congressional testimony, because the agency never put out a clearcut statement. I would say that frequently their failure to do so may have been for self-protective reasons. What I mean by "You get what you pay for" is this: One of the major desired outcomes in treating people who are drug abusers is for them to reduce, and hopefully eliminate, their drug abuse. However, there are other important outcomes that involve rehabilitation and return to normal social living; that is, getting productive jobs, having a normal home life with a family, and becoming good self-sufficient citizens. If you look at the budgets across the treatment programs, you will find that there were some treatment programs that were staffed only to concentrate on the reduction of drug use. Their clients may well have been unemployable, without learned employment skills, without resources to find a place to live, and with severely disrupted family life. In order to deal with these problems and to provide rehabilitation services in these other areas, the treatment programs need other kinds of services beyond those that focus only on drugs. Unfortunately, they frequently do not have them. One program at Yale University in New Haven, Connecticut, and another one in Chicago did have comprehensive services, and they frequently produced the expected good results. However, across the board, in many different states and cities across the country, treatment budgets have been greatly restricted. With restricted budgets, and frequently no professional staff in the program except the nurse who administers the methadone, or something like that, there is no encouragement for those other outcomes. Notwithstanding all this, our study of drug abuse treatment provided support for the continuation of these programs. In addition, it appears that the mere willingness to enter into treatment represents a change of attitude which is part of the therapeutic process. In general, we found that treatment, even with bare-bones budgets, is productive and I have recommended that such programs receive continued support.

Dr. Evans:

Well, let us elaborate a little more. Look at all the different programs and evaluate the recidivism that I have also found in alcoholism, smoking, and other addictive behaviors. As I understand it, using your multivariate approach, you said in some cases the outcome might be that there is actual reduction in the use of drugs, and maybe the person might not use them

at all. Another outcome might be that the person might
still be using drugs, but at least he or she can now
function better in society.

Dr. Sells:

...or is using less serious drugs.

Dr. Evans:

Yes, or is using less serious drugs. You also said
that the attitude of the person entering treatment is
critical.   What do you think about making drugs
available and allowing people free use of them?   It
would be less costly and might lead to less crime.   If
most of them can function reasonably well, what would
be wrong with that? We let them have cigarettes to go;
we let them have alcohol to go. Why not let them have
drugs?   This seems to me to be in question with your
work. We would like you to give us some insights into
this question because you are aware of the different
types of options.

Dr. Sells:

As you undoubtedly recall, we did have prohibition for
alcohol, years ago, and it was not successful. At the
same time, you cannot say that license has been
successful when alcoholism is our number one substance
abuse problem. I am not convinced that decriminalizing
drugs and taking them off the banned list and letting
them flow in the supply and demand of society would be
worse than what we have now. However, we could never
get the politicians to approve it, nor do I think a
study of this procedure could ever be funded on a scale
that would provide definitive data--not in this
country. The data from England, where they tried this,
indicated that it was not successful. In my opinion,
the only way that we are ever going to get rid of drug
abuse and other abuses and basic social ills, is to
address the causes. We have a cancer in our society
related to rejection and unequal distribution of
opportunity.   I do not want to sound political, but
just to mention the problems that we have and see how
these function within individuals.   Under the

circumstances of many lives, drug abuse is sometimes a
very satisfactory way of coping with almost impossible
situations. It is not widely recognized, but many
people who use drugs enjoy it. It is the only
pleasure they get in a life where all the doors are
closed. If we could open the doors, things might be
different. We need to look at that.

I think we have a polarization in our society. I
read this week in the *Fort Worth Star-Telegram* that a
study here in Fort Worth showed that 40% of our
population is living below the poverty level. One of
my students, Debra Murphy, is completing a dissertation
using data provided by Lee Robins on American soldiers
in the Vietnam war. She has very convincing evidence
that in our society, social class, or more specifically
low social class, is a strong predictor of drug abuse--
preservice, in service, and in Vietnam in the war zone.
I do not know that we are going to cure that, but as
long as we have it we are going to get backsliding,
even when the programs are working.

Dr. Evans:

Well, now moving to another area of your contributions,
we have one of your former colleagues, a very fine
investigator, Allan Jones, in our psychology
department. I notice, looking at his work, that he
certainly fits into the mold of what may be called
organizational psychology and I am intrigued by how you
are taking your interactionist approach not only to
things like drug abuse, but also to organizational
behavior. Could you summarize, as you see it, how you
have approached the work place and where you think
research in the work place is going? It has seemed to
me that a lot of organizational psychology sounds like
early sociology plus early social psychology and has
lacked sophistication.

Dr. Sells:

I will be very brief on this. I think that there is at
the present a special interest in the United States in
the so-called Japanese management system. The Japanese
system is said to be beating the pants off of us in the

manufacturing and distribution of automobiles and many
other kinds of goods. Many times we have asked the
question, "Why?" Back in World War II and immediately
after, Japanese goods were always looked at as *ersatz*
and of poor quality, and the Japanese were said to have
just copied everything. How have things changed? If
there is one thing that Japanese management has
learned, and which we have learned, and which some of
the most successful corporations in this country are
practicing, it is how to manage their people in their
work place. However, such practice is very limited in
the United States. One of the things that has been
noticeable as I have dealt with businesses and
industrial executives right here in our own community
is that they have a different attitude toward their own
positions than they do toward their subordinates. "Do
not step on me, but it is all right to step on them".
There is a great need to educate managers to realize
that if they can treat people fairly and understand
that workers have the same needs that managers have,
and if management can satisfy those needs in some
reasonable way, the result would be improved
production, as well as satisfaction. Then a manager
might be able to take off some week and go fishing and
not worry about the business and people when he gets
back. That is putting it rather crudely, but, I think,
correctly. During the 1970s a tremendous amount of
interest evolved in what is now called the
organizational climate There is extensive literature
on this. The universe of organizational climate
variables, which is a subdomain of the total
environment, represents those aspects of the
organizational environment, the organizational
situation, that have impact on the behavior of people
working in the organization. The variables involved
include such factors as job importance, conflict,
challenge, openness, opportunity for advancement,
monotony, standards, warmth and friendliness, and
others. A climate that encompasses openness of
expression, for example, is important. In some
situations, people are afraid to speak out because of a
fear of recrimination, whereas in others, people are
encouraged to speak their minds freely. There are even

some people who are so enlightened that they say, "I do not want yes-men; I want people to disagree with me so we can really get at the answers." I was visiting with Joe Hunt yesterday, and he was talking about Charles Sanders Pierce's theory of abduction. This is an important issue in decision making; we need people who are willing to find fault with an idea so that when we make a decision and on balance realize that nothing is perfect, we come out with the wisest decision we can make. We have to encourage people to think this way. Many people are afraid to express their opinions because they fear criticism and loss of face. Without being pedantic or dogmatic about it, I believe we are talking about universal variables here which have to do with the way people perceive their work environment and the extent to which variables constructed from such data can be used to formulate better principles of management which would increase productivity of the work force, their satisfaction with the job, their tenure on the job, and their ability to function effectively on the job.

Dr. Evans:

Well, I served as a consultant to the Control Data Corporation in a program that was moving into what is called *Matrix*. This had apparently led to many problems for CDC. I am sure you are familiar with it. I have seen exactly what you are talking about and have been trying to deal with it with an approach modelled somewhat after the Japanese. Do you think the answer is to model our efforts after other systems and cultures or other approaches that seem to be working in one situation or another? Would that work in the complex industrial patterns we have in this country?

Dr. Sells:

I believe there are two answers to that--one is "yes" and the other is "no." The "no" is that you cannot take a procedure literally and transplant it and expect it to work. However, if you can understand the principle that is involved and adapt it to a different set of circumstances, then "yes" it might work. The culture of this country is different from that of

Japan. We cannot do things in exactly the same way they do. However, some of the relationships are similar and can be adapted. There is now some good literature on this. I would say that Americans are beginning to understand that we can learn from the Japanese by learning the principles that are involved in their work, but not necessarily applying them the way the Japanese do.

Dr. Evans:

This was demonstrated to us earlier about the specific situation, the culture, the environmental factors, the behavioral spectra, especially environmental, in determining the operation at Control Data in Minneapolis and Exxon in Houston.

Dr. Sells:

I am glad you brought that up because there is a point I have wanted to emphasize. Because most of the research we do in the United States involves a single culture, all of these culture variables are dropped out, since there is very little variance. If you look at the complete list that is available in my *Stimulus Determinants of Behavior*, you will see many factors that should be taken into account but are ignored for this reason. These include family size, marital customs, religion, social status, and so on; it is about a 20 page list. When all this drops out, we become community centered. It is inappropriate for us in view of the concerns of our sponsors, who support our research, to try to do cross-cultural research on a grand world-wide basis. I will not pursue that further here. However, in relation to the Japanese management systems, we have to be careful when we go from one culture to another, because it usually does not transfer.

Dr. Evans:

Now, in the time remaining, I would like you to give your opinions of factor analysis. I wish you would get a lot more specific than we have been so far because I think you will have an even better opportunity to expound on your views on this method, which is

prominent in much of your work. As I understand it, a
distinction can be made between what might be called a
deductive use of factor analysis as compared with the
more inductive approach that appears to characterize
your work. Have you violated any of the statistical
assumptions of this method? Some people say that
factor analysis has lost its value, and some people say
it is still important, some people say that it can be
manipulated. What can you tell us about this?

Dr. Sells:

There are two people in the audience here who have
written textbooks on factor analysis. I am flattered
to be asked to discuss it in their presence.

Dr. Evans:

I ask the question of you.

Dr. Sells:

Then I guess I will give you my naive views. In one
sense, factor analysis is merely a method of crunching
numbers. However, you must make some assumptions and
there are a number of different approaches. You can
use it to test hypotheses; you can use it to reduce the
number of variables, and you can use it for other
purposes. Many years ago, I discussed this with Phil
DuBois while we were reviewing some factor analytic
studies in our Air Force program. He said he had
concluded that factor analysis had much in common with
psychoanalysis. In the hands of many naive people who
collect data and send it to a computer center to be
processed, he was probably correct. However, in the
hands of skilled scientists, who follow a number of
rigorous requirements before they even touch their
data, there is a different story. Factor analysis
provides a means to achieve a degree of simplicity in
complex data sets. We often need what I will call
least-common-denominator types of variables   to
understand relationships where the original variables
are very complex. Then there are issues of hypotheses
with which you are dealing--the definitions of the
variables you are putting in. At least one other point
that is very important is that if you take the salient

variables in four or five different data sets, they may not look the same to different investigators and there are issues of interpretation. I have a pragmatic view toward factor analysis. Debra Murphy and I recently wrote a chapter called "Factor Analytic Theories Of Personality" which will appear in Norman Endler's revision of Joe Hunt's *Personality and the Behavior Disorders*, to be published this year. We pointed out here that there are a number of disagreements among the leading authorities in this field that are almost impossible to resolve--Eysenck is one, Cattell is another, and Guilford must also be mentioned. If you compare the approaches taken by these three leaders, they reflect differences that I see no empirical way to resolve. We have to recognize that problems of this kind exist. Notwithstanding this, for pragmatic purposes, reducing large data sets to smaller numbers of homogenous variables to test hypotheses, to understand the data better, to explore the implications of extracting different numbers of factors on various rationales, can be extremely valuable. But there is no generally accepted cookbook that gives you all the answers. It still requires skill, and this is what I think DuBois had in mind, because the skill of the clinicians in studying individual cases and the skill of very capable statisticians in studying data matrices both involve some degrees of uncertainty for which the cookbook is not yet available.

Dr. Evans:

Well, Saul, I think that we have heard you comment on a lot of things. Over your career and your many contributions, what do you yourself view as some of your most important contributions to psychology and science?

Dr. Sells:

I am not sure that any of them is of value. Nevertheless, they are available in my books and in several of my papers that have been reprinted in anthologies. The ecology paper and the interactionist papers have appeared in perhaps 20 different anthologies and collections. To the extent that they have been selected, I suppose they are important. We have received some awards for work that we did in the Air Force on pilot selection and stress, and from the National Institute on Drug Abuse on drug research, and I suppose that is important. Most of them were shared with other people and I really thought of them more as institutional awards than as personal awards.

I still think that, although it was a box office failure, my textbook of psychology was a very fine book. I still think that that is the way psychology should be taught!

Dr. Evans:

Saul, I want to thank you very much for your remarks, and judging from the audience response on the real importance of the issues you have covered, I think the feedback is positive and rewarding.

Dr. Sells:

Thank you, Dick. I feel that having joined others, I mean interviewed by you, I can now go back to the armchair with a feeling of satisfaction.

3 Contributions of a Behavioral Scientist to a Public Health Administrator

Lois R. Chatham
National Institute on Alcohol Abuse and Alcoholism

We have heard about Dr. Sells' many contributions to measurement, to personnel selection, to understanding the workplace, and to the efficacy of treating the addicted. His contributions to psychology and science have likewise been acknowledged. Dr. Simpson (chapter 12) indicated that I would be discussing policy implications of DARP, but I think Dr. Barry Brown (chapter 13) has covered that issue well. I want to talk about how Dr. Sells contributed to one public administrator's career. I want to talk about Saul, the man, as I know him. To do this, I talk about the contributions he has made to my career--knowing full well mine is one of the least illustrious careers he has influenced.

   I first met Saul when I was a medical psychology intern being supervised by Dr. Ivan Mensh at Washington University Medical School in St. Louis. I can still

---

*This chapter was the last paper presented in the symposium and was partially a discussion of the papers by Dwayne Simpson (chapter 12) and Barry Brown (chapter 13). Therefore, the reader may want to refer to those chapters first.

visualize my desk in the Malcolm Bliss Hospital
Outpatient Unit. I was working on my dissertation,
quantifying the complaints of aging patients when my
supervisor announced we were being visited by Dr. Saul
Sells. For some reason I believed that Dr. Sells was
checking to see if I was using my NIMH grant funds to
good advantage. The only thing that prevented me from
having an acute anxiety attack was the fact that I was
given only 5 minutes' warning.

When the hulk of a man, as he seemed to me then
and still does today, came in smoking a pipe, he bowed
in his continental way and chuckled. That chuckle has
characteristically smoothed many an otherwise tense
moment in our relationship.

My next encounter with Dr. Sells occurred when I
attended a symposium in Fort Worth entitled
Rehabilitating the Narcotic Addict. I was then working
for the National Center for Health Statistics, where I
had come to view violence as the number one public
health problem. To me, it seemed that addiction might
somehow be related. I show you the book edited by Saul
and published in 1966, which is the report of this
symposium, to emphasize Saul's early imprint on the
treatment of addiction.

My next contact with Dr. Sells occurred when, as
the individual responsible for advising on the
psychological components of a National Health
Examination Survey, I found myself possessing thousands
of TAT responses. Now while the selection of
measurements included standard intelligence tests and
questions whose validity at least were apparent, two of
the tests selected caused me problems--the Draw-A-
Person Test and the TAT. It should be pointed out that
these tests had not been chosen without due
consultation with psychologists of eminence--but I was
left to develop norms, etc. I shall forever be
grateful to Dr. Dale Harris who provided consultation
on the drawings. However, it was Dr. Sells that I
called for help in quantifying the mass of TAT
responses. I shall be grateful forever that at that
particular point in my career he did not chide me for
collecting answers before I knew the questions--but he

chuckled a lot. Saul not only developed a method for analyzing the data, he also did the scut work of transcribing all the verbal responses. I suspect that this indirectly supported science because the wives of many Ph.D. candidates were employed by Saul as secretaries at IBR.

During my stay in the National Center for Health Statistics (NCHS), I became concerned that there was no operational definition of mental health, yet we were attempting to measure it. To whom did I turn? To Dr. Sells, of course. Under his leadership, the following voices addressed this issue: John A. Clausen, John R. P. French, Jr., Elmer A. Gardner, John C. Glidewell, Ernest A. Gruenberg, Jane Loevinger, Benjamin Pasamanick, M. Brewster Smith, Leo Srole, and Joseph Zubin. Libraries of this Nation now save space for the book, *The Definition and Measurement of Mental Health* You will note that by then I knew how to raise the questions and he helped me get the answers--an improvement on my part!

Dr. Simpson has talked about the early history of the development of the management information system that would contribute to the science of treatment research. This pleased Saul, Barry, and me. But, as manager of the Nation's Narcotic Treatment Addict System, what Dr. Sells did contributed to making that system one of the most accountable treatment systems in the Nation.

Now, let's step back a little. Having left NCHS, I went to NIMH in a research capacity, and discovered that some service programs existed along with research units. These service units were the two narcotic hospitals, Lexington and Fort Worth, whose research activities I attempted to at least enumerate for the Institute. But, a new act was passed that would eventually lead to the phase-out of institutional care for addicts in favor of treating them in their own communities--preferably in a non-institutional setting. As an additional task, my administrator, Dr. Sherman Kieffer, asked me to see what was happening with those patients committed under the Narcotic Rehabilitation

Act.   Even   a   cursory review sent   me   scurrying   to
advise him that most likely we would lose the   patients
if   we   did   not set up some   tracking   system.   While
others, such as Karst Besteman, saw to the logistics of
contracting   for services, working with courts,   and   a
myriad   of other details, a medical   records   librarian
and I set up a tracking system.

Having   read   some   of   the   testimony   that   had
resulted   in the enabling legislation, I realized   that
treating   addicts   on   an   outpatient   basis   in   their
communities   was, at best, "clinical wisdom"   based   on
very limited information, let alone research.   At   that
point,   I attempted to introduce logic into   decisions.
I later learned to accept some decisions for what   they
are--political   maneuvers.   With   all of my   persuasive
powers   I argued that if this were to be   a   treatment-
only   program, it would have been administered   by   the
Department   of Social and Rehabilitative   Services   and
not   by   the   National   Institute   of   Mental   Health.
Because   it   was   to be administered   by   the   National
Institute on Mental Health, Congress certainly intended
that   it   be   studied   to   see   whether   this   type   of
treatment   indeed   did   work.   I   had   an   easy   job
persuading   Dr.   Sherman Kieffer on the   importance   of
evaluating treatment of narcotic addicts because he had
worked   at both the Fort Worth and Lexington   hospitals
and was deeply interested in knowing how effective   his
treatment was, largely due to his work with Dr. Sells.

Through   a series of reorganizations, I   ended   up
administering the Narcotic Addict Rehabilitation Branch
where,   with   the power of withholding funds   from   any
contractor   who   would not provide the   information   we
requested, treatment evaluation was underway.

Parallel   to this event was the growth of a   small
grant   program where addicts would be   treated   without
being   civilly   committed.   Dr.   Simpson   has   identified
the   first six programs and has told how Dr.   Sells   was
proposing to evaluate their effectiveness.   After   some
bureaucratic maneuvering, it turned out that,   although
I   was the administrator of both programs, it   was   the
grant   program   that turned out to be the one   so   well

studied by Saul, and the Civil Commitment program was evaluated less rigorously as an in-house effort.

When one decides on a career in public administration, one closes off some other opportunities. To me, the decision to administer programs meant I would aid science but not conduct it. My contribution was to keep the data coming in--and that I did. That is probably why until this day when I meet some of the grantees they say, "Okay, okay, I'll send in the TCU forms!"

Hence my long-term association with Dr. Sells and DARP. Soon we developed a management-by-exception program. I still remember the items that I, as administrator, always looked for when I made a site visit. I looked to see if the deaths had increased. I looked to see if there was a great underutilization or overutilization of capacity, and I looked for dramatic changes in staffing patterns. These indicators could tell me that a program was in trouble. I think it is not accidental that some of these are things I was later to look for when administering alcohol treatment programs.

In those days it was Saul's responsibility to report regularly on each program in the system, and he did so with great vigor. The volumes he submitted to us came to be known as the "Purple Monsters." I hold one up with affection! Some have said that Saul has a data reduction problem. I would like to correct that misunderstanding. Saul just gives one more than one has paid for.

Now, I would like to talk about some of the findings contained in Dwayne Simpson's (Chapter 12) and Barry Brown's (Chapter 13) chapters because of the significance I think they have in the field of addiction in general. We tend to think of the abuse of alcohol and drugs as different phenomena, but they really are not. They are both drug dependencies. As a result, it may be that the findings of the DARP may, at least sometimes, be generalizable to the alcohol abusing population. I noted with interest that how long one stays in treatment is a predictor of how drug-

free one will be. Such is the case for the treatment
for alcohol also. I once thought a lot about why it is
so difficult to define "treatment" for the alcoholic in
terms other than its setting. We tend to talk about
halfway house treatment, outpatient treatment or
inpatient treatment rather than to describe what
happened within the treatment setting. I think,
perhaps, we concentrate on settings because of the
Mental Health Center Act that dictated the five
essential services of inpatient, outpatient, partial
hospitalization, emergency care, and consultation and
education. Perhaps we were unduly influenced by the
location rather than content of treatment. This also
was encouraged by our reimbursement system.

In terms of operational definitions, I have come
to the conclusion that for me "the treatment of
alcoholism is any support system that reinforces the
individual's decision not to drink." I am wondering if
this could be the underlying factor in the studies
reported on by Barry and Dwayne. Maybe it does not
matter which support system is used as long as that
support system reinforces an individual's decision not
to use drugs, not to commit criminal acts, and to get a
job.

I bring in my present interest in alcohol research
because I hope I shall be able to entice Dr. Sells into
yet another field of endeavor; namely, looking at the
treatment for alcoholism to help us discover "what
works for which alcoholic patient, at what risk, and at
what cost?"

For someone who is sometimes described as "not
suffering fools gladly"--I remind you that Saul
chuckled at this young fool. For someone who is
sometimes described by envious, less competent
individuals as "merely a research entrepreneur"--I say
he is the living proof of the "G" factor in
intelligence. For someone who prides himself in doing
"only rigorous research"--thanks for helping this
public servant be accountable, be successful, and be
able to contribute to science through you.

And finally, all who know Saul know he is one part of a two-person team. My division is responsible for writing *Alcohol And Health V*. In the process of negotiating for editorial services, I heard myself say: "Put in some money for indexing. It's the most important part of the book." I was quoting Helen Sells, and she was right!

4 Atmospheres in Sentences and Narratives

J. W. Mann
University of the Witwatersrand

Saul Sells was right. There is an atmosphere effect. It might seem strange that, after nearly 50 years of pertinent research, such an assertion should need to be made at all. Yet, in one area of that research, some doubt has been cast on the extent or even existence of the atmosphere effect.

This area is the one centering on the use of reason. Most research about atmospheres seems to have been done in this area; and some of the conclusions drawn from the research have been negative. Results have been found difficult to explain in terms of atmospheres (Ceraso & Provitera, 1971). Hypotheses based on atmospheres have been treated as inadequate (Johnson-Laird, 1975). The usefulness of an explanation based on atmospheres has been doubted (Dickstein, 1978). The part played by atmospheres has been seen as limited and the very possibility that atmospheres are effective has been questioned (Wason & Johnson-Laird, 1972).

Of course, all these negative points derive from work on reasoning; and what must be remembered is that Sells by no means confined the atmosphere effect to its workings in syllogisms. He cast his net widely and generously included other areas in which an atmosphere might be effective, such as in the pronunciation of words or in perceptual processes (Sells, 1936).

One of the types of atmosphere originally considered by Sells was a grammatical one. Here is an example: The value of the old, well-tried approaches to the problems facing the investigators were considerable.

In this sentence, the verb "were" agrees with the plural atmosphere of the subject phrase "of the old, well-tried approaches to the problems facing the investigators". To be grammatically correct, it should agree, of course with the subject noun "value" which is in the singular.

The plural-saturated subject phrase, "of the old, well-tried approaches to the problems facing the investigators", is supposed to conjure up a plural atmosphere; and it is this atmosphere that the verb, "were" apparently agrees with, rather than the subject noun.

Plenty of experimental evidence has been adduced recently in support of the view that the grammatical atmosphere really does exert an effect.

It may not be a very powerful effect, and it seems to be rather volatile; but appropriate ways have been found to coax it forth successfully.

Last year, for example, there was a report of a simple experiment that clearly disclosed the workings of the grammatical atmosphere effect (Mann, 1982b).

The experiment depended on the use of ambiguous subject nouns, that is to say, subject nouns like "deer" and "Siamese" that are ambiguous in number, in the sense that they take the same form whether they are singular or plural.

A subject noun like "deer" would be followed, say, by a string of nouns in the plural atmosphere effect. The verb would be left out of the sentence and the respondent would have to supply it: for example, in the incomplete sentence "The deer photographed by the

technicians   during   the   investigations   for   the
scientists   from the laboratories ... undernourished".
If the plural nouns engendered a plural atmosphere, a
respondent should be encouraged to supply a verb in the
plural form, like "were".   In contrast, if the nouns
after "deer" were all changed into the singular, a
respondent should be encouraged to supply a verb in a
singular   form,   like   "was".   The   results   of   the
experiment   indeed brought out the contrast that   would
occur if there is a grammatical atmosphere effect.
Respondents completing sentences that contained   plural
nouns   were more likely to supply plural   responses   (a
mean of .84) than the respondents completing   sentences
that contained singular nouns (a mean of only .08).

Several   similar   experiments carried   out   earlier
also   supported   the   existence   of   a   grammatical
atmosphere effect (Mann, 1982).

The effect that Sells had been concerned with   was
one   that is strong enough to trap the respondent   into
error, as in the example cited earlier:The value of the
old,   well-tried approaches to the problems facing   the
investigators were considerable.   Here the subject noun
"value" is in the singular and the   plural   atmosphere
has to be sufficiently powerful to swing the respondent
toward   a plural and mistaken response.   This seems   to
have been the case in an experiment reported last   year
(Mann, 1982a).   In that experiment, sentences like   the
value   sentence were significantly more   successful   in
producing erroneous plural words than variations on the
sentences that contained singulars instead of plurals.

Altogether, sufficient evidence has been collected
to show convincingly that there is indeed an atmosphere
effect of the grammatical sort.   The kind of grammar
under   scrutiny, however, has been the grammar   of   the
sentence.   The experiments referred to have   been
concerned with the nouns and verbs contained within a
single   sentence.   There is another kind of   grammar
and   it has to do with whole passages containing   many
sentences: text grammar (see for example, Martindale,
1981).

One might well inquire whether the atmospheres already shown to be effective in the sentence are effective also in broader contexts involving a number of sentences which are knit together into a narrative whole.

As a tribute to Dr. Sells, I carried out an experiment the month before last on atmospheres in narratives.

The experiment involved 433 first-year students of psychology. They served as subjects in what was designed to be an experiment of the 2 X 2 factorial type.

Every respondent received a booklet containing a narrative or story made up of nine sentences. In one of its versions (the plural unbroken version), the narrative read as follows:

1. The general conditions has .... terrible. The .... officially-appointed observers or investigators .... described the conditions concluded performances had .... before been worse. .... extremely negative conditions prevailed .... eventually the results .... regular samplings of performances allowed the observers .... report to their national heads or superiors .... significant changes had occurred. .... the transitional stages .... to have been gradual; .... the changes of the features that mattered because .... obvious .... the observers repeated their measurements. The .... figures commented on .... the reports of performances presented .... the transitional phases should convince the national heads .... the situations that had to .... reckoned .... could be considered to be .... new. The new international conditions could be characterized as gratifyingly ....

Appreciative comments will come surely
.... the observers. right now, the
observational series .... ready to be
finally designated as good. Considered
nationally, the Maltese .... expected
to perform most effectively.

The task of the respondent was to fill in the words that were missing from the sentences.

The narrative had an underlying form of the "metafunctional" type (Martindale, 1981). The first two sentences conveyed a state of disequilibrium: Specifically, an unpleasant state of affairs was described. The next three sentences described a transitional state. The last four sentences conveyed a state of equilibrium: This time, a pleasant state of affairs.

The last two sentences of the narrative were the critical sentences on which the results of the experiment depended. Each of these critical sentences had as its subject a noun that was ambiguous in number, that is to say, a noun that could be interpreted as either singular or plural: "series" and "Maltese". Immediately after the ambiguous noun, there was a dotted line indicating that a word was missing. The missing word was actually a verb. The point of the experiment was to find out whether the word filled in on the dotted line was in a plural form or another form.

In one of the four treatments, a great many plurals appeared in the sentences preceding the two critical sentences with ambiguous nouns. In other words, an attempt was made to conjure up a plural atmosphere. The opposite type of atmosphere, the singular type, was intended in another treatment, to achieve which the words that had been plural were changed from plural to singular.

As a further variation, the narratives were presented in either an unbroken form, or in a broken form. When the narrative was broken up, the last two sentences (the critical ones) were separated by a wide gap from the preceding sentences, and given the number 2 as though a second narrative were being presented.

So there were two stories containing plenty of plurals: one story unbroken, the other broken; and two stories containing plenty of singulars, one unbroken, and the other broken.

Each respondent was allocated by a random method to one of the four treatment groups. There were 102 respondents in the plural/unbroken group, 117 in the plural/broken group, 108 in the singular/unbroken group, and 106 in the singular/broken group.

A score of 1 was given for each plural-type verb used to complete a critical sentence. Typical plural-type responses were "are" and "were".

Mean scores were: plural/unbroken, .72; plural/broken, .70; singular/unbroken, .58; singular/broken, .47. An analysis of variance for unequal groups (Winer, 1971) brought out only one significant result. Plural-verb output depended on whether narratives had plenty of plurals or plenty of singulars (SS, 3.46; SS within groups, 213.95; F, 6.93; F of 3.86 required for rejection of null hypothesis at .05 level). The output of plural verbs did not depend on whether narratives were unbroken or broken (SS, .43; F, .87); and the effectiveness of numerous plurals or singulars did not depend on whether a narrative was broken or not (SS, .32; F, .65).

There is thus clear evidence that an atmosphere effect was at work. It could be said that the atmosphere of the plurals spread its influence into the critical sentences, where no words were clearly singular or plural, and led to a relatively high mean of plural responses. It could be said likewise that the atmosphere of the singulars led to a relatively low mean of plural responses.

Atmospheres seemed as it were to jump the gap when a narrative was broken into two parts, and to spread from one narrative into the next. This was evident from the result that showed that atmospheres in broken narratives were not significantly different in effect from atmospheres in unbroken ones.

A secondary finding deserves mention. It might be wondered whether the first of the two critical sentences was not more susceptible to atmospheres than the second, seeing that the first was closer to the atmosphere-bearing words. In fact, both critical sentences seemed more or less equal in their susceptibility to atmospheres. this emerged from a scrutiny of the treatment group that had the largest mean output of plural verbs (.72). The relevant treatment group was the one that received an unbroken narrative containing plenty of plurals. Scrutiny of this treatment group revealed that respondents who gave a plural response to the first critical sentence were not especially likely to change their responses when confronted with the second critical sentence. Twenty changes, compared to 25 who changed to a plural responses for the second critical sentence from some other response for the first sentence (McNemar test, Everitt, 1977; (two-tailed x^2 of 3.84 required for significance at .05 level).

To return to the evidence supporting the existence of a grammatical atmosphere effect, it should be noted that exactly why atmospheres are influential is still a fairly open question. Explanations that have been suggested recently (Mann, 1982a) are in terms of familiar cognitive processes.

One of these processes fails to account for the atmosphere effect observed in narratives. The process is one of short-term memory. Long ago, the linguist Jespersen (1924) speculated in passing that memory for the number of a subject noun might fail if the verb followed too long after that subject noun. A relevant example is the sentence cited earlier, The value of the old, well-tried approaches to the problems facing the investigators were considerable. A long string of words came after "value" and before "were", so that the singular nature of "value" could have been forgotten by the time a choice of a singular or plural form for the verb had to be made. However, short-term memory cannot easily explain the atmosphere effect in the narratives. There were no words at all between "series" and the verb that had to be filled in immediately after it, or between "Maltese" and the verb that had to follow it immediately.

For convenience in considering the other two explanations, I shall consider only the plural type of atmosphere. One of these explanations is in terms of attention. It could be argued that a strong plural atmosphere so compels the attention that the respondent tends to react to it when required to choose a singular or plural form for the verb, and so chooses a plural.

The third explanation hinges on interpretation. The argument here begins by noting that an ambiguous noun like "series" or "Maltese" can be interpreted as singular or can be interpreted as plural. Confronted by an ambiguous noun, the respondent is likely to rely on some kind of set to guide him or her in choosing whether to interpret the noun as singular or a plural. The plural atmosphere provides such guidance. so the respondent interprets the noun as a plural and accordingly puts the verb in a plural form to agree with that noun.

This explanation works well in respect to the narratives experiment, which involves ambiguous nouns. Of course, it would not explain effective atmospheres in material that contains, say, an unambiguously singular subject-noun.

Perhaps no one explanation will account for all instances of the grammatical atmosphere effect. What is needed now is for research to turn to explanations of the grammatical atmosphere effect, and to stipulation of conditions under which it will appear, rather than to remain concerned with confirmations of its existence, which surely has been adequately established.

ACKNOWLEDGMENT

The author is grateful for the help received from Mrs. H. Mann.

REFERENCES

Ceraso, J., & Provitera, A. (1971). Sources of error in syllogistic reasoning. *Cognitive Psychology*, *2*, 400-410.

Dickstein, L. S. (1978). The effect of figure on syllogistic reasoning. *Memory and Cognition*, *6*, 76-83.

Everitt, G. S. (1977). *The analysis of contingency tables*. London: Chapman & Hall.

Jespersen, O. (1924). *The philosophy of grammar*. London: Allen & Unwin.

Johnson-Laird, P. N. (1975). Models of deduction. In R.J. Falmagne (Ed.), *Representation and process in children and adults* (pp. 7-54). Hillsdale, NJ: Lawrence Erlbaum Associates.

Mann, J. W. (1982a). *Effects of number. Experimental studies of the grammatical atmosphere effect*. Johannesburg: Witwatersrand University Press.

Mann, J. W. (1982b). Atmosphere or red herring? *The Journal of General Psychology*, *106*, 159-163.

Martindale, C. (1981). *Cognition and consciousness*. Homewood: Dorsey Press.

Sells, S. B. (1936). The atmosphere effect: an experimental study of reasoning. *Archives of Psychology*, No.200.

Wason, P. C., & Johnson-Laird, P. N. (1972). *Psychology of reasoning. Structure and content*. London: Batsford.

Winer, B. J. (1971). *Statistical principles in experimental design*. (2nd ed.). New York: McGraw-Hill.

II MODELS OF INTERACTIONIST STRATEGIES

5 Relevance to Educability: Heritability or Range of Reaction

J. McVicker Hunt
University of Illinois at Champaign-Urbana

I first met Saul Sells when he was a graduate student at Columbia University, and I was a first-year postdoctoral, National Research Council Fellow in Psychology at the New York Psychiatric Institute and Hospital. My mentor there was Professor Carney Landis who was then both head of the psychology department at the New York Psychiatric Institute and professor of psychology at Columbia University. Each Friday afternoon, we at the Institute took the subway from 168th Street down to 116th Street to attend the colloquium of the department of psychology at Columbia University. Saul Sells was in regular attendance as were all the graduate students of the department of psychology. So, in the course of time, I met Saul Sells. We have kept in touch ever since. Following a 5 year stint at the Office of Price Administration in Washington, where he was first chief statistician and then associate director, he spent 2 years as assistant to the president of the A.B. Frank Company in San Antonio, and then he became the professor of medical psychology and the chief of the department of the department of medical psychology for 10 years at the School of Aviation Medicine at the Randolph Air Force Base, here in Texas. Saul invited me to become a psychological consultant to the School. Illinois had its first big snowstorm early in November, and I looked forward to my first visit to Texas. When Saul came to the airport to meet me, the Texas weather seemed fine. When I wakened the next morning, I looked out to see palm trees, but as I looked closer, I could see that they were covered with sleet and ice. But iciness of the weather could not spoil the warmth of the greeting I received from Saul and Helen. I congratulate Saul on a splendid career; a career filled with contributions of importance in several domains, and those he has made since 1958 when he came to Texas Christian University.

In Saul's honor, I discuss a topic of special importance to the science of psychology for the technology of education, namely, the relevance to educability of the heritability of intelligence and the range of reaction for intelligence.

The validity of my message is dependent on what I believe to be a proper relationship between science and values. There are several aspects of this relationship. First, the validity of knowledge demands that the investigative processes of science must be value-free. By that, I mean that the logical analyses, the selection of data, the collecting of data, the processing of data, and the drawing of conclusions in science must be as free as possible from our wishes, our preconceptions, and our prejudices. The goal of science is to determine "what actually *is* what," and not what we wish it to be. Values and needs are a major source of wishes and prejudices. One utterly essential reason for keeping the processes of science value-free is to obtain accurate knowledge. The occurrence of our knowledge, in turn, is very important for the effectiveness of our efforts to achieve the adaptive and civilizing goals that we value.

On the other hand, it is inevitable that human needs and human values will influence whether and with what vigor various domains are investigated. Crowther's (1941) book *The Social Relations of Science*, documents the validity of this proposition for the most recent, roughly 500 years, of human history. He shows that the challenging demands prevalent in each age since the Renaissance have dictated those domains of reality calling for inventive action, and the efforts to create new means of coping have figured heavily in what was investigated. This means that the kinds of problems demanding solutions, lest we suffer, figure heavily in what we investigate and what we investigate with vigor.

Second, values can quite properly combine with knowledge to influence the choice of strategies for research within a given domain. The argument that follows presumes a second relationship between science and values.

Third, and finally, new knowledge can also make established values relevant to domains for which they have previously had no relevance. In so doing, new knowledge may become a major basis for social change. It should be added that whenever knowledge results in social change, it is typically if not always, tied up with social values.

This third relationship of science to values is illustrated by the roles of knowledge and values in the launching of Project Head Start. So long as the social Darwinism of Herbert Spencer and William Graham Sumner held sway in the United States (see Hofstadter, 1945), people generally presumed the view promulgated by Francis Galton (1869) that intelligence is essentially determined by an individual's heredity and the view promulgated by G. Stanley Hall and his student, Arnold Gesell (1954) that the rate and course of psychological development are determined by heredity.

Parenthetically, what has been called *social Darwinism* should have been called *social Malthusianism*, for it was Parson Thomas Malthus who produced the clearest value statements behind this view in his *An Essay on the Principle of Population* (Malthus, 1914). The time was the latter third of the 18th century. Malthus was responding to the revolution going on in agriculture and the misery associated with the migration of displaced peasants from the farms to the cities as the Industrial Revolution got underway in

England.   Here are a few quotations Malthus' famous essay.

> We are bound in justice and honor formally to disclaim the *right* of the poor to support. (p. 201)

> To this end, I propose a regulation to be made, declaring that no child born from any marriage, taking place after the expiration of a year from the date of the law, and no illegitimate child born two years from the same date, should ever be entitled to parish assistance. (p. 201)

> The infant is, comparatively speaking, of little value to society, as others will immediately supply its place. (p. 203)

> All children born beyond what would be required to keep up the population to this [desired] level, must necessarily perish, unless room be made for them by the deaths of grown persons. (p. 179)

From such observations, Malthus concluded with a statement of policy:

> We should facilitate, instead of foolishly and vainly endeavoring to impede the operations of nature in producing this mortality; and if we dread the too frequent visitation of the horrid form of famine, we should sedulously encourage the other forms of destruction, which we compel nature to use. Instead of recommending cleanliness to the poor, we should encourage contrary habits. In our towns, we should make the streets narrower, crowd more people into the houses, and court the return of the Plague. In the country, we should build our villages near stagnant pools, and particularly encourage settlements in all marshy and unwholesome situations. But above all, we should reprobate specific remedies for ravaging diseases; and those benevolent, but much mistaken men, who have thought they were doing a service to mankind by

projecting schemes for the total extirpation of particular disorders. (p. 179)

In his autobiography, Darwin credited Malthus as the source of his idea of competition for survival, and its corollary, the survival of the fittest.   Darwin's focus of application, however, was on the survival of the species; Malthus' focus was on the survival of the individual.

So long as such beliefs prevailed, the value of equality of opportunity, handed down by the founding fathers, had no relevance to the inequities of the preschool years for those children who had the bad luck to be born to parents in poverty without education.   On the other hand, assembling the evidence of plasticity in early psychological development and combining it with evidence of class differences in childrearing clearly made the value of equality of opportunity highly relevant to these inequities of the preschool years.   In *The Children's Cause*, Gilbert Steiner (1976) (and I confess being glad to have someone to cite for this point) credits my book, *Intelligence and Experience* (Hunt, 1961) and Benjamin Bloom's (1964) *Stability and Change in Human Characteristics* with assembling the evidences of plasticity and of the role of early experience in psychological development in such a way as to make them reasonably convincing. Although such knowledge clearly made the value of equality of opportunity relevant to the inequalities of development-fostering experience across the social class structure, the influence of these books in the political sphere was largely a matter of accident. First, it depended on President John F. Kennedy's having launched a War on Poverty for reasons I need not go into here.   Second, it depended on the fact that Kennedy had a mentally deficient sister. Parenthetically, because they are often used interchangeably, I would like to distinguish between *mentally deficient*, a deficiency in development and competence due to pathology, and *mentally retarded*, a descriptive term for delayed development without reference to presumed causation.   I wish to keep these two terms separate with these differing meanings.   Now,

President Kennedy appointed his sister's husband, Sargent Shriver, to the directorship of the Office of Economic Opportunity. The Sargent Shrivers had chosen as their pediatrician a physician who had fathered a mentally deficient child. This physician, Dr. Robert F. Cooke, was asked to chair the White House Task Force on early child development, which recommended the establishment of the National Institute of Child Health and Human Development to promote research and, at the same time, recommend Project Head Start as an agency for action in this domain. At the time (1964), Cooke wrote President Kennedy that, "There already exists adequate understanding of the problems and processes involved to permit an immediate and massive intervention in the poverty cycle." Congress approved this recommendation, and Project Head Start was launched in 1965. The knowledge of plasticity and of class differences in the development-fostering quality of early experience made the value of equality of opportunity highly relevant to the inequalities of infancy and the preschool years. Family relationships with persons mentally deficient augmented the importance of this domain. The advent of men with such a family relationship coming into political power, the augmented importance of the value, brought support for both research and social action.

It is, however, the fate of Project Head Start that gives me the springboard for my message. Project Head Start had three main goals. One was health. Toward this goal, what Frankenberg would consider to be largely untested screening devices were devised and deployed. The second goal concerned community action. An effort was made to provide people from the poverty sector with more opportunity for influence on their own lives and their own institutions than they had ever had before. The third goal was education. Here the hope was to compensate the children, and particularly those from the poverty sector, for the deficiencies in the development-fostering quality of the experience of their first 4 years, and to do it in a summer or a year of nursery schooling. This, in gist, was the arrangement. It was also mandated that the program was to be evaluated for its effectiveness.

Now, when the evaluative studies were made, first by the Civil Rights Commission in 1967--which was not a very strong study--and then by the Westinghouse Report by Cicarelli's (1969) group at the Ohio University, the focus concerned only the educational goals. I dare not take the time here to recite the details. The upshot is that participants in Head Start programs exhibited greater scholastic progress than did non-participants from similar backgrounds while the programs were in progress. On the other hand, they failed to achieve the unrealistic goal of catching up with those from middle-class families. Moreover, those gains made during the Head Start year tended to dissipate and nearly all were lost by the end of the first grade. Against the unrealistic hopes from Project Head Start, these outcomes tended to damn the whole enterprise.

The principal reasons for this so-called failure[1] are easy to see. It is one thing to have knowledge that a given kind of reform should be possible; it is quite another one to know with precision how to effect it successfully. What we did in Project Head Start was to deploy the most prevalent kind of nursery schooling available. This kind had been developed under the

---

[1]I say "so-called failure" because at the time it was not yet known that participation on Project Head Start had a "sleeper effect" manifested as reduced assignment to classes in special education, reduced frequency of repeating grades, and reduced involvement in delinquency with court records (Lazar & Darlington, 1982). An economic analysis of such effects by Weber, Foster, and Weikart (1978) has shown the cost to be effective in the long run, for the savings more than equaled the costs of the early education of the Ypsilanti Perry Preschool Project.

influence of psychoanalytic thought for the children of
affluent parents, who could pay for it. The goal was
to enable such children to escape for part of the day
from their overcontrolling mothers so that they would
not develop such strong superegos as to make them
neurotic. This statement may be somewhat unfair, but
it helps make the point that the nursery schooling
deployed was poorly fitted to achieve the compensatory
educational goal of Head Start. When Head Start was
launched, no tested technology of compensatory
education existed. A good many of us feared that the
goals and expectations for the project were
unrealistic. We would have preferred to begin with a
program with a goal of developing a tested technology
of compensatory education before launching such a large
scale program of service.

A second reason for the so-called failure was
based on our attempt to achieve the community-action
goal by means of a "grass-roots" administrative
philosophy that brought parents from the poverty sector
directly into the Head Start programs as
paraprofessional aides in administration, teaching, and
transportation. The result, all too often, was chaos
(see Payne, Mercer, Payne, & Davison, 1973). This is
another reason that the kinds of experiences provided
to the children of Head Start programs were poorly
calculated to achieve the compensatory goal.

A third factor is moot, but I believe it has to be
taken seriously as an hypothesis. It is Epstein's
(1974a, 1974b) hypothesis of *phrenoblysis*--the
welling of the brain and the mind--for which there
are two kinds of evidence. The examinations of the
gains that children make in head size show spurts that
occur during ages 2-4, 6-8, 10-12, and 14-16 years of
age. Epstein has found similar spurts of gain in the
IQ that come during the same periods of those for head
size. From such evidence, Epstein has suggested that
there are periods in the course of development in which
the brain grows more rapidly than does the soma as a
whole, and that it is during these periods of
especially rapid growth or welling, that a child can
most rapidly achieve new knowledge and skills. I have

taken this hypothesis seriously enough to examine the
evidence   from   the Parent and Child   Centers   and   the
evidence from the Follow Through Program of Head Start.
It is true that the size of the gains one finds   during
the   period from 4 to 6 years of age are   smaller   than
those gained earlier or those gained later.   Although
other   factors   could well account for   such   consonant
findings,   it may well be that Project Head   Start   was
launched at the least fortunate age possible to achieve
its   educational goals.   Now the hopes created   by   the
combination   of   the knowledge of plasticity   in   early
development   and   the   appreciation   of   experiential
inequities   that   launched   Project   Head   Start   also
launched a renaissance in developmental psychology with
investigations   of the variations in   early   experience
across   the social classes and attempts to improve   the
technology   of compensatory education.   These are   not,
strictly speaking, part of Project Head Start, but they
do   represent   social   gains   from   the   Zeitgeist.
Moreover,   any   gains toward the Head   Start   goals   of
health   and community action have never been   assessed.
When   I wrote Julius Richmond in 1964 to   question   the
wisdom of launching such a large-scale service   program
as Project Head Start without first developing a tested
technology of compensatory education, he answered   that
the   health   gains   alone   would   easily   justify   the
project.   It seems to me that there is a lesson for the
policy makers.   Those making policy should demand   that
evaluative   investigations obtain evidence   of   effects
relevant to all of the goals of a reform.

REACTION TO THE SO-CALLED FAILURE
OF PROJECT HEAD START

Despite   such   weaknesses,   this so-called   failure   of
Project   Head Start has prompted a revisiting of   these
old beliefs in intelligence being essentially fixed and
development   being predetermined by heredity.   In   his
wellknown paper entitled "How Much Can We Boost IQ   and
Academic   Achievement?,"   Arthur   Jensen   (1969)   opened
with   this   sentence: "Compensatory education has   been
tried   and   it apparently has   failed"   (p. 2).   The
remainder   of his paper is   concerned with why.   In   a
long discourse on heredity and heritability, he finally

comes up with the proposition traditional in textbooks of psychology before World War II, namely, approximately 80% of the variance in the IQ is hereditary. Hence, only 20% of the total variance is left, so not much of an effect can be expected to result from compensatory education. This is the gist of his argument. Of course, Jensen also argues that racial and social class differences in performance on tests of intelligence and academic achievement are also largely hereditary. This argument from Jensen (1969, 1972, 1973) supported by the authority of Nobel Prize Physicist William Bradford Shockley and the partial support of Richard Herrnstein (1971, 1973), has rearoused the emotionality of the old harangues of the relative influences of heredity and environment that I had thought to be "by the boards." Not so, for I have been told on good authority that this paper of Jensen's was discussed by the Nixon cabinet in some detail, and that it was important in reducing the Nixon administration's enthusiasm for both the Office of Economic Opportunity and for compensatory early education. Furthermore, it has produced some vitriolic debates and aroused tremendous hostility on campuses (Herrnstein, 1973; Jensen, 1972). We now turn next to some definitions and definitional discussions.

SOME DEFINITIONS

Heredity is the process through which living beings that reproduce sexually pass the determiners of their basic characteristics from generation to generation. *Genetics* is the science through which this process is investigated. I make no attempt to give a course in genetics here, but a few concepts are important. These determiners of characteristics are *genes*, the units of genetic material. Each gene controls a biochemical step in metabolism. Genes (DNA and RNA) are arranged in linear chains called *chromosomes*, and their arrangement regulates the sequences of metabolic paths that lead in still poorly understood fashion from a fertilized ovum to a mature member of a species. The historical story of the gene from its introduction as a logical construct, termed a *Merkmal* by Gregor Mendel (Krizenecky, 1965), a *factor* by William Bateson (1916), and finally, a *gene* by Johannsen (1909), through its physical identification with the electron microscope, to the double-stranded model of DNA of Watson and Crick (1953) is one of the most dramatic stories of modern science. In human beings, each nucleus of each cell contains 22 pairs of chromosomes called *autosomes* with an additional pair of sex chromosomes. In women, the two sex chromosomes are similar, but in men they are different. One of these sex chromosomes in the male is full size, and it determines femaleness. The other is minute and determines maleness. As somatic cells divide, each chromosome of each pair divides and reduplicates itself. In the production of germ cells, ova and sperms, on the other hand, there is a reduction process in which the chromosome number is exactly halved. Each sperm and each ovum gets one of the chromosomes from each of the pairs present in each of the somatic cells. When a sperm enters an ovum in fertilization, each brings its compliment of 22 autosomes plus the sex chromosome into a new pairing. It is through this reduction and coming back together that the fertilized ovum which constitutes the beginnings of a new human organism has a genotype composed of chromosomes and genes from both parents. Whether the new human organism will be female or male depends on which kind of sex chromosome carried by the sperm enters the ovum.

The *genotype* is the compliment of chromosomes and genes that hold the determiners that guide the metabolic sequences in the maturation of the new individual. It was Johannsen (1909) who distinguished the *genotype* from the *phenotype*, which is the compliment of observable and measurable characteristics of the new individual. Traditionally, we have treated such measures as the IQ as if they concerned inherent genotypic potential. Actually, of course, all tests measure only the phenotype that is the product of the individual's genetic constitution as it has been modified through the changes elicited in efforts to adapt to the circumstances, biochemical, physical, and social, encountered in the course of living and developing. It is not the environmental circumstances per se that influence development; rather it is the changes that occur within the organism in the course of the adaptive efforts which are important. These adaptive efforts constitute the experience of the developing organism. It is thus that I dislike using the term *environment*; I much prefer to use the term *experience*. If the term *environment* is used, it means what I have described as experience. Thus, the so-called effects of environment are the accumulation of the modifications in sensorimotor organizations, knowledge, and skills that come about through these adaptive efforts.

Heritability, a key term for my message, is the term for that proportion of the variance in any observable or measurable phenotypic characteristic in the progeny from a population of individuals that is attributable to heredity, or, more precisely, to the variation of genotypes within the population. This is merely a definition. The process of assessing heritability calls for a methodology with assumptions. These assumptions are tricky because the influence of heredity and of experience are typically confounded in families. Superior genotypes are likely to go with the provision of experience with high development-fostering quality, and vice versa. In view of this tangle, various methodologies for separating the influences of heredity and experience have been used.

Perhaps the most direct is one employed in animal husbandry where the idea of heritability has a long history. I grew up on a farm. One of our operations was a dairy. There we were continually concerned to improve the milk crop. A standard method is to select for breeding purposes those cows of a breed with milk production well above average: say, for example, the top 3% that give, on the average, five gallons a day. To make the illustration simple, let us say that the average yield for the breed is three gallons a day, and that the standard deviation of the yield is one gallon. This means that our sample selected for breeding purposes averages two standard deviations above the mean in yield. We find that their offspring yield an average of four gallons of milk a day. Thus, they remain well above the average for the breed; in fact, their yield is one standard deviation above the average. This direct assessment of heritability is obtained by dividing the *selection gain* (i.e., one standard deviation) by the *selection differential* (i.e., two standard deviations). The result, for these illustrative data, is .5 or 50%. Such a direct measure of heritability could be expected to hold, however, for only an identical sampling of genotypes reared under exactly the same set of conditions.

With human beings, investigators have employed an indirect strategy for separating the intertwined influences of heredity and experience. In essence, this indirect strategy consists of statistical comparisons of the size of correlation between pairs of individuals with differing degrees of genetic relationship. Those most commonly used for such comparisons are the correlations between monozygotic or identical twins with the correlations for heterozygotic or fraternal twins. I make no attempt here to go through the mathematics of the formula for heritability (h^2). Instead, I refer the reader to the papers of Erlenmeyer-Kimling and Jarvik (1963) and Jensen (1967). Values of heritability indices for the intelligence quotient obtained through various assumptions about the degree of assortive mating range from a high of 93 to a low of 42 (see Jensen, 1967). These indices of heritability may be thought of as the percentages of the variance in the IQ attributable to heredity. The mean value of these heritability indices is 68. This mean is based on the assumption of a genetic correlation of 0.25 between two parents and, therefore, a genetic correlation between siblings of 0.55, is 0.68. Nevertheless, Jensen (1967), revisits the traditional estimate of 80 by taking as "most representative" those based on the data summarized by Erlenmeyer-Kimling and Jarvik (1963) "which represent the median values of all of the twin studies reported in the literature up to 1963" (p. 301). Thus, according to Jensen, the variance in the IQ contributed by heredity is four times that contributed by environment. Parenthetically, by using a somewhat different set of statistical assumptions to examine the overall pattern of correlations between relatives and non-relatives, Jencks (1972) came up with a value of 45 as seeming to more closely explain that pattern than does either a higher or lower estimate, but debates over values of heritability are irrelevant to my message.

Two statements can be made about estimates of educability based on indices of heritability: First, they are at best indirect when a direct approach to the assessment of educability exists, as we see later. Second, and at any rate, such estimates of educability are meaningless because indices of heritability are essentially irrelevant to educability. I explicate these statements.

Estimates of educability based on indices of heritability are indirect because they are derived from subtracting the percentage of variance due to heredity from the total variance in the IQ. Thus, such estimates of educability must come indirectly from subtracting an indirect assessment of the influence of heredity on the variance in the IQ from the total variance in the IQ. This strategy assumes the additivity of these influences of heredity (H) and of experience (E). Put in mathematical form, $H + E = 100\%$, so $100\% - H = E$. If $H = 80\%$, then $100\% - 80\% = 20\%$, and the influence of heredity is of the order of four times that of experience.

This approach to the assessment of educability not only piles indirect assessment on indirect assessment, but it assumes the additivity of the influences of heredity and experience. This assumption, originally made by R. A. Fisher (1918), is itself highly questionable (Hogben, 1939; Loevinger, 1943; McGuire & Hirsch, 1977). It is highly questionable because, as I have pointed out elsewhere (Hunt, 1961), neither heredity nor environment operates directly on such measures of behavior as the IQ, and because "it is highly unlikely that either heredity or environment are properly regarded even as scales, not to say scales based on family income, the vocabularies of father and mother, the Whittier scale, etc." (p. 329). As already noted, each of the various genes must influence behavioral measures indirectly through the metabolic paths that each of the genes is considered to control (Beadle, 1945). It is conceivable that genes may influence what is measured by tests of intelligence in affecting, for instance, the proportion of the brain that is unconnected with either receptor inputs or motor outlets (something akin to Hebb's, 1949, A/S ratio) or biochemical balances that help determine the ease with which cerebral systems are modified by experience. But such influence need be no monotonic function of the proportion of the genes shared by related individuals. Moreover, the presumption of additivity assumes, in turn, the absence of interaction between the influences of heredity and experience, and genetic research has turned up many findings, beginning with the original ones of Johannsen (1909), to disprove this assumption. In general, these findings show that the influence of differing environments varies with different genotypes (see Hirsch, 1972; Hunt, 1961). At best, then, any statement about the educability of individuals based on assessments of heritability is doubly indirect, and each indirection involves assumptions that are palpably false.

The educability of individuals or groups is basically irrelevant to assessments of heritability because the latter, by their very definition, hold only for the particular sample of genotypes and of environments or life histories on which they are based. The term *educability*, on the other hand, signifies potential for the achievement of competencies. This potential need not, and inevitably will not derive from either the average of or the variation in the development-fostering quality of experience represented in any conceivable sampling of genotypes and phenotypes to be obtained empirically for the purpose of correlating the IQs of identical and fraternal twins for comparison. Educability depends on the ingenuity of those who try to invent development-fostering experiences through childrearing procedures and those who set about to improve the technology of education.

Educability can be evident in either the rate of developmental achievement or the ultimate level of competence attained in any behavioral domain. No particular measures of heritability, based upon any given sampling of genotypes and environments or life histories, can possibly yield through subtraction from the total variance of the IQs in any population the ultimate level of achievement attainable through man's ingenuity in the educational domain (see also Hirsch, 1972).

There is yet another reason for the irrelevance of assessments of heritability to educability. Measures of heritability concern the contribution of the variation in genotypes to the variation in any phenotypic characteristic, including intelligence as measured by the IQ. Thus, the emphasis is on what causes variance in the phenotype. Educability is concerned with attaining those abilities, attitudes, kinds of knowledge, kinds of skills, and values demanded by the standards of a culture. When he introduced the measurement of twins into the investigative strategy for determining the relative importance of heredity and environment, E. L. Thorndike (1905) made this statement: "In the actual race of life, which is not to get ahead, but to get ahead of somebody, the chief determining factor is heredity" (p. 553). This notion that life is a race to get ahead of somebody reflects the idea of the struggle for existence that emerged from the first studies of human population in relation to the food supply made during the 17th century in the stormy society of pre-revolutionary France. This idea of the struggle was formulated most clearly in his famous *An Essay on the Principles of Population* by Malthus in 1798. It figured heavily in Darwin's *Origin of the Species* in 1859. It was central to Francis Galton's study of *Hereditary Genius* in 1869, the work that launched the study of individual differences and put the emphasis on heredity in their causation. Although it is hard to escape evidences of such a struggle, one can also readily find a political basis for the emphasis on heredity as a defense against the democratization of class privileges by attributing them to nature. Although competition plays a role in life, I believe the goal of living is much less "to get ahead of somebody" than it is to achieve a respectable and rewarding outlet for one's talents in the scheme of things. Thus, the relevant standard is less one of competition and variance than one of level of achievements required for productive participation in the mainstream of one's culture. Thus, the goal of educability is not to be defined competitively in terms of position in a sample or population, but by the attainment of those abilities, attitudes, kinds of knowledge, kinds of skills and values required for productive and respected participation in the mainstream of a culture. Thus, what is important for education is not individual differences in achievement reflected in measures of the variance, but rather the achievement of a functional and specifiable level of performance or standard of excellence in performance. Because measures of heritability aim to account for variance in performance or achievement, they are irrelevant for a second reason to the functional standards of educational achievement.

THE RANGE OF REACTION

Now, do geneticists have anything to say about educability? The answer is: They do indeed. Their answer resides in their concept of the "range of reaction" authored by Richard Woltereck in 1909. Woltereck was a botanist. A major share of the work on the range of reaction has been done by botanists, probably because they have the advantages of plants that clone. This permits control of heredity because an investigator has a substantial number of plants with the same genotype. Samples of plants from a given clone can be reared under differing conditions, and various resulting phenotypical characteristics can be observed and measured. In fact, it was through such a strategy that the Danish botanist, William Johannsen (1903/1959) demonstrated that plants with the same heredity would differ in physical appearance if they are reared under differing circumstances, and that the amount of difference is a function of the strain (genotype). It was such findings that led him to his distinction between the *genotype* (i.e., genetic composition) and *phenotype* (i.e., the observable physical characteristics of the organism) and his idea of interaction between heredity and environment. Such findings also led Woltereck to his concept of the range of reaction. Although educators and psychologists have not often used it, this concept is far from new.

By definition, the *range of reaction* is that variation in any observable, measurable phenotypic characteristic that a given genotype can produce in response to variations in the environment--or life experience. Botanists typically investigate the effects of variation in such environmental factors as altitude or chemistry of the soil. In the case of abilities and motives in human beings, what is relevant is not such distal factors as parental income, number of books in a home, and other social-class variables, but rather the intimate, proximate experiences which determine the sequence of adaptive modifications in abilities, motives, understandings, and values as the infant becomes a toddler, and the toddler becomes a child. What strategies of investigation does this definition of the range of reaction suggest?

One would consist of rearing homozygotic or identical twins apart. Such studies have been done, but they have usually employed the correlational strategy. One by Holzinger (1929), however, reported the maximal difference between pairs of such twins reared apart to be 17 points of IQ. He also reported the correlation of pair differences in IQ with the amount of contrast between the environmental circumstances in the respective homes of the twins being reared apart to be 0.70. According to correlational logic, this finding would suggest that approximately half of the variance ($r^2 = .49$) in the IQs of the sample of identical twins would be attributed to these differences in environmental circumstances. Actually, however, even for that pair of twins in Holzinger's sample with a difference in IQ of 17 points, only a moderate degree of difference is evident in the development-fostering quality of the experiences in their life histories. The twin version of the investigative strategy suggested by the range of reaction would have one of a pair of identical twins reared in an orphanage such as that in Iowa from which Skeels and Dye (1939) transferred their sample of infants to a ward for moron women or such as that discovered by Dennis (1960) in Tehran where 60% of the infants in their second year were not yet sitting up and 80% of those in their fourth year were not yet walking. The other twin in each pair should be reared through toddlerhood, according to my methodological fantasy, in the fashion that Myrtle McGraw (1935) reared Johnny. This twin would also have experiences to foster vocal imitation and semantic mastery such as we employed with our fifth wave at the Tehran Orphanage (Hunt, Mohandessi, Ghodssi, & Akiyama, 1976). Thereafter through the first decade, this other ' twin would be provided with the kind of educational experiences that James Mill and his wife provided for their son, John Stuart. Who knows how large the differences in the IQs from pairs of identical twins with such widely differing life histories might be? For reasons ethical and humanitarian this is but an idle fantasy. It is worth noting in passing, however, that I would expect the genotypes of the various pairs of homozygotic twins to make a substantial contribution to the size of the difference obtained (see Hunt, 1961, p 323ff).

Because the investigative strategy of deliberately rearing pairs of homozygotic twins apart with markedly differing life histories is out of the question, let me turn to an alternative approach. This alternative consists of comparing the means and standard deviations of such measures of phenotypic competence as the IQ in groups of children from the same population who are reared under differing circumstances. There can be, of course, no single value for the range of reaction. Just as any index of heritability holds only for the particular sample of genotypes and the particular sample of environments on which it is based, so does the range of reaction. The range of reaction must be at least as large, however, as the maximum obtained difference between the measures of phenotypic achievement for any two groups of children from the same population who are reared under differing conditions. By increasing the difference in the development-fostering quality of the experience induced in groups of children, one can always hope to increase the difference between the means for the phenotypic achievement. You will see that such differences between the means of phenotypic achievements have the essence of relevance for educability. What I wish to do next is to present some illustrative data based on this strategy of investigation. Because there are as yet very few data from this strategy that I am suggesting for the investigation of educability, I present some of my own.

Findings from the Strategy Suggested by the Concept of the Range of Reaction

These data are outcome findings from our interventions in the childrearing at the Orphanage of the Queen Farah Pahlavi Charity Society in Tehran (Hunt et al., 1976). The purpose of our interventions was to foster psychological development in the successive samples, or waves, of infant foundlings who served as our subjects. In the terms of the categories of public health programs I would call our program a pilot study despite the fact that it took place over a period of 8 years. It is merely a demonstration of what can be done, but it is not a demonstration of all that can be done, by a long shot.

In terms of the requirement for "informed consent," I do not know how our program would fare. All 66 infants who served as subjects in our program were foundlings. There were no parents or relatives to give consent. The people who actually consented to have them serve as subjects were Mrs. Khozeimeh Alam, Vice Chairman of the Queen's Charity Society, the Queen Mother, and my collaborator, Mehri Ghodssi, who directed the orphanage in which our program was conducted. Despite problems with this matter of informed consent, we were not unmindful of ethical issues. Because we questioned the ethics of withholding arrangements that might elicit development-fostering experiences, we have not employed contemporary control and experimental groups.   Rather, we have used what I like to call "wave design."   We started with a control group of 15 infants who were reared according to the customary childrearing practices of the orphanage.   The only intervention consisted of repeated examination with our ordinal scales (Uzgiris & Hunt, 1975). These examinations were made every other week during the first year of the infants' lives, and every fourth week thereafter until they were transferred to another orphanage for toddlers or young children.   The 15 infants in this control wave were selected by Mehri Ghodssi, the director, with the counsel of a pediatrician. They were selected from those no more than a month old in the Municipal Orphanage of Tehran to be without detectable pathology. The infants in each successive sample or wave were obtained in this same fashion, so all the infants do come from the same population, but they were not randomly selected. We had to take all available infants over a period of 2 months each time we needed a new sample or wave. Unfortunately, we have no information about the characteristics of either parent of any of the foundlings.

Now for the independent variable. Wave I, the controls, consisted of these 15 foundlings who got only the repeated testing common to all waves. Wave II consisted of 10 foundlings. These got what was intended to be audiovisual enrichment, but it proved to be abortive because the person who was then my resident director failed to keep the equipment operating.   I fear we actually did some damage to these infants. Wave III also consisted of 10 foundlings. These got untutored human enrichment. Instead of providing only a single caretaker for 10 infants, we provided three, but we gave these caretakers no instruction in how to foster development in the infants under their care. They simply did whatever came naturally, and all three were equally responsible for all 10 infants. Wave IV consisted of 20 foundlings who received the schedule of audiovisual enrichment intended for Wave II. The audio portion consisted of tape-recorded music and mother talk. The infants could obtain 15 seconds or so of this input at will by moving their arms, which were connected with plastic bracelets and strings to switches that turned on the speakers attached to the sides of their cribs. The visual portion consisted of motion in mobiles hung over the cribs which the infant could obtain by jiggling her or his body. There were also other responsive toys provided for these infants. Wave V consisted of 11 foundlings who received the "tutored human enrichment." The infant-caretaker ratio was reduced from 10/1 to 3 or 2/1 and the caretakers were taught Badger's (1971a, 1971b) learning programs for infants and toddlers. These programs were supplemented, however, with instructions for experiences calculated to foster both vocal imitation and semantic mastery (ability to name) those parts of the body and items of clothing and actions involved in the caretaking operations. Thus, the independent variable consists of these interventions in the caretaking operations. Each wave followed the preceding by a little more than a year and a half.

The dependent variables derived from the repeated testing with our Piaget/inspired ordinal scales: (I) Object Permanence, (II) Obtaining Desired Environmental Events, (III-A) Vocal Imitation, (III-B) Gestural Imitation, (IV) Operational Causality, (V) Object Relations in Space, and (VI) Schemes for Relating to Objects. These scales are ordinal in nature in the sense that they consist of sequences of progressively more advanced behavioral landmarks elicited by situations arranged in standard fashion. Since they are ordinal in nature, they permit a strategy for assessment that differs from that of mental age and intelligence quotient. In the testing, the examiners start each infant with steps on each scale on which they succeeded in the preceding testing. The examiner then proceeds with successive landmarks on each scale until the infant has failed two in succession. Repeated examining with such a longitudinal strategy as we have employed permits one to use the age at which each child first demonstrates achievement of each of the landmarks on each of the scales, or in the case of a longitudinal strategy with a single testing, we have used the mean and the standard deviation of the ages of children at a given level defined as having passed all steps below, and failed those above.

Those interested in the overall outcome findings from this program of research should consult the paper describing it (Hunt et al., 1976). Here, I limit my concern to the means and standard deviations of the ages in weeks at which the top steps on these Uzgiris/Hunt Scales were achieved by the controls (the infants in Waves I and II), the mean ages at which these same steps were achieved by the foundling in Wave V who got the tutored human enrichment, and the differences between the means. These appear in Table 5.1.

The performance of the foundlings in Wave V differ in two ways from those in Waves I and II. First, whereas all of the 11 infants in Wave V demonstrated achievement of the top step on each scale, substantial portions of those in Waves I and II failed to do so before they were transferred at an age of approximately 169 weeks. Thus, before transfer only 15 of the 25 managed to demonstrate the retrieval of a desired object that had been hidden in a container after the container had disappeared under three covers by reversing the order of search. Only 10 of the 25 demonstrated genuine imitation of the pronunciation of unfamiliar words. And, for Scale VI, only 2 of the 25 spontaneously named an object. Second, even those who demonstrated the critical behaviors for the top steps on these scales did so at average ages older than did those of Wave V. In order to make overall age comparisons, I devised an estimate that used the mean age of transfer for the age of achievement of each child who failed to demonstrate achievement of the top steps on these Scales. Because these infants had not yet demonstrated these top steps, this is a very conservative estimate on which to base comparisons. Even so, the mean ages at which the infants of Wave V achieved these top steps differ much from the estimated mean ages of their achievement by the controls in Waves

TABLE 5.1

Mean Ages in Weeks of Achieving Top Steps on Uzgiris-Hunt Scales by Waves I, II, and Wave V with the Differences Between Them

		Waves			Difference in Mean Age	Saving in Mean of Attainment	Difference in Mean IQ-ratio
	I & II		V				
Scales	Estimated[b] N[a]	Mean Age	N	Mean Age			
I. Object Permanence	15	127.2	11	93.0	34.2	26.73	32
II. Development of Means	12	148.2	11	94.0	54.2	36.57	41
III-A. Vocal Imitation	10	155.6	11	93.0	62.6	40.23	49
III-B. Gestural Imitation	8	157.6	11	71.0	86.6	54.95	83
IV. Operational Causality	14	138.2	11	85.0	53.2	38.49	40
V. Object Relations in Space	12	140.3	11	88.0	52.8	37.50	35
VI. Schemes for Relating to Objects	2	169.0	11	90.0	79.0	46.75	45

a The number that actually demonstrated the critical behavior for the top step.

b In estimating the mean age, the mean age of transfer (169 weeks) has been used in the averages of the mean ages for achieving the top step.

I and II.   These differences range from a low of   34.2
weeks   for the Scale of Object Permanence to a high   of
86.6 weeks for gestural imitation, and 79 weeks   for
schemes   for   relating to objects.   The mean   of   these
mean age-differences in weeks is 60.37.

Before I continue, it should be noted that the top
step   on   the Scale of Object Permanence for   which   we
have the smallest difference in mean age of   attainment
(34.2   weeks) at the Tehran Orphanage is   actually   the
one on which we have the largest obtained difference in
mean   age   when   all of the studies we   have   done   are
considered   (see Hunt, Paraskevopoulos, Schickedanz,   &
Uzgiris, 1975).   The largest mean age at which this top
step   of   object permanence has been   attained   is   184
weeks, and that by children of the Municipal   Orphanage
in Athens, Greece.   The youngest mean age at which this
landmark   has been attained is 73 weeks, and that by   8
consecutive   children   born to the parents   of   poverty
served   by the Parent and Child Center in Mt.   Carmel,
Illinois.   Thus,   the maximum obtained   difference   in
mean   ages of attaining top-level object permanence   is
111   weeks   rather than the 34 weeks   obtained   in   the
Tehran Orphanage.

Inasmuch   as   it   is commonly presumed that   the
development-fostering quality of experience in   middle-
class   homes   approximates or at least approaches   the
optimum   (see e.g., Jensen, 1969), it is   worth   noting
that   the   educational daycare at Mt.   Carmel   enabled
these   8 consecutive infants born to the   parents   from
the   poverty   sector   served by the Parent   and   Child
Center to attain top-level object permanence at a   mean
age (73 weeks) 25 weeks younger than did 12 home-reared
infants (mean = 98.31 weeks) from predominantly middle-
class families in Worcester, Massachusetts without such
an intervention.   Thus, these infants of unskilled   and
often   unemployed   parents   had experience in   their
educational   daycare that served to advance   their
attainment of top-level object permanence ahead of that
by infants from predominantly middle-class families   by
nearly half a year (25 weeks).

A   digression   concerning   the   nature   of   the

experience that seems to have produced this advance may be of interest. The educational daycare at Mt. Carmel was based upon Badger's (1971a, 1971b) training programs for infants and toddlers. The mothers who served as the teacher-caregivers at the Parent and Child Center had been taught by Badger to arrange situations for their infant pupils to keep them interested rather than either bored or distressed by overmatching. In retrospect, the surprising advancement in object permanence appears to have been a serendipitous outcome of experience with a shape box. During a visit when this educational daycare was being initiated, Badger and I found the infants in cribs along the wall as are typically seen in orphanages. We looked at each other with dismay. When we noted that the floor was well carpeted, I suggested, "Let's get them on the floor." In a search for something of interest, I happened to select the shape box. The infant whom I was tending could not manage to hold the round block sufficiently vertical to get it through the round hole in the top of the box. It seemed to me that he might be able to manage a ping-pong ball, so we got one. At first, I helped him hold it over the round hole. It disappeared, making a noise as it hit the bottom of the box. Then I helped the infant use his left hand to lift the hinged top. When he saw the ping-pong ball, he went for it immediately. With several such repetitions, he learned to lift the top and retrieve the ball on his own. Thereafter, it became his preoccupation, and he persisted long after I ceased to be interested. Neither Badger nor I thought much of this incident until after the bi-weekly testing had uncovered the surprisingly rapid development of object permanence. Then, during a regular teaching visit, one of the caregivers remarked on the avid interest of the infants in the shape box. With the increasing complexity of the task afforded by round holes, square holes, rectangular holes, and triangular holes with blocks of corresponding shapes, these boxes proved a favorite preoccupation of these infants from the time they could sit up at about 25 weeks.

After the fact, it is easy to see that the

experience provided by this shape box could readily foster object construction. From the ping-pong ball to the cylindrical block to the square block to the rectangular block, and so on, the disappearance through the hole in the top of the box makes a noise. The child can then act to lift the lid, and this act enables him to see again the block that had disappeared. Insofar as this generalizes, and it certainly generalized not only to the regular testing situation, which constitutes the criterion of top-level object construction on our Scale of Object Permanence, but also to others in which a desired object was made to disappear into a little chalk box which, in turn, was made to disappear in a series of tall wastebaskets, it fosters the development of object permanence.

Now let us return to the significance of these differences in mean ages of attaining the top steps on our sensorimotor scales. What does it mean to say that the maximal obtained difference in mean age of attaining the top step on the Scale of Object Permanence is 111 weeks, which is approximately 26 months, or more than 2 years? How large a gain is this?

Because we have no ready-made frame of reference for such answers, I have sometimes, for communication purposes sake, transformed such differences in mean ages to one of difference in points of the IQ-ratio for attaining top-level landmarks on these Scales. In order to do this, we use as the norm, or mental age, the mean age at which those home-reared children without intervention attained the top-levels of object permanence. The mean age of top-level object permanence for such home-reared children as we have tested from working-class families in Athens, Greece, and from predominantly middle-class families in Worcester, Massachusetts, rounds to 110 weeks. This is a mental-age equivalent. If one divides this 110 weeks for attaining top-level object permanence, for example, by the mean chronological age of 73 weeks at which top-level object permanence was attained by those infants receiving educational day-care at Mt. Carmel, and then multiplies by 100, one obtains a mean IQ-ratio of 150. When one also divides this mental age of 110 weeks by

184 weeks, the mean age of attainment for the children
of the Municipal Orphanage in Athens, their IQ-ratio
for top-level object permanence averages approximately
60.   Now, by subtracting the latter from the former,
one obtains a maximal obtained difference (150 - 60 =
90) of 90 points of IQ-ratio for attaining the top step
on the scale for this branch of sensorimotor
development. Because the children at the Municipal
Orphanage in Athens do not come from the same
population as do the eight offspring of the unskilled
parents served by the Parent and Child Center of Mt.
Carmel, this difference fails technically to fulfill
the definitional requirements for the range of
reaction. On the other hand, it is hard to see why one
should expect the genotypic potential for object
construction in these children from the bottom of the
socio-economic-educational scale in Mt. Carmel to be
any greater than that of the largely illegitimate
children at the Municipal Orphanage in Athens, Greece.

Because it is common to believe that the quality
of development-fostering experience provided by
educated families of the middle-class approaches the
optimum, it is of interest to note that the education
day-care enabled the Mt. Carmel infants to attain the
top step on the Scale of Object Permanence at a mean
age (73 weeks) only 74.5% of that (98 weeks) of the
infants from predominantly middle-class parents in
Worcester. We can also compare the estimated mean IQ-
ratios for top-level object permanence in the Mt.
Carmel children with that of the Worcester children.
Because the IQ-ratio for the former is 150 and that of
the latter is 114 (110/98), the educational daycare at
Mt. Carmel appears to have advanced the rate of object
construction in these offspring of uneducated parents
of poverty served by the Parent and Child Center at Mt.
Carmel, by 38 points of IQ-ratio ahead of that for the
home-reared offspring of predominantly middle-class
families in Worcester.

Now look again at Table 5.1 and this time at the
IQ-ratios derived from the differences in mean ages of
attaining the top steps on our ordinal scales. These
range from 32 points for object permanence to 83 points

for gestural imitation. The infants in Wave V show an average superiority of 46 IQ points over the controls (Waves I and II).

These transformations have been made only to permit the use of a familiar frame of reference in order to get a sense of how much variation in experience can modify the average rate of development in groups of infants.[2] These IQ-ratios indicate only variations in average rates of achievement from past experience in groups of infants. Such performances of the infants on our ordinal scales are useful for determining the kinds of experience that are development-fostering. Knowledge of what fosters and what does not is necessary for developing a pedagogy for infancy and early childhood. On the other hand, these IQ-ratios should not be considered to have implications for the rate of future achievement nor for the ultimate level of the competence to be achieved. Although it appears to become progressively more difficult to make up deficiencies of achievement as the years pass, future development depends on the pedagogic quality of the experience to be elicited by those circumstances these children will encounter in their lives.

VARIATIONS IN LANGUAGE AND
MOTIVATIONAL ACHIEVEMENT: TEHRAN

Now consider the variations in language and

---

[2]Please note that this IQ-ratio is not an equivalent of a ratio-IQ, for the latter is based on the mean ages of attaining a sampling of items on the standard tests where the means are based on substitutive averaging (see Coombs, 1950), whereas the IQ-ratio is based on attaining a given landmark on a single branch of sensorimotor development. Since the first version of this chapter was written, my collaborator in developing these ordinal scales, Ina Uzgiris, has convinced me that this way of achieving communication probably contributes as much or more error and confusion than valid communication.

motivational   achievement   associated   with   the
interventions in the childrearing at the orphanage   in
Tehran.   For these we have no metrics to manipulate.

Perhaps I should make clear that I did not start
the program in Tehran in order to study the development
of language.   As a matter of fact, I started it in
order to test some of my notions about intrinsic
motivation (see Hunt, 1960, 1963a, 1963b, 1965, 1966a,
1966b).   The significance of the program for language
development emerged gradually.   The most   relevant
comparisons are those among the controls (Waves I and
II   combined),   Wave III,   with   untutored   human
enrichment, and Wave V with tutored human   enrichment.
It is the dramatic influence of a deliberate effort to
facilitate language acquisition by fostering vocal
imitation and semantic mastery through what we taught
the caregivers of the infants in Wave V that is most
significant for theory of language   development.
Serendipitously, this experience provided by   the
caregivers whom we taught resulted also in marked
improvements in facial expression,   motivational
initiative and social attractiveness.

In the controls (Waves I and II), both expressive
and   receptive language were essentially absent at the
time of transfer from the orphanage for nurslings to
one for toddlers at an age of 169 weeks, which is more
than 3 years of age.   The absence of expressive
language was evident from two facts.   First, these
children almost never vocalized unless they were in
distress.   Then they cried.   They did not, with the
exception of two who had become special pets of a
caregiver during illness, use vocal means to obtain
their desires in their interaction with   either
caregivers or each other.   Second, only the two who had
been pets ever spontaneously named an object in the
examining situation.

My evidence for saying that receptive language was
also essentially absent at 3 years is somewhat less
solid, and is based on what I like to call "horseback
research." During one of my visits when these children
were in the latter part of their third year, I would

stand before them in the playroom and ask one of their
familiar caregivers or examiners to tell a child to "go
to the man." I would stand there passively while
looking at the target child with an expression intended
to show interest. Only the two who had been pets ever
moved toward me in this crude test of receptive
language. On the other hand, if I pointed to one of
the children and extended my arms in inviting fashion,
the child would either come forward or her or his
countenance would droop and she or he would withdraw
further. Either way, they seemed to respond with
understanding to the gesture, but not to spoken
language. In another such crude test, I would place a
piece of paper on the floor beside one of the low
tables. Then I would request one of the examiners or
caregivers to tell a child to "pick up the paper and
put it on the table." Again, they failed to respond.
On the other hand, if I could get one of these children
to come to me by gesturing, I could then point to the
paper, point to the table, and make a motion from the
paper to the table, and perhaps repeat the sequence two
or three times. I could thereby get about half of the
children to pick up the paper and put it on the table.
From the standpoint of the theory of language, I am
inclined to feel that what Norm Chomsky (1965, 1969)
has termed *deep structure*, is really cognitive
understanding of a situation and of the action in that
situation. It is this cognitive understanding that the
child symbolizes in language. In the hierarchy of
acquisition, semantics is fundamental before syntax.
Moreover, phonemics is fundamental before semantics.
These children of Waves I and II showed some
understanding of what can be symbolized through
gesture, but they had essentially no semantic mastery
of these cognitions, no understanding of language
symbols.

Next, consider the linguistic behavior of the
children in Wave V. All 11 of them had spontaneously
named a familiar object in the testing situation before
age 21 months, and several of them at ages considerably
younger. Their average age of achieving this top
landmark on the Scale of Schemes for Relating to

Objects was 90 weeks, or 20.76 months. I can dramatize this contrast by relating some of the experiences with these children in Wave V when I first saw them.

When I arrived for what proved to be my last planning visit in October of 1974, it was the Shah's birthday. The next day was his son's birthday, so I had to twiddle my thumbs for 2 days before I could go to this orphanage of the Queen Farah Pahlavi Charity Society to see these youngsters whose performances I had been following through monthly reports. When I finally got to the orphanage, the customary tea ceremony was prolonged inordinately. When Miss Sakhai, the principal examiner, finally came for me, she took me to the door of a playroom in which the pairs or, in one case a triad, of youngsters were arranged in a semi-circle in front of their respective caregivers. As I entered the room, a signal was given, and in unison they called out "ahllo." Then I learned why the tea ceremony had been so prolonged. The caregivers had been trying to get the children to say in unison, "Hello, Dr. Hunt." Five syllables turned out to be too many, so they settled for "hello." Even so, this was a startling contrast with anything I had ever seen and heard before.

Immediately after the greeting, Cambiz, then at 22 months and the oldest, came to me requesting in both language (Farsi, the language of Iran) and gesture, to be picked up. Here was evidence of such trust as I had never seen before in an orphanage-reared child. When he resisted being put down as I was invited to see the new examining room, I carried him along. Through a window opposite the door through which we entered the examining room, there was an irrigation sprayer. Cambiz saw it and immediately began to cry out with enthusiasm: "Ab, ab, ab." *Ab* is the Farsi word for water. Cambiz was naming spontaneously with a vengeance at 22 months of age. Cambiz was said to be a very good imitator, so, impulsively, I attempted to teach him to say "water." I called his name, and once he was attending, said, "water." But Cambiz's attention to me was brief. Instead, his left arm was reaching toward the sprayer as he continued to say,

"Ab, ab, ab." After several such efforts had demonstrated that keeping his attention on the imitation game would be impossible so long as he could see the sprayer, I carried him back into the hall out of sight of the sprayer. Then, I repeated, "Cambiz, water." Cambiz looked at me and replied, "awter." He omitted in his imitation the sound of the initial consonant symbolized by the letter w; yet once I had modeled the syllable, "wuh, wuh," a few times, with him responding, and then returned to "water," he responded with a pronunciation of the word water as plainly as my own with almost the same intonation. Later, my spectacles intrigued Cambiz. He quickly picked them off my face while saying, "Enack, enack, enack." Again, spontaneous naming of the Farsi word for spectacles. He also attempted to put my glasses on his own face. Again, impulsively, I attempted to teach him to say the English word, "glasses." It was impossible to get his attention on the imitation game so long as he was preoccupied with manipulating and naming "enack." Putting my glasses into their case and the case out of sight in my pocket was to no avail. Cambiz quickly demonstrated top-level object permanence by searching under my jacket for the glasses case, all the while saying, "enack, enack, enack." After giving the glasses to someone else and moving out of sight of the person holding them, it was possible to get Cambiz interested in the imitation game. I would say, "Cambiz, glasses." At first, Cambiz responded with, "asses." When I slowed my vocalization of the word, glaaasses, on the second and third presentations, Cambiz responded with "lasses." Because he had omitted the double consonant combination of gl, I modeled repeatedly, "Gl, gl, gl," and then "glasses," with the double consonant combination followed by a prolongation of the a sound and then the ses. Cambiz responded, "Glaaasses." After this, I could shorten the duration of the aaa, and Cambiz pronounced the word glasses as clearly as I had. At this point, Professor Mohandessi noted, with some surprise at Cambiz's performance, that such a consonant combination as gl does not exist in Farsi, and that it is especially difficult for Persians to combine two consonants without a vowel between them.

My reply came with a grin. "Cambiz does not yet know your phonetic rule; he managed to get it in no more than a dozen presentations."

Now an experience of a few minutes later with Shabnam, a little girl in her 18 month. I was holding her, while Miss Sakhai, the chief examiner, was showing me that she could imitate the names of all the children in the group. Although my Farsi is almost nil, Shabnam's imitative responses seemed to match the sounds modeled by the examiner almost perfectly. Finally, in naming her playmates, they came to Yass. Because Yass had been adopted the week before my arrival, I never saw her. When the examiner said, "Yass," Shabnam's manner changed abruptly. She dropped the imitation game, twisted her body in my arms, and reached her arm out toward the door behind me and said, "Yass rafteh." This is the Farsi equivalent of "Yass gone." It is a sentence. Moreover, it reflected an actual state of affairs. Yass, Shabnam's closest friend, had been taken by her adoptive parents, with father in the diplomatic service, to England a week or two earlier.

Shabnam had never been taught to say a sentence. Her caregiver had done her best to keep the infants in her charge interested, and she was said to have followed well the instructions for fostering vocal imitation and semantic mastery.

Our effort to facilitate language acquisition was based on a hypothetical scenario. According to this scenario, the acquisition of phonetics is based heavily on imitation and imitative skill. Semantics derive from a combination of association of objects and events with the phonetic patterns heard as the object appears or the event happens. Syntax begins as a creative act on the part of the infant in which her or his achievements in phonetics and semantics are combined in the interest of an intention to communicate something of which the child has cognitive appreciation.

Imitation has an epigenesis of its own (Uzgiris & Hunt, 1975), in which the infant first becomes familiar with sound patterns, is attracted by the familiar

patterns, responds vocally to them in what is termed
vocal pseudo imitation, gradually becomes interested in
unfamiliar patterns, responds to them, approximates
examiner modeling of them, and finally becomes able to
produce good copies of modelings of several unfamiliar
syllables with little or no repetition.

The easiest way to start this process of
development is to imitate nondistressful vocalizing of
infants. The fact that the infant has just uttered a
sound renders it familiar. Hearing another person
imitate her or his utterance is highly reinforcing, and
is the easiest way to initiate interactive games with
an infant. Thus, the caregivers in Tehran were taught
to imitate the spontaneous vocalizations of the
foundlings in their charge in order to get vocal games
going. They were to imitate first the cooing sounds,
and then the babbling sounds.

When an infant had mastered several babbling
patterns, the caretaker was to introduce into the
imitation game a procedure of "follow-the-leader" (see
Hunt, 1981). In this procedure, the caregiver got a
vocal game going with one of the familiar babbling
patterns, shifted to another, and then as the child
followed, the examiner shifted to yet another.

Once an infant in her care had achieved skill at
following the leader, the caregiver was to introduce
new phonemic combinations that she had not yet heard
the infant make. This change gave the caregiver an
opportunity to lead rather than merely respond to the
vocalizing of her charge. It also led to genuine
imitation through which she could increase the phonemic
repertoire of the infants in her charge.

The procedure for fostering semantic mastery
consisted chiefly of sharpening up the bases for
association of the sounds of heard words with concrete
experiences. We considered an experience of feeling a
part of her or his body touched to be maximally
discernible. The illustrative paradigm involved ear-
washing. The caregiver was to say: "Now, I am going
to wash your ear." As her vocal emphasis hit the word
ear, she was instructed to have the washcloth contact

the anatomical ear. Such procedures were to be used throughout the caregiving operations.

Because I observed just these procedures in operation after operation, I am confident that these children had very little or no tutelage in sentence structure. Yet, when Shabnam heard the examiner say the name, Yass, it prompted her to leave the imitation game, and to symbolize in language her understanding that Yass was no longer in their midst. Even though this sentence demonstrated the top-level of object relations to space, it was several months before Shabnam was credited with this achievement because the eliciting situation arranged by the examiner called for indicating the whereabouts of familiar persons rather than the absence of familiar persons.

As the examiner was showing me that Shabnam could imitate the names of her features and the parts of her body, and so on, she pointed to the various parts of her body and the various pieces of clothing that she was wearing. Because the examiner's English was shallow and I have almost no command of Farsi, we had some difficulty with communication. Finally, I asked how to say: "What is it?" What I heard can be transliterated as three syllables: "In chi aay?" When I gently pulled Shabnam's hair and asked, "In chi aay?" she replied, "muh." The examiner nodded, for *muh* is the Farsi word for hair. In this fashion, I learned that Shabnam at less than 18 months of age, had a vocabulary of the order of 50 words for objects involved in caregiving. In the course of a few days, I was able to demonstrate in similar fashion that all 10 of the remaining 11 knew the names not only of the parts of their bodies, but the names for the pieces of clothing they wore, the foods they ate, and also for a good many of the actions involved in their caregiving. They all demonstrated expressive vocabularies of at least 50 objects without any effort to test their limits.

A few days later, I found the caregiver of Monee picking up the rings of the stacking toy. As she picked up each ring, she named its color for Monee to

imitate.   I   wondered   immediately   if   Monee   was
developing semantic mastery of colors.   After   learning
how to ask in Farsi: "What color is it?" I   proceeded
to hand Monee each of the rings on the stacking toy   as
I   asked   the   question, "What   color   is   it?"   Monee
responded   correctly   with   the   names   for   red,   yellow,
green, and blue.   I wondered if these were merely names
for   these   rings, or if Monee   had   achieved   semantic
mastery of the elementary abstraction of color.   So,   I
proceeded   to   carry him to the hall where   there   were
colorful   pictures   on the walls.   There   I   pointed   to
spots in the pictures and asked, "What color is   that?"
Monee   responded   correctly for   these   four   primaries
repeatedly.   He had clearly achieved semantic   mastery
for   color. Cambiz and Parviz also named   colors,   but
not   correctly   so   consistently as   Monee.   When   one
considers   that only about a fourth of the   4-year-olds
participating   in   Head   Start   classes   show   such
expressive   semantic mastery for colors (Kirk, Hunt,   &
Lieberman,   1975),   semantic   mastery   of   such   an
elementary   abstraction   at the age of 2 years   may   be
seen   as   no   mean   achievement,   and   especially   in
orphanage-reared foundlings.

Although   we   have no nice quantification   of   the
degree   to   which   the   language   achievements   of   the
controls   (Waves   I and II) differ from   those   of   the
infants   in Wave V, it is obviously tremendous.   It   is
also worth noting that at about age 2, the children   of
Wave   V   were also equal to or superior in   clarity   of
imitative   pronunciation to those in Wave III   who   got
untutored human enrichment in language skills and   were
older   by between 2.5 and 3 years than those of Wave   V.
These facts suggest that what we taught the   caregivers
to   do in order to foster vocal imitation and   semantic
mastery   did indeed provide experiences   important   for
language acquisition.

MOTIVATIONAL INITIATIVE
AND SOCIAL ATTRACTIVENESS

The   experiences that we taught the caregivers   of   the
children   in   Wave   V to provide also   had   a   marked
influence   on   the   facial   expressions,   the   motivational

initiative, and the social attractiveness of their charges. Comparing the facial expressions and the gestures in pictures of some of the control infants (Waves I and II) with some of those of Wave V helps to bring out the contrast. A sample of four of the former over a sample of four of the latter appears in Figure 5.1.

These pictures were originally taken on the wards in color merely to enable me to recall the individual children. They were taken with fast film to avoid the disturbing shock of a flash. They were also taken in each case after I had been around the orphanage for considerable time and was becoming a familiar figure. The expressions of the infants in the upper four pictures in Figure 5.1 are typical for children in Waves I and II. Evidence of the proverbial exuberance of toddlerhood is clearly absent. Their facial expressions are glum, and they went with a marked lack of initiative and activity that betoken apathy. These children appeared to expect nothing and to seek nothing. It is difficult to see these children of Waves I and II as individuals. Their names will not stick with me.[3]

---

[3]Later, as I learned more of the investigations of "learned helplessness" in the canine (Overmier & Seligman, 1967; Seligman and Maier, 1967), I came to feel that the situations of these foundlings who were reared on a ward with between 30 and 40 foundlings under the care of three caregivers were analogous to those of the dogs submitted to inescapable shock. The human infant is helpless at birth. Her or his only means of coping with the pain of hunger, thirst, and the other discomforts is to cry. When the infant/caregiver ratio is of the order of 30 to 3, and no caregiver has responsibility for any specified infants, crying must often fail to bring any response before the infant gives up. When this happens often, it must inevitably result in a weakening or even an extinction of striving. Thus, the "glum lumps" show something of the depressive lassitude described in the dogs (Seligman, 1975); their lack of initiative and

Consider the lower four pictures in figure 5.1. The first one on the left shows Cambiz in the arms of his caretaker hitting a ball that hangs on a string attached to a ring in the ceiling. His exuberant enthusiasm for this enterprise is evident. The second shows Shabnam in the arms of her caretaker. Her outgoing manner is evident in the gesture of waving. The third shows Parviz busy with the rings of his stacking toy. The fourth shows Monee with arm extended and a facial expression that requests something of the adult standing beside him.

These children show motivational initiative. They expect and demand notice and aid from adults they encountered. They are anything but apathetic and their expressions, gestures, and actions express the joy of life. Moreover, they are socially attractive. This is a judgment validated by the fact that seven of the eleven in Wave V were adopted by families characterized by the chief examiner as "very high people." Of the 57 children involved in the four earlier waves, only 2 were ever adopted, and they were adopted when they were a little less than 6 months old because they were pretty babies. Seven of these 11 were adopted because they were attractive 2-year-olds.

It would appear that the experiences involved in the vocal games prescribed to foster vocal imitation as a means of achieving a phonemic repertoire had also an important influence on facial expression, motivational initiative, social expectations, and social attractiveness. This effect may well have derived from the fact that participation in the vocal

---

spontaneity correspond to the activity deficits in the dogs and rats, and their retardation in cognitive development is at least reminiscent of the associative deficits in the dogs (Overmier & Seligman, 1967) and rats (Jackson, Maier, & Rapaport, 1978). In such a situation, the human infant has no opportunity to develop an attachment to a special adult (Bowlby, 1969) and certainly not a "secure attachment" (Ainsworth, Bell, & Stayton, 1971).

Wave I & II

Wave V

FIG. 5.1.   Wave I II and Wave V children

games enabled the utterances of the children to elicit responses from their caregivers. Uncontrolled, however, is the fact that in Wave V, each child had a continuing relationship with a caregiver, whereas in Wave III, all three of the caregivers were equally responsible for all 10 infants. Whatever the details of the causation, the contrast in motivational initiative and social attractiveness appears to be as great as that in language achievement, but again, we have no metric with which to quantify it. The largest obtained difference in a quantified dimension of development at the Tehran Orphanage is that in the mean age of attaining top-level gestural imitation. This is a difference of 86.6 weeks. In terms of percentage of mean age of attainment saved, it is 54.95%. In terms of difference in IQ-ratios for top-level gestural imitation, it is 83 points. Recall, however, that the largest obtained difference in the mean age of attaining top-level object permanence was 111 weeks which was a saving in mean age of attainment of 60%, and in terms of mean IQ-ratio, was a difference of 90 points. These contrasts in language achievement and facial expression and motivational initiative are unquantified, but I believe you will agree that they are also impressive.

OTHER DATA

These data from my own research are limited to the first 3 years of life. Let us turn to other data for a strategy of investigation suggested by the range of reaction, based on somewhat older children. One set comes from a study by Wayne Dennis (1966) in which he summarized the results obtained from giving the Goodenough Draw-A-Man test to samples of typical children, aged between 6 and 13 years, whose experiential histories were those of typical families in some 50 cultures over the world. Because this study is cross-cultural, the children do not come from the same population, so the data do not fulfill the definitional requirement for a range of reaction. Nevertheless, given the paucity of data from this strategy, they are suggestive.

The highest mean Draw-A-Man IQ was 125, and it came from a sample of middle-class American children. Mean Draw-A-Man IQs of 124 and 123 were obtained for Japanese children of Kyoto and mean IQs almost as high for poor children from a Japanese fishing village. A mean Draw-A-Man IQ of 115 was also found for Navajo Indian children. At the lower end of the range was a mean Draw-A-Man IQ of 53 for a sample of nomadic Shilluk children of the Sudan, and a mean IQ of 56 for the children of nomadic Bedouins of Syria. If one subtracts 53 from 125, the maximal obtained difference in Draw-A-Man IQ for children from 6 to 13 years of age is 72 points. Even though population is not controlled, this is a difference clearly associated with the amount of meaningful experience with representative graphic art. A difference of 72 points in older children clearly shows that what was originally presumed by Goodenough (1926) to be culture free is far from it.

Other evidence can be obtained from combining the results from different studies. First, the damage from orphanage rearing appears to be of the order of 50 IQ points. This statement is based on the evidence in Dennis' (1973) *Children of the Creche* and in Skeels' (1966) follow-up study comparing the IQs of children who remained in orphanages with those of children who were transferred from the Iowa orphanage to the ward of moron women in an institution for the mentally deficient, and then later adopted. Second, educational daycare has been found to increase the IQ substantially. In their Milwaukee study, Heber, Garber, Harrington, Hoffman, and Falender (1972) started with 40 Black mothers with IQs of 75 or below. The 20 infants in the treated group got home visits during their first 6 months, and thereafter were taken 5 days a week to a center where each child had a tutor. The tutors were provided with curricula designed to foster cognitive development and language skills. The infants of the other 20 mothers were reared at home. Home visitors maintained contact with the untreated families, counseled the mothers in home management, but not in childrearing. The treated and untreated children got the same schedule of repeated testing. At 66 months of age, the IQs of the treated group averaged 124, whereas those of the untreated group averaged 94. Thus, the effect of the treatment would appear to be of the order of 30 points, but let us take only the 24 points of advance of the treated group above the norm of 100. If we then add the 50 IQ points of damage from orphanage rearing to these 24 points of advance from educational daycare, one obtains a maximal obtained difference of 74 IQ points. Such evidence suggests that the effects of experience in the traditional terms of the IQ is of the order of 75 points. Heber (1976) followed the school progress of these children for 6 years.   Once   their development   became   entirely dependent on the experiences afforded by their homes and standard schooling and they lost the help of educational day-care, the average IQ of the treated group dropped from 124 to 109. At the same time, those of the untreated group dropped from 94 to the upper 70s. Thus, although both lost IQ points with time, the treated group maintained their 30 IQ points of superiority over those in the untreated group.   The loss that follows the termination of educational daycare illustrates the fact that plasticity cuts both ways.

Another experiment, one done by Scarr and Weinberg (1976) to estimate the "range of reaction" in the IQ, should also be mentioned. It employed as the norm the mean IQ (90) attained by Black children reared by their biological parents in the North Central Region of the United States. They compared with this norm the mean IQ of 130 Black/interracial children who were being reared in White families of educational and economic status well above the average. Adoption offers a human analogue of the cross-fostering design employed in experiments on behavioral genetics with animal subjects. The mean age of adoption for all these children was 22 months, but the median was 6 months, and 99 of the 130 had been adopted before their first birthday.

Both adoption and the age of adoption had significant effects on the mean IQ.   The mean IQ attained by all 130 of the Black children adopted into White homes was 106.3, but that for those adopted early attained a mean IQ of 111. Scarr and Weinberg wrote as follows:

> In other words, the range of reaction of socially classified black children's IQ scores from average (black) to advantaged (white) environments is at least 1 standard deviation. Conservatively, if we consider only the adopted children with two black parents (and late and less favorable adoptive experiences), the IQ reaction range is at least 10 points between these environments. If we consider the early-adopted group, the IQ range may be as large as 20 points. The level of school achievement among the black and inter-racial adoptees is further evidence of their above-average performance on standard intellectual measures. (p. 737)

Note also that even though the White parents who adopt Black infants tend to be above average in education and economic status, they are people without special knowledge of pedagogy for infancy and early childhood. Nevertheless, the experience they provided those Black infants whom they adopted early increased their IQs by as much as 20 points on the average.

CONCLUSION

Nothing I have said should be taken to deny the existence of individual genetic differences. On the other hand, this evidence does show that the cumulative effects of experience that individual children have with their physical and social circumstances in the course of their life histories makes a very substantial difference in the intellectual competence they achieve. From such evidence, I am inclined to believe that all children born without pathology have the genotypic potential to acquire all the knowledge, motivation, skills, and values required to participate productively in the mainstream of any society in this world. This is not to say that any infant can be made into an intellectual giant, an outstanding concert pianist, or a great athlete. For productive participation in the mainstream, no society demands such specialized excellence of achievement. Yet, if we take seriously our value of equality of opportunity, even such limited evidence as we have from the strategy of investigation suggested by the range of reaction demands that the welfare of the children of the future should not be endangered by social policies based on the indirect and irrelevant assessments of educability obtained by subtracting indices of the percentage of heritable variance in the IQ from 100. It is a shame that we have so few data from the direct strategy of investigation suggested by the concept of the range of reaction. It is high time that we undertook to make more use of this strategy.

REFERENCES

Ainsworth, M.D.S., Bell, S.M.V., & Stayton, D.J. (1971). Individual differences in strange-situation behavior of one-year-olds. In H.R. Schaffer (Ed.), *The origins of human social relations* (pp. 17-52). New York: Academic Press.

Badger, E. (1971a). *Teaching guide:Infant learning program*. Paoli, Pa: The Instructo Corp.

Badger, E. (1971b). *Teaching guide: Toddler learning program*. Paoli, Pa: The Instructo Corp.

Bateson, W. (1916). Problems of genetics. New Haven, CT: Yale Univ. Press.

Beadle, G.W. (1945). Biochemical genetics.*Chemical Review, 37*, 15-96.

Bloom, B. S. (1964). *Stability and change in human Characteristics*. New York: Wiley.

Bowlby, J. (1969). *Attachment and loss. Vol. 1: Attachment*. New York: Basic Books.

Chomsky, N. (1965). *Aspects of the theory of language*. Cambridge, MA: MIT Press.

Chomsky, N.(1969). *Deepstructure, surface structure, and semantic interpretation*. Bloomington, IN: Indiana University Linguistics Club.

Cicarelli, V. G. (1969). *The impact of Head Start: An evaluation of the effects of Head Start on children's cognitive and affective development* (2 vols.) Bladensburg, Md.: Westinghouse Learning Corp.

Coombs, C.H. (1950). Psychological scaling without a unit of measurement. *Psychological Review, 57,* 145-158.

Crowther, J. G. (1941). *The social relations of science.* New York, NY: The Macmillan Co.

Darwin, C. R. (1965) On the origin of species. Cambridge, MA: Harvard Univ. Press. (Originally published in 1859)

Dennis, W. (1960). Causes of retardation among institutional children:Iran. *Journal of Genetic Psychology, 96,* 47-59.

Dennis, W. (1966). Goodenough scores, art experience, and modernization. *Journal of Social Psychology, 68,* 211-228.

Dennis, W. (1973). *Children of the Creche.* New York: Appleton-Century-Crofts.

Epstein, H.T. (1974a). Phrenoblysis: Special brain and mind growth periods. I. Human brain and skull development. *Developmental Psychobiology, 7(3),* 207-216.

Epstein, H.T. (1974b). Phrenoblysis: Special brain and mind growth periods. II. Human mental development. *Developmental Psychobiology, 7(3),* 217-224.

Erlenmeyer-Kimling, L., & Jarvik, L. F. (1963). Genetics and intelligence: A review. *Science, 142,* 1477-1479.

Fisher, R. A. (1918). The correlation between relatives on the supposition of Mendelian inheritance. *Transactions of the Royal Society, Edinburgh, 52,* 399-433.

Galton, F. (1869). *Hereditary genius: An inquiry into its laws and consequences.* London:Macmillan.

Gesell, A. (1954). The ontogenesis of infant behavior. In L. Carmichael (Ed.), *Manual of child psychology* (pp. 335-373). New York: Wiley.

Goodenough, F. L. (1926). *The measurement of intelligence by drawings.* Yonkers-on-Hudson, NY: World Book Co.

Hebb, D. O. (1949). *The organization of behavior.* New York, NY: Wiley.

Heber, R. (1976). Research in prevention of socio-cultural mental retardation. In D.G. Forgays (Ed.), *Environmental influences. Proceedings of the 1976*

Vermont Conference on the Primary Prevention of Psychopathology (Vol. II), Burlington, VT:University of Vermont.

Heber, R., Garber, H., Harrington, S., Hoffman, C., & Falender, C. (1972). *Rehabilitation of families at risk for mental retardation*. Madison, WI: Rehabilitation Research and Training Center in Mental Retardation, University of Wisconsin.

Herrnstein, R. (1971). I.Q. *The Atlantic Monthly*, *228*, 43-64.

Herrnstein R. (1973). *IQ in the meritocracy*. Boston, MA: Little, Brown.

Hirsch, J. (1972). Genetics and competence: Do heritability indices predict educability? In J.McV. Hunt (Ed.), *Human intelligence* (pp 7-29). New Brunswick, NJ: Transaction Books.

Hofstadter, R. (1945). *Social Darwinism in American thought*. Philadelphia, PA:University of Pennsylvania Press.

Hogben, L. (1939). *Nature and nurture* (2nd ed.). London: Allen & Unwin.

Holzinger, K. J. (1929). The relative effect of nature and nurture influences on twin differences. *Journal of Educational Psychology*, *20*, 241-248.

Hunt, J. McV. (1960). Experience and the development of motivation: Some reinterpretations. *Child Development*, *31*, 489-504.

Hunt, J. McV. (1961). *Intelligence and experience*. New York, NY: Ronald Press.

Hunt, J. McV. (1963a). Motivation inherent in information processing and action. In O.J. Harvey (Ed.), *Motivation and social interaction: The cognitive determinants* (pp. 35-94). New York, NY: Ronald Press.

Hunt, J. McV. (1963b). Piaget's observations as a source of hypotheses concerning motivation. *Merrill-Palmer Quarterly*, *9*, 263-275.

Hunt, J. McV. (1965). Intrinsic motivation and its role in psychological development. In D. Levine (Ed.), *Nebraska Symposium on Motivation* (Vol. 13, 189-282). Lincoln, NB: University of Nebraska Press.

Hunt, J. McV. (1966a). Toward a theory of guided learning in development. In R. H. Ojemann & Karen Pritchett (Eds.), *Giving emphasis to guided learning* (pp. 98-160). Cleveland, OH: Educational Research Council.

Hunt, J. McV. (1966b). The epigenesis of intrinsic motivation and early cognitive learning. In R. N. Haber (Ed.), *Current research in motivation* (pp. 355-370). New York, NY: Holt, Rinehart & Winston.

Hunt, J. McV. (1981). The experiential roots of intention, initiative, and trust. In H. I. Day (Ed.), *Advances in intrinsic motivation and aesthetics* (pp. 169-202). New York, NY: Plenum.

Hunt, J. McV., Mohandessi, K., Ghodssi, M., & Akiyama, M. (1976). The psychological development of orphanage-reared infants: Interventions with outcomes (Tehran). *Genetic Psychology Monograph, 94,* 177-226.

Hunt, J. McV., Paraskevopoulos, J., Schickedanz, D., & Uzgiris, I.C. (1975). Variations in the mean ages of achieving object permanence under diverse conditions of rearing. In B.L. Friedlander, G. M. Sterritt, & G.E. Kirk, (Eds.), *The exceptional infant* (Vol. 3): *Assessment and intervention* (pp. 247-262). New York, NY: Brunner/Mazel.

Jackson, R. L., Maier, S. F., & Rapaport, P. M. (1978). Exposure to inescapable shock produces both activity and associative deficits in rats. *Learning and Motivation, 9,* 69-98.

Jencks, C. (1972). *Inequality: A reassessment of the effect of family and schooling in America.* New York, NY: Basic Books.

Jensen, A. R. (1967). Estimation of the limits of heritability of traits by comparison of monozygotic and dizygotic twins. *Proceedings of the National Academy of Science, 58,* 149-157.

Jensen, A. R. (1969). How much can we boost IQ and scholastic achievement? *Harvard Educational Review, 39,* 1-123.

Jensen, A. R. (1972). *Genetics and education.* New York, NY: Harper & Row.

Jensen, A. R. (1973). *Educability and group differences.* New York, NY: Harper & Row.

Johannsen, W. (1959). Om ARvelighed i Samfund og i rene Linier. Oversigt over det Kgl. danske videnskabernes selskabs forhandlinger #3 forelagt i modet den 6 Feb. 1903. in J. A. Peters, (Ed.), *Classic papers in genetics*. Englewood Cliffs, NJ: Prentice Hall, 1959. (Originally published in 1903)

Johannsen, W. (1909). *Elemente der exakten erblichkeitslehre*. [Exact elements of genetics] Jena: Fischer.

Kirk, G. E., Hunt, J. McV., & Lieberman, C. (1975). Social class and preschool language skill: II. Semantic mastery of color information. *Genetic Psychology Monographs, 91*, 299-316.

Krizenecky, J. (1965). Fundamenta genetica. Prague: Publishing House of the Czechoslovak Academy of Sciences.

Lazar, I., & Darlington, R. B. (1982). Lasting effects of early education: A report from the consortium for longitudinal studies. *Monographs of the Society for Research in Child Development,47*, (2-3), Serial No. 195.

Loevinger, J. (1943). On the proportional contributions of differences in nature and nurture to differences in intelligence. *Psychological Bulletin, 40*, 725-726.

Malthus, T. R. (1914). *An essay on the principle of population*, Vol. 2. London: J. M. Dent & Sons, Ltd.

McGraw, M. B. (1935). *Growth: A study of Johnny and Jimmy*. New York: Appleton-Century.

McGuire, T. R., & Hirsch, J. (1977). General intelligence (g) and heritability (H^2, h^2). In I.C. Uzgiris & F. Weizmann (Eds.), *The structuring of experience* (pp. 25-72). New York: Plenum Press.

Overmier, J. B., & Seligman, M. E. P. (1967). Effects of inescapable shock upon subsequent escape and avoidance learning. *Journal of Comparative and Physiological Psychology, 63*, 28-33.

Payne, J.S., Mercer, C.D., Payne, R.A., & Davison, R.G. (1973). *Head Start: A tragicomedy with epilogue*. New York, NY: Behavioral Publications.

Scarr, S., & Weinberg, R. A. (1976). IQ test performance of black children adopted by white families. *American Psychologist, 31*, 726-739.

Seligman, M.E.P. (1975). *Helplessness*. San Francisco, CA: Freeman.

Seligman, M. E. P., & Maier, S. F. (1967). Failure to escape traumatic shock. *Journal of Experimental Psychology*, *74*, 1-9.

Skeels, H. M. (1966). Adult status of children with contrasting early life experiences. *Monograph of the Society for Research in Child Development*, *31* (3; Serial No. 105), 1-65.

Skeels, H. M., & Dye, J. B. (1939). A study of the effects of differential stimulation of mentally retarded children. *Proceedings of the American Association on Mental Deficiency*, *44*, 114-136.

Steiner, G. (1976). *The children's cause*. Washington, DC: The Brookings Institute.

Thorndike, E. L. (1905). The measurement of twins. *Journal of Philosophy, Psychology, and Science Method*, *1*, 547-553.

Uzgiris, I. C., & Hunt, J. McV. (1975). *Assessment in infancy: Ordinal scales of psychological development*. Urbana, IL: University of Illinois Press.

Watson, J. D., & Crick, F. H. C. (1953). A structure for deoxyribosenucleic acid. *Nature*, *171*, 737 & 964.

Weber, C. U., Foster, P. W., & Weikart, D. P. (1978). *An economic analysis of the Ypsilanti Perry Preschool Project*. Ypsilanti, MI: High/Scope Educational Research Foundation.

Woltereck, R. (1909). Weitere experimentelle Untersuchurgen über Artveränderung, speziel über das Wesen quantitativer Artunterschiede bei daphneiden. *Verhandlunged der Deutschen Zooligschen Gellschaft*, *19*, 110-173. (From L. C. Dunn, *A short history of genetics*, Mew York:McGraw-Hill, 1965).

Discussion of "Relevance to Educability"

Goldine C. Gleser
University of Cincinnati

Dr. Hunt has presented some very convincing evidence that psychological development in infancy and early childhood is highly plastic. The evidence has been of two types: the first is that occurring by virtue of "experiments of nature" in which children of low socioeconomic status have been adopted at an early age into middle-class or professional families; and the second is evidence involving experimental intervention procedures in daycare centers or institutional settings.

I would like to make three points with regard to these data: First, the data on plasticity of cognitive development are not necessarily incompatible with genetic studies indicating the heritability of intelligence, although interpretations of heritability by educators and others make it advantageous to emphasize range of reaction.

Second, these data do not imply that current psychometric techniques for measuring aptitudes and intelligence are inappropriate, provided it is recognized that what is being measured is "learned abilities" and not "ability to learn" at a given point in time.

Third, the work of Dr. Hunt on language acquisition in the first 2 years of life is an important step in the direction of increasing our understanding of children's cognitive development. However, there is much more we need to know before we can implement effective educational programs for young children who remain in their natural home environment. Indeed it is questionable whether sizeable gains can be made in a single generation unless we are willing to remove children from such environments.

HERITABILITY AND RANGE OF REACTION

Let us consider what range of reaction can be expected using the heritability model. Heritability assumes that what is measured by intelligence tests is an estimate of the phenotypic response of an individual of a given genotype. According to Jensen (1980) the phenotypic response is "the final product, at any given time in the individual's life span, of the genotype and all the environmental factors that have interacted with the genotype since the moment of conception" (p. 184). For individuals of the same genotype, the range of values in performance obtained under the existing population of environmental conditions is termed the *reaction range*. Note that this distribution of environmental conditions is assumed to remain constant and independent of genotype.

Estimates for heritability of intelligence range from 0.50 to 0.90 with a central tendency of around 0.75. Problems with the separation of genetic and environmental effects probably make this estimate too high, but let us assume 0.75 for the sake of the argument. Because effects are assumed to be additive, if we take the proportion due to heritability as 0.75, that due to environment is 1 - 0.75 = 0.25. Now, making the usual assumption that the standard deviation of IQ for a reliable intelligence test is 15 and hence the variance is 225, we find that variance due to range of reaction is 56.25; the standard deviation is 7.5.

Although standard deviation is a measure of variation, it is not the same as range. If we want the range of scores of 95% of the phenotypes that could arise from a given genotype we need to double the standard deviation and add and subtract it from the hypothetical genotype. Thus 95% of children with average genotypic intelligence might obtain scores of from 85 to 115 depending on their environment; a range of 30 points. Even a range of 45 points is quite possible from this model in approximately 1 out of 1,000 cases. It would appear that high heritability is not as restrictive of range of reaction as many might think.

Now let us look at some of the findings on adopted children. Scarr and Weinberg (1976) found that Black children adopted into middle class families during the first year of life had average IQs of 110 compared to a 90 IQ average for Black children raised in the north central region of the country. These figures are quite compatible with the hypothesis that the Black children were of average genetic intelligence and differences in environmental conditions produced a range of reaction of ± 10 points. Schiff and her collaborators (1978) found a difference of approximately 14 points between the IQs of French children adopted into families of high socioprofessional status and those siblings reared by their lower educated parents, again well within the calculated range. Even the findings of Heber (1978) indicated a difference of 34 points between the 20 children in his control group and the 20 given one-on-one tutoring until they entered public school is not unreasonable when one considers that such a total push involving perhaps 35 hours of special tutoring a week for several years occurs but rarely, even in professional homes.

ABILITY TESTING

What is unfortunate about the genetic model from the standpoint of education and social policy, as Dr. Hunt has pointed out, is that it has tended to encourage passive acceptance of the idea that since most differences among people are genetic, little can be done to change the matter. It has also encouraged the thinking, among those who would do away with social differences, that the real villain is ability testing.

They reason that social differences arise because IQ
tests are biased against the socially disadvantaged.
Bias is not the culprit, however, according to the
report of the Ability Testing Committee of the National
Academy of Science (Wydor & Garner 1982). Intelligence
and other ability tests serve many useful purposes,
particularly in determining who is in need of special
educational intervention, gauging the results of such
programs, and in predicting achievement under unchanged
environmental conditions. What such tests do not do is
assess genetic capacity nor areas of deficiency in the
developmental process. Thus, they tell us something
about "learned ability" but not about "ability to
learn" under appropriate educational intervention. For
this purpose tests such as those developed by Reuven
Feuerstein (1979) for use with adolescents may be more
appropriate. His tests provide tasks that can be used
in a teaching process, thus enabling the examiner to
evaluate the ability of the examinee to learn to deal
with new situations. He has used such tests in Israel
to diagnose and develop instructional techniques for
reversing deficiencies in culturally different and
deprived adolescents from Afro-Asian countries judged
irreversibly retarded according to conventional tests.
For much younger children, some of the tasks that
Gelman (1979) has devised to study cognitive
functioning in preschoolers in the area of numerical
conservation might be useful as diagnostic and
instructional tools.

PLASTICITY A TWO-EDGED SWORD

Turning now to Dr. Hunt's report of his experiments in
Tehran, one cannot help but be impressed by the results
of his program of vocal games and pseudoimitation with
the fifth wave of children. Such a program was
undoubtedly of value for children who otherwise would
be reared in the sterile environment of an orphanage in
which vocal interplay between caretaker and child were
absent or at a minimum. I would have liked, however,
to have heard the outcome of his audio-visual
enrichment program. I can understand why Dr. Hunt has
compared the Wave V children to those for whom
intervention was at a minimum because his major point

was   to demonstrate range of reaction.   However,   from the   standpoint of gaining a better idea of the   effect of   tutored   human enrichment   per se, it would   be   of interest to compare them with the Wave IV children   who received   audio-visual enrichment.   Such   a   comparison might   be more helpful in assessing the   usefulness   of his   approach for the training of young mothers in   low socioeconomic households in this country where there is exposure to verbal and other auditory stimuli, although certainly not under the infant's control.

In   accord with Dr. Hunt, I believe that   children born   without pathology have the genotypical   potential to acquire the knowledge, motivation, skills and values required to participate productively in the   mainstream of   society.   I am not optimistic, however, that   these results can be achieved in a single generation or   with intervention at any one age.   Perhaps, this is   because I   am more concerned than he seems to be with the   fact that   plasticity is a two-edged sword.   The   plasticity that   makes   it   possible   to   improve   motivation   and cognitive functioning with enrichment seems to work   in reverse   when   the child returns   to   the   discouraging atmosphere of his or her family and neighborhood peers. Thus   when   Heber's   experimental   group   of   tutored children, who had an average IQ of 124 at age 5½,   were retested   at   age   9, their scores had   dropped   to   an average   of   109.   True, the untreated group   had   also dropped,   so that a difference of 30   points   remained, but   it   is   the drop in both groups with   which   I   am concerned.   Results of the Head Start program also tend to   confirm   the   view   that   unless   children   can   be maintained   in   a steady, improved   environment   little headway   can   be made.   In this context we   might   note that   there were not particular differences in   average IQ between younger and older adopted Black children   in the Scarr-Weinberg (1976) study.   We need to know   much more   than   we   do   now   about   the   environmental deficiencies that cause the drop in IQ in children from low socioeconomic families.

Some   clues   are   available   in   the   literature. Sroufe (1979) noted that children from poor homes often experience fluctuating environments such as changes   in parent's job status, residency, caregivers, and living group arrangements. His evidence indicates that such fluctuating circumstances are linked to the child's quality of attachment at 12 and 18 months as indicated by the Ainsworth Test of Infant-Caregiver Attachment. Lower socioeconomic mothers less often use techniques such as expansion and elaboration of the young child's telegraphic utterances than do middle-class mothers, according to de Hersch (1980). Such matters as excessive noise and distraction, lack of space in which to study and difficulty in maintaining the privacy of one's possessions, all play a role. Feuerstein (1979) lists a number of the deficiencies found in socioeconomically and culturally disadvantaged children. Among them are unplanned, impulsive, and unsystematic exploratory behavior; lack of need for precision and accuracy in observation and data gathering; inability to select relevant versus nonrelevant cues in defining a problem; poor strategies for hypothesis testing; trial-and-error or impulsively arrived at responses. It is doubtful that these problems can be overcome in a single generation by educational means alone in the absence of a changed home environment. The radical proposal that these children be maintained in a residential setting apart from their families as Feuerstein has done in Israel is not likely to be accepted in this country. Therefore, changes will probably be slow, with successive generations inching forward on the gains made by the previous generation. In the meantime, we need to push ahead to learn more about the development of cognitive functioning and it's interaction with experience and to implement the insights we gain, as was so well indicated by Dr. Hunt.

REFERENCES

de Hersch, D. (1980). Early language development. In S.I. Harrison & J. F. McDermott, Jr. (Eds.), *New directions in childhood psychopathology*, (Vol. I, pp. 146-158). New York: International Universities Press.

Feuerstein, R. (1979). *The dynamic assessment of retarded performers: The learning potential assessment device, theory, instruments, and techniques.* Baltimore, MD: University Park Press.

Gelman, R. (1979). Preschool thought. *American Psychologist, 34,* 900-905.

Heber, R.F. (1978). Sociocultural mental retardation: A longitudinal study. In D. Forgays (Ed.), *Primary prevention of psychopathology, Vol. 2: Environmental influences* (pp. 39-62). Hanover, NH: University Press of New England.

Jensen, A.R. (1980). *Bias in mental testing,* New York: The Free Press.

Scarr, S., & Weinberg, R.H. (1976). IQ test performance of black children adopted by white families. *American Psychologist, 31,* 726-739.

Shiff, M., Duyme, M., Dumaret, A., Steward, J., Tomkiewicz, S., & Feingold, J. (1978). Intellectual status of working class children adopted early into upper middle class families. *Science, 200,* 1503-1504.

Sroufe, L. A. (1979). The coherence of individual development: Early care, attachment, and subsequent developmental issues. *American Psychologist, 34,* 834-841.

Wydor, A.K., & Garner, W.R. (1982). *Ability Testing, Uses, consequences, and controversies.* Washington, DC: National Academy Press.

Response to Dr. Gleser's Discussion

J. McVicker Hunt
University of Illinois

Nothing Dr. Gleser has said in her discussion of my chapter is unacceptable to me. But I do wish to emphasize the difference in emphasis. In a sense, this difference is analogous to the proverbial diverse reactions to a 4-ounce wine glass with 2 ounces of wine in it. Her reaction to the traditional estimates of heritability in this context seems to me to be "half full," mine has been "half empty." Moreover, in the terms of my third aspect of the relationship between science and values, I believe the welfare of children in our society calls for an emphasis on the potential range of reaction for healthy human genotypes rather than the one evident from existing societal conditions. I want us to look at psychological development in terms of what might and ought to be rather than in terms of what exists under prevailing conditions of childrearing.

Yet, I agree that ability testing, per se, is not the villain. The villain is the interpretation of test results as inevitable because it is believed that heredity *determines* the rate and course of development rather than merely *influences* the process of interaction with circumstances underlying development.

Ever since Francis Galton published his book on
Hereditary Genius in 1869 and established his
anthropometric laboratory to measure human faculties,
the idea that such tests measure hereditary potential
has been tied to ability testing. Alfred Binet (cited
in Stoddard, 1939) tried to untie the conceptual knot,
but ironically, his technique of substitutive averaging
to obtain a single metric with which to measure the
intelligence that he regarded as a single faculty,
mental age, undid his argument. Once Wilhelm Stern hit
upon the idea of dividing the mental age by the
chronological age to obtain the ratio-IQ, it provided a
measure of ability tied only to the individual-for-life
and provided those with Galton's views a metric that
fit so beautifully that it has been exceedingly
difficult to demonstrate the defects. It was largely
this conceptual relationship between tested
intelligence and heredity that motivated my wish for a
new approach to assessment in infancy. The
implementation of this wish has been more the work of
Ina C. Uzgiris than mine (Uzgiris & Hunt, 1975).

Dr. Gleser admits that problems with the
separation of genetic and environmental effects
probably make even the estimate of the heritability of
intelligence of 0.75 too high, and that is lower than
Jensen's revised estimate of 0.80. I question whether
we can fruitfully separate genetic and environmental
effects for human beings. Only in agriculture where
one can measure directly the separate effects, as did
Wilhelm Johannsen and Richard Woltereck, are measures
very meaningful. Moreover, in human development, we
have not only statistical interaction, but a
continuous, on-going dynamic form of interaction
between the demands of situations and the achieved
competencies that individuals bring to their encounters
with these demands to contend with. Fortunately, Dr.
Gleser has agreed with me that children born without
pathology do have the genotypical potential to acquire
the knowledge, motivation, skills, and values required
to participate productively in the mainstream of
society.

Dr. Gleser and I agree that plasticity is indeed

a double-edged sword, but the rate of maturation and
development moderates with age. The greatest effects
of experience are obtainable with that coming in the
preschool years and especially in infancy.   Thus,
while Project Head Start was a societal step that
helped in a variety of ways, it began too late to
capture the opportunity for getting the maximal
effects of experience on intellectual and motivational
development.   Nevertheless, I, too, learned that a
single generation is inadequate to achieve what I
believe is possible over time, but this will have to
be approached gradually. And I also agree that we
need to know much more than we do about the ways in
which child-rearing in the homes of the poorly
educated people of poverty hampers children's
development. Yet this does not necessarily mean that
infants must be separated from their parents, for
parents can also learn.

    What is needed is for both parents and political
leaders to realize how great the plasticity in
cognitive and motivational development is during
infancy and later preschool years.   We need more
evidence concerning how much the competence of
children can be modified. We need to know more about
the specific relationships between kinds of experience
that hamper and facilitate early development. We need
to know more about the specific relationships between
kinds of experience and kinds of developmental
advance.

    I want to emphasize that in view of the
democratic values that we inherited (speaking
socially, not biologically) from our American
forefathers, it is incumbent upon us to emphasize
modifiability of competence to be obtained from
various kinds of experience. This is the import here
of the range of reaction. Thus emphasis on it is not
misplaced even though the range of reaction is
ultimately a function of the genotype.

    Although I dislike borrowing a slogan from the
Army Recruiters, I must confess that I both like and
find appropriate here the words of their song that

comes nightly on television: "Be all that you can be."
Applied here, it becomes: "Help our children become
all that they can be." Do not succumb to the ancient
dogma that "What is must have always been and will
always be." As Dr. Gleser has admitted, the
"interpretations of heritability by educators and
others make it advantageous to emphasize range of
reaction."

REFERENCES

Galton, F. (1869). *Hereditary genius: An inquiry into
    its laws and consequences*. London: MacMillan.
Stoddard, G. D. (1939). The IQ: Its ups and downs.
    Educational Record, 20, 44-57).
Uzgiris, I. C., & Hunt, J. McV. (1975). *Assessment
    in infancy: Ordinal scales of psychological
    development*. Urbana, IL: University of Illinois
    Press.

6 Measuring to Understand and Understanding Measuring

Donald W. Fiske
University of Chicago

Science progresses by examining its assumptions--often finding that they are faulty. Although this proposition was originally stated for substantive knowledge, it also applies to measuring in the social-behavioral sciences. In fact, our measuring processes are behavioral processes: Almost every datum is produced by a person--a subject or an observer. Although we assume we know what is going on in the process leading to a datum, we have little established knowledge or theory about the process. Hence we need mini-theories or rationales, one for each type of measuring. That theorizing can--in fact, should--draw upon general substantive theory but should be carried beyond such theory to describe and explain the behavior in the measurement context. The behavioral process in the person making a recorded measurement is behavior generated by the research process and would not have occurred if research were not being done. Even when archival or other records of behavior are used, someone takes the behavioral step of producing measurements from those records.

A better understanding of the behavioral process in measuring should improve the quality of our measurements and of our empirical findings. In addition, as Adams, Smelser, and Treiman (1982) stated, "As in the physical and biological sciences, the history of the social and behavioral sciences has been one of constant interaction between improvements in measurement and improvements in theory" (p. 22). Understanding measuring will help to improve conceptualization by clarifying our constructs as they are measured. For example, having identified several typical steps in the process of answering an item on a test of mental ability, we can endeavor to determine to what extent each step contributes to individual differences in intellectual performance: Do all steps show variation in performance or are some steps correctly executed by most persons, leaving only one or two to carry the burden of differentiating people with high and low ability?

We also need to determine whether the processes we are measuring are the processes we want to measure. Are subjects and other data-producers doing what we think and expect them to do? But just what do we expect them to do? What do we think should go on in the head of a data-producer to make the obtained data of maximum value to our research? For what measuring operations for a concept is the process in the data-producer (subject or observer) the same as the process implied by the concept and by its definition or explication? When is it a different process? The examination of measuring processes should lead not only to the evaluation of the adequacy of our procedures but also to the identification of the linkage between the measuring and the referent of the construct being studied. By such analysis, we should be able to locate and remove contamination in our measurements due to the occurrence of irrelevant processes. It is still true that, as Campbell (1969) noted some years ago, many of the laws that are operative in a given measuring situation are yet to be discovered.

In the history of social-behavioral measurement, new problems, new sources of confounding and biasing have continually been uncovered, including response biases and other forms of reactivity in the people producing our data and also experimenter effects and other artifacts (Cook & Campbell, 1979; Rosenthal, 1976). We have recognized these problems and have tried to cope with them but only in a patchwork fashion. We have not focused directly on the basic task of reexamining our assumptions, our procedures, and their rationales. If we are to do a good job of measuring to understand, we need to understand our measuring more fully. We need theory and facts about three principal topics: (a) The elements present throughout the entire measuring process (i.e., the data producer--subject or observer--and the constant conditions); (b) the behavioral process involved in measuring the variables for each type of construct; and (c) transformations of the data obtained from the data-producer into scores or indices for the construct.

The Constant Elements in Measuring. Any measuring in social-behavioral science involves, at some stage, a human instrument, a data-producer. We need to understand that instrument better; we need to know what it is like at the beginning of measuring. What sets and orientation have been given to the data-producer when introduced into the measuring situation and instructed about the task to be carried out? How does the data-producer react to the physical setting, to the person giving the instructions, and to the task as perceived? In everyday terms, the data-producer should understand the assigned measuring task, must be motivated and competent to carry it out, and should not be distracted or diverted by any conflicting purposes.

Also evident throughout the measuring are the physical and psychological conditions, which may have unintended effects, and the other people present. In particular, there is the overseer, the experimenter or investigator, who we know has effects on experimental subjects as well as on subjects producing self-reports. The data-producer has the set given in the research instructions. In addition, that person and the others present have their personal interpretations of the total situation and their several expectancies. We have some inferred knowledge about these factors but need a more systematic understanding. More generally, the constant conditions may be created and manipulated by the experimenter or may be unalterable. In either case, they provide boundary conditions that must be taken into account in judging the reproducibility and generalizability of the data and the findings derived from the data.

The Ongoing Process in Measuring a Variable. The behavioral process in the data-producer that generates each datum is the core of measuring. Yet we know less about it than other aspects of measurement, probably because it has seemed so obvious to us. For example, we ask the data-producer to carry out mental operations that, we believe, are familiar to the data-producer because they are so much like the perceiving, cognizing, and deciding that goes on in everyday living. Yet we have found that the task assigned in measuring has aspects specific to measuring, as well as intrusions from uncontrolled sources.

Just how does a subject decide to report that he or she prefers stimulus A over stimulus B? How does a respondent choose an answer to the survey question, "How many friends and relatives do you feel close to?" How does a rater go about marking a rating scale to indicate the degree of ambition perceived in a friend?

What is the course of the behavior that goes on in the data-producer? (In this chapter, *behavior* refers not only to manifest action, physical movement in time and space, but also to internal activity, to mental processes.)

We need to develop an explicit mini-theory linking the process in measuring to the conceptualization of the construct at which the measuring is aimed. More exactly, how is the process in measuring related to the behavioral process to which the construct refers? An ideal model is the measuring of temperature in physics. Each device for measuring temperature is designed on the basis of physical theory about changes in things associated with changes in temperature. Each of the many types of device is built upon an established part of physical theory. Kuhn (1977) has argued that "a quite highly developed body of theory is ordinarily prerequisite to fruitful measurement in the physical sciences" (p. 201); later, he makes the seemingly paradoxical assertion that "to discover quantitative regularity one must normally know what regularity one is seeking and one's instruments must be designed accordingly" (p. 219).

The preceding paragraph is oriented toward the direct measurement of properties of behavior. The general argument also applies to the less direct measurement of such characteristics as "urban" and "rural" (Bradburn, 1982). Whenever the measuring process is not conceptualized as directly reflecting the construct of interest, we need a rationale for the links between the process used and the construct. To develop that rationale, it is evident that the target construct itself must be well specified. Given the present state of the social-behavioral sciences, the investigator must often develop his or her own theory for the construct in interaction with the conceptualization of the measuring process, the interaction between measurement and theory to which Adams et al. (1982) refer.

The Transformation of Data into Indices for the Construct. Each unit of the activity of the data-producer yields a datum. The several data form a protocol that is transformed by the investigator to a score or index on a variable. The term *variable* is used here to identify the product of the measuring process occurring in the data-producer. That product may itself be the score on a variable, as in the rating of a trait or other attribute, or several products may be combined to obtain such a score. After obtaining scores and using them in statistical analyses, the investigator interprets the variable as related to the construct of interest: The variable may be taken either as indicating the whole construct or as indicating an aspect of the construct. The measurement of the construct is thus interpreted as assessing a property or attribute of the actor. In the personality area, it is taken as a relatively enduring property. In experimental work, it is usually viewed as a property of the actor's behavior in the immediate experimental context, taking into account any experimental manipulation. In this step, there is implicit generalizing from the assessments of the variable to assessments of the construct. (The term *construct* is used here to remind us that the target concept is the construction of the investigator, the construction antedating the measuring.)

For analytic purposes, the three topics--the constant conditions, the process, and the transformation of data--are designated as distinct. It is, however, difficult to draw a sharp line between them (e.g., answers to ability items are scored as correct or incorrect, so the clerk or the machine scoring an answer sheet may produce the scores to be analyzed). Again, the distinction between the data-producer as a constant throughout the measuring process and the tendency of subjects making self-reports to give socially desirable answers is rather artificial. In effect, when we have some information about how characteristics of a data-producer affect the data, it may be undesirable to view the data-producer as a factor differentiated from the actual measuring process. Finally, the concern of psychometricians with relating item responses to constructs has led them to consider the determinants producing correct responses. For instance, Embretson (1983) has proposed that construct validity be seen as including construct representation, the identification of the theoretical mechanisms underlying item responses.

WHAT IS OUR CURRENT UNDERSTANDING OF MEASURING?

Our assumption that we understand our measuring is based not only on our use of everyday processes of perceiving and cognizing but also on the partial knowledge that we have developed about our measuring. What do we know? We have a lot of conceptualization and knowledge about the third topic, the steps from a datum to the construct. Psychometric theory and its ramifications deal with that phase. We also know a lot about the first topic: Much attention has been devoted to the data-producer, whether observer or subject. For example, we have postulated and measured response sets (by rescoring the data). We have inferred the existence of evaluation apprehension (Rosenberg, 1969). We have demonstrated experimenter effects on the data generated by our data-producers and on the subsequent processing of those data. The willingness of subjects to give verbal reports about whatever they are asked to tell has been highlighted by Nisbett and Wilson (1977), with their argument leading to the careful examination by Ericsson and Simon (1984) of the conditions under which such reports can appropriately be used (see also Fiske, 1980). We have, however, little systematic knowledge about the second topic, about the actual process of producing a datum.

More generally, when we look at what we know about our measuring, we see two main features. First, most of our understanding is negative knowledge, findings about things that can go wrong, sources of error, bias, distortion in measurement. In the present state of the social-behavioral sciences, we can more confidently identify deficient measurements than veridical or valid ones. This feature should not surprise us--much of what is clearly established in social-behavioral science is negative knowledge. We often agree better on what is not so (contrary to untutored beliefs) than on what is so. From his broad perspective on "Psychology as Science," Koch (1974) writes: "Throughout its history as 'science,' the *hard* knowledge which it has deposited has usually been *negative* knowledge!" (p. 19). Negative knowledge is a kind of progress. As Boulding (1980) put it, "Knowledge increases by a kind of relentless bias toward the perception of error" (p. 381). But rather than wait for the discovery and identification of further confounds, additional sources of systematic error in our measuring, we should examine our measuring processes more directly to determine exactly what goes on in each type of measuring operation.

The other prevalent feature in our contemporary understanding of measuring is its basis in inference from the products. Under the influence of the behavioristic mores, we have concentrated primarily on analyses of our standard data (i.e., on recorded responses). We have thoroughly examined the relationships between aggregated scores and various criterion measures (that are themselves subject to measuring problems). To a lesser degree, we have manipulated conditions and stimuli to see how these affected the data. But we have rarely turned our attention to exploring what goes on between item and response. It is possible to carry out research on that topic, as we shall see later.

We cannot, of course, observe directly the process occurring in the data-producer, any more than we can observe any other perceptual or cognitive process. We have to make inferences from traces or other products, as is frequent in the natural sciences (e.g., the paths of particles observed in cloud chambers). As some of my colleagues have suggested, what we will be doing is substituting smaller and smaller black boxes for the gross black box now standing between the presentation of the stimulus and the observed response.

COGNITIVE PROCESSES IN MEASURING MENTAL ABILITY

To understand the operation of the measuring process, we need a conceptualization, a minitheory for what goes on in measuring, for the processes in the data-producer. Although we have much informal speculation and some a priori theory, we have little conceptualization with a firm empirical base. An excellent example of what is needed can be found in Sternberg's work on the cognitive processes in answering items reflecting mental ability (Sternberg, 1977, 1979, 1980, 1983). Although he views his work as substantive, as determining the nature of mental ability as it is manifested in general behavioral functioning, his research illuminates the process in measuring such ability. Thus, he is not only finding out to what our constructs for abilities refer but he is also uncovering the operation of mental ability as it is measured in tests. When we understand the nature of mental ability, we will also understand its measurement because testing for mental ability involves performance on tasks requiring the application of such ability.

Rather than just taking a gross black box approach and looking for relations between the stimulus input and the response output, Sternberg analyzed the process into a series of components and ingeniously devised procedures for looking at each separately.

It is obviously impossible to summarize here Sternberg's creative and complex theory of mental ability. Instead, one can point out aspects of that conceptualization that are pertinent to the discussion of measuring and mention relevant features of his empirical work. As Sternberg (1979) stated, "The theory organizes mental abilities into four levels-- composite tasks, subtasks, information-processing components, and information-processing metacomponents. Composite tasks can be decomposed into subtasks, and subtasks into components. Metacomponents control the use of components in composite tasks and subtasks" (p. 214). Composite tasks correspond approximately to quite specific types of intelligence tests. Subtasks can be thought of as stages in responding to an item, each stage involving information processing. Although Sternberg views the upper levels of this hierarchy as somewhat arbitrary, the information processes are not.

Information-processing components include encoding, inference, mapping, application, justification, and response. Of these, the last three are of particular importance in other measuring contexts because they refer to the processing when the subject finds that none of the available alternative responses exactly fits the answer he or she feels would be correct. The step from the data-producer having decided on a solution of the presented task to the choosing of the response to give seems crucial in a variety of measuring procedures, especially those in which considerable inference, interpretation, and judgment are required of the data-producer, as in rating a trait or deciding on the strength of an attitude.

Sternberg's work is of major significance for its

contribution to understanding mental ability.   It   is examined   here   for   several   reasons.   First,   it illustrates   how   the measuring process can   be   finely analyzed   into   its cognitive components.   Second,   it shows how substantive theory and theory about measuring interrelate.   Note also that Sternberg's work considers not   only   behavior   elicited   by   a   task,   but   also individual differences in that behavior.   Finally,   his theory is not just speculation: it both guides and   is modified   by   empirical   work.   By   such   experimental manipulations   as pre-cueing and partial tasks,   he   is able   to   isolate   the   separate   components   in   the information processing.

Less well investigated are the metacomponents that control   what   happens   at   the   component   level. "Metacomponents   are   the   processes by   which   subjects determine   what   components,   representations,   and strategies   should   be   applied   to   various   problems" (Sternberg,   1979, p. 226).   Although   these   decisions are   of major importance to   understanding   performance involving   mental ability, they seem to be of equal   or greater   importance to understanding the   processes   in data-producers in work on preference, attribution,   and other   topics.   The empirical   investigation   of   such metacomponents presents a real challenge.

Sternberg's distinction between metacomponents and information-processing   components is similar   to   that between   executive   functions   and   control   processes. Butterfield   and   Belmont (1977)   identified   these   as follows: "...control   processes   are seen   to   be   the operations   by   which   we   work   on   the   information available,   or   retrieve it from memory,   in   order   to perform   a cognitive task.   By contrast, the   executive function   is   the means by which we   select,   sequence, evaluate,   revise,   or abandon these   operations" (p. 281).

MEASUREMENT AS PROBLEM SOLVING

The   awesome   complexity   of the   processes   in   mental ability   should   make us careful   and   judicious   about investigating   the   processes   in   measuring   other variables.   Perhaps we should begin   by   investigating performance on more simple tasks, such as discrimination or recognition. Perhaps it will prove possible to start studying some measuring processes by identifying stages at a more gross level than information-processing components, stages that can subsequently be broken down more finely. The history of research on problem solving suggests that such an approach may be fruitful. The earliest work divided the process into a few very broad steps. Later, Newell and Simon (1972) have carried out very detailed analyses of various kinds of problem solving. They hold that a few characteristics of the human information-processing system are invariant over task and problem solver although each kind of task has its particular process characteristics.

Similarly, Sternberg indicates that the particular information-processing components used in a given mental-ability task vary with the task, or rather with the type of task. Some are common to one class of tasks but not to the other. In contrast, the metacomponents are involved in a wide variety of tasks.

Suppose we looked at all observing and measuring as problem solving. The data-producer is given the problem of making a judgment, an estimation of the value (or "score") to be assigned to something. In carrying out that task, the data-producer will generate a process involving various information-processing components appropriate to the particular kind of task, such as direct observation of a segment of behavior or rating a peer. We can anticipate that it will turn out that many of the difficulties in such estimations, difficulties evident in poor agreement between observers, will come from using inappropriate components.

But in all such tasks, or in any given broad class of tasks, we can expect to find the same metacomponents operating, the same "higher-control processes used for planning how a problem should be solved, for making decisions regarding alternative courses of action during problem-solving, and for monitoring solution processes" (Sternberg, 1980, p. 573).

My proposal for applying Sternberg's theory, extending it (as necessary) to the rather general production of data in social-behavioral science is not very radical: Sternberg (1983) and his associates have already done empirical work, within the general theoretical framework, analyzing classifications, metaphorical understanding and appreciation, and the prediction of future events. They have also worked on social-practical settings, and the decoding of nonverbal cues. Sternberg (1985) sees intelligence as adaptation to one's environment. Perhaps we should construe all our data-producers as adapting to the specific measuring situation.

What we need to do, then, is to develop subtheories, one for each kind of data-producing, and then test empirically whether these applications help us to understand our measuring. Such research will not be easy and our efforts may yield disappointing results because most of our measuring tasks are not as well specified as a task manifesting a mental ability. Instead, they are what Sternberg (1981) called *nonentrenched* tasks. The stimulus materials are typically heterogeneous and complex, rather than explicit and restricted. For producing many kinds of data, the steps in the process are not implicitly directed. In the usual case, several alternative strategies may be available and used. Simon (1975) noted that, even for simple experimental problems, any of several solution strategies may be employed. Because ratings and other judgments that we use as data are the answers given to rather complex problems, we must expect to find much variety in the processes producing such measurements. Thus, for the production of a given kind of data, it may be necessary to identify and adjust for each of several processes used by various observers or raters. Ideally, we should find ways of guiding them toward a single way of proceeding. And perhaps discovering how to instruct data-producers more explicitly, how to delineate the general strategy to be followed, may contribute to the overall improvement of the quality of our data.

Such work will be in a normative context. In

studying the nature of intelligence, Sternberg is locating steps in the process of being intelligent that are associated with individual differences. In studying data-producers, our aim would be roughly similar but the emphasis would be different. We need to identify the components and metacomponents used in generating what we judge to be the best data, and then find ways of getting our data-producers to use such optimal processes. In the ideal world, when our data-producers are generating data about the behavior of others, they will not show individual differences in the processes used. (Of course, when we are obtaining data about the data-producers, as in assessments of their mental ability or their behavioral dispositions, the processes used by a self-reporting data-producer can be expected to vary with the level or strength of the attribute being measured.)

In studying manifestations of intelligence, we have a good criterion for the right answer, and so can determine what process leads to the right answer. But in studying other data-producing, such as the judgments in making attributions, we do not have a really good criterion. So perhaps we will have to decide a priori what the appropriate processes are.

For example, Banks (1982) has an Instantaneous Report of Judgments procedure for studying the process in rating others. Subjects watch a videotape and press a button to record the level of any tentative judgment, and then verbalize the basis for that impression. She has found that both the latency of the first judgment in this procedure, and the making of a few such reports, correlate with quality of the final rating, using expert judgment as the criterion (something that others have reported for different contexts). But is expert judgment of, say, leadership the correct criterion? One gain from the study of data-producing processes is that it will force us to decide what our target concept really is. What is the correct solution to the "problem" given to an observer? In attribution and many other instances, it will be just that--someone's judgment. Leadership is not a constant property of a person, like eye color.

BEHAVIORAL PROCESSES
AND MEASURING PROCESSES

In some domains, the investigator elicits a behavioral process that is itself the measuring process. Ability is measured by having subjects exercise or demonstrate their ability, the investigator subsequently making a simple judgment about an aspect of their product-- classifying the product as correct or incorrect, or timing the duration of that process. The measuring of some other types of constructs can be viewed as similar: The investigator may ask the subject to manifest a preference between two designs or two political candidates; he or she may ask the subject which of two values is more important. If the meaning of the stimulus words is the same for the investigator as the subject, and hence for all subjects, then the process is appropriately used as the measuring process for the variable, its relevance to some construct being the measuring process for the variable, its relevance to some construct being the only area of uncertainty. Once again, the investigator makes a judgment about the datum--usually a simple clerical classification.

In other domains, the investigator uses naturalistic behavior, as in going to a home to observe a mother interacting with a child. Alternatively, the mother and child may come to a laboratory where the mother is instructed to leave the room for a period. Somewhat similar is the generation of behavior by assembling subjects and asking them to reach a group decision about a question posed to them. In all these instances, there is a behavioral protocol from which measurements are obtained by a separate process. Observers record occurrences of specified behaviors that have been classified a priori as *manifestations of a construct*. Observers may also be asked to estimate the strength of a behavioral disposition on the basis of the impressions formed during the observation period. Going further, the investigator may ask for inferences, the observers using bits of the observed behaviors to reason about the actors' dispositions in all other conditions.

Finally, there is measurement where the behavioral protocol is only implicit, where no actor behavior is generated for the purpose of measurement. Ratings of self or of others are frequently requested by the investigator, the implicit instruction being to recall the subjects' prior behavior and the data producers' impressions of that behavior. The measuring process, the making of the ratings, is then quite distinct from the behavioral processes on which they are based.

In social-behavioral science, then, the measuring procedure involves several phases. One element of the ongoing process in measuring, previously discussed, is the segments of behavior that are to be measured. There is also a processing of that protocol by a data-producer, yielding separate bits of data. Finally, there is the processing of the bits to obtain the values that are entered into statistical analyses. Because our measuring procedures are so heterogeneous, the identification of these phases may not have fixed rules or criteria. The critical point is that there are, at the very least, two stages: something behavioral must occur; then an aspect or property of that protocol must be extracted and converted into a datum. And in certain instances, the data obtained from one process provide the protocol processed by a subsequent data-producer. For instance, a letter of recommendation is the product of one evaluation of the candidate for a position, with such a product itself being integrated with other letters and materials by someone making the final decision. Again, in clinical personality research, the judgments made on the basis of processing some specific protocols may be integrated into an overall judgment about the mental health status of a patient.

CONCEPTUALIZATION AND MEASUREMENT

The measuring process varies with aspects of the conceptualization of the construct being measured. Many of our difficulties in social-behavioral research stem from our failure to identify and specify our constructs adequately. We have to begin with a clear view of the level of conceptual analysis at which we are working, the view of behavior that our construct requires. These levels range from neuropsychological or physiological phenomena, such as heart rate or pupil response, through overt movements, such as shifting the gaze or starting to smile. Beyond these, there are levels of a different kind, such as segments of behavior taken as integrated, purposive actions and, at the extreme, perceived enduring dispositions.

The identification of levels is not sharp because that identification may be based on one or more underlying dimensions. One basis may be temporal duration of the behavioral protocol to which the measurement refers, ranging from fractions of a second to years. Another is from fairly objective, explicit protocols to less explicit ones. Again, levels may be specified in terms of the processes in data-producers, from simple cognitions or recognitions to complex cognitive inferences and judgments. Finally, the concepts themselves can be ordered from specific and concrete to general and abstract. It is obvious that the measuring processes in data-producers vary with the level of conceptual analysis at which the investigator is working.

There is a peculiar dilemma, a trade-off involved in the choice of level. The investigator working at lower levels has firm, dependable data but is left with the problem of interpreting them, of assigning meaning to them. The controversial aspect of such a measuring process is the inference from the data to the construct of interest. For example, response latency can be measured quite well, but does a larger value indicate that the process has an additional step not present in another process that has a shorter latency? In contrast, the investigator working at higher levels of analysis takes the variable and its measurements more or less at face value, as indicating the target construct; there is no apparent problem of interpretation of the data. For example, when peers are asked to rate leadership, the data are taken as assessments of leadership. The cost, of course, is the necessity of assuming that the complex judgments, the unknown processes in the data-producers, are appropriate: If the raters have never observed instances of actual leading, they may have based their judgments on inferences from apparent self-confidence or assertiveness or social skills, singly or in some combination.

Whatever the level at which investigators choose to   work,   they   must   make   explicit   a   full conceptualization of each construct.   (For extended discussions of such explications, see Fiske, 1971, 1978.)   The conceptualization of a construct should expose the behavioral process to which the construct refers and should enable the investigator to derive an appropriate measuring process. The choice of process will vary with the level of the construct, that level being determined by the behavioral protocol deemed relevant to the construct.

Take dominance as an illustration. If *dominance* is defined as an aspect or quality of specified actions (i.e., if dominance refers to dominating behaviors) then the measuring process has to be based on direct observation, the data-producer identifying actions that have the designated aspect. Such measurement is at a relatively low level and uses a particular kind of behavioral protocol--one where the actor is actively interacting with others.

Dominance can also be taken as an attribution that one person makes about another: X sees Y as a dominating person. With this view, the investigator needs   to   determine   how   the   rater   processes recollections of the subject's behavior and carries out a decision process. Working in this framework, we might be able to identify the information-processing components associated with rater disagreements.   Do some raters decide on the basis of their observation of one or two very salient instances, while others decide on the basis of a pervasive, consistent quality in the subject's actions? Again, perhaps all raters agree on the relevant protocol (e.g., all have observed the same segment of behavior) but they integrate the material in ways that lead to different ratings.

In   still   another   construal,   dominance   is   a

disposition to act in certain specified ways. Is there a single appropriate measuring process for assessing such a construct? Does a set of self-report response-data to questions provide the appropriate process? For example, the items might be of the form: "When I am in a (particular situation), I tend to (tell others what to do, take charge, etc.); or, "If I were in (a particular situation), I would feel inclined to (do certain things)." As the illustrations suggest, disposition can be construed as that which results in certain actions or as the inclination to engage in certain actions. Which does the investigator see as congruent with the preferred definitions of dominance?

These illustrative levels, of course, reflect the fact that in the world outside, psychologists and others process social information on several levels, as examined by Wiggins (1984). But note the contrasts among these construals. When the construct refers to perceived behaviors, the measuring process is linked directly to the behavior processes. When it refers to an attribution, the appropriate measuring process involves actual attributing. But when the construct is taken as referring to a property of a person without any explicit restrictions, it is quite unclear what the measuring process should be. Many of the constructs in social-behavioral science are so abstract and vague that their measurement is problematic and empirical work can contribute little to our understanding of them.

PROCEDURES FOR GETTING
AT THE MEASURING PROCESS

We cannot directly observe the measuring process going on in the data-producer, any more than we can observe problem solving and other perceptual-cognitive activity. In their work on problem solving, Newell and Simon (1972) used "think-aloud" procedures. My exploratory use of such procedures with raters suggests that they can furnish us with some leads as to what is going on. The protocols of such verbalizations do not, of course, include everything that goes on--all the images, encoding, and so on. Similar to think-aloud methods is the Instantaneous Report of Judgments procedure (Banks, 1982), discussed earlier.

Post hoc reports have been used by Simon (Ericsson & Simon, 1984). A few years back, Kuncel (1973) studied such reports about what went on while answering items on personality questionnaires, identifying a variety of processes. Minor and Fiske (1976) obtained evidence that similar processes occur in describing other people. Think-aloud and post hoc reporting provide us with hunches for further empirical work. They enable us to replace the big black box between stimulus input and response datum with a series of smaller black boxes, as in Sternberg's analyses of the processes in manifesting mental ability while responding to an item in an intelligence test. As discussed earlier, he devised ways to break down those processes into stages, measuring duration or response latency for each (see also Rogers, 1974a, 1974b). Latency has proved to have great value in much current work in cognitive psychology generally--and so should continue to be of value in studying the cognitive activity in measuring processes.

None of those techniques provides information on the process from moment to moment. It may be possible to devise procedures closer to the physiological or neural level. For example, Hess (1965) has traced pupil size while a subject carried out mental arithmetic, solved a problem, checked the answer, and simply held it in mind. What might other indices of activation or arousal show us? And are there unobtrusive behavioral manifestations that could give us clues to the measuring process? For example, Newell and Simon (1972) used eye movements in some of their work. The task of examining the measuring process poses a challenge to our ingenuities.

CONCLUSION

In spite of the generality of the title, a chapter of this length cannot provide a comprehensive treatment of the measuring process in social-behavioral science. It has neglected measurement in laboratory research because there usually are few difficulties there, unless complex judgments are required of the data-producer. It has ignored the measuring of reactions in field experimentation. It has not considered the process in the subject making a judgment in an Asch-type experiment on conformity to group pressure. It has also omitted the complex problems in the cognitive processing of semantic material, as in the diverse meanings that data-producers give to the words in our instruments. It has not cited many who have thought about the strategies of subjects responding to ability or to personality items. It has not mentioned the affective processes involved in much measuring. Finally, it has not developed the implications for understanding the measuring process and the decisions of data-producers that can be found in much current cognitive psychology, especially in conceptual and empirical work on making inferences and decisions. Except in cognitive psychology, there has been little relevant research that empirically analyzes the stages in the processes producing judgments and data.

To measure and understand behavior, we must understand what we are doing, we must learn what goes on in our measuring processes. Such understanding may not be essential in applied measurement, where we can evaluate the adequacy of our measuring procedures against the pragmatic question: Does it work as we want it to? (How many of us understand the principles underlying the speedometer or the temperature gauge in our car?) But such understanding is necessary in basic research.

Measurement is, of course, instrumental; it is a means to an end. We measure in order to understand our constructs and their interrelationships. The diversity of our constructs requires a variety of measuring procedures, each with its own process. We must decide what process or processes are appropriate for each type of construct, and adapt our measuring procedures to elicit those processes. By this route, we will come to a better understanding of our measuring and be able to measure better. We will also come to understand our constructs better. The final product will be gains in our understanding of behavior.

REFERENCES

Adams, R. McC., Smelser, N. J., & Treiman, D. J. (Eds.). (1982). *Behavioral and social science research: A national resource* (Part 1). Washington, DC: National Academy Press.

Banks, C. G. (1982, August). *Behavioral indices of raters' cognitive processing in performance appraisal.* Paper presented at the Annual Meeting of the American Psychological Association, Washington, DC.

Boulding, K.E. (1980). Science: Our common heritage. *Science, 207,* 831-836.

Bradburn, N. M. (1982). Discrepancies between concepts and their measurements: The urban-rural example. In W.H. Kruskal (Ed.), *The social sciences: Their nature and uses* (pp. 137-148). Chicago: University of Chicago Press.

Butterfield, E. C., & Belmont, J. M. (1977). Assessing and improving the executive cognition of mentally retarded people. In I. Bialer & M. Sternlicht (Eds.), *The psychology of mental retardation: Issues and approaches* (pp. 277-318). New York: Psychological Dimensions.

Campbell, D.T. (1969). Definitional versus multiple operationalism, *Et al., 2,* 14-17.

Cook, T. D., & Campbell, D. T. (1979). *Quasi-experimentation: Design and analysis issues for field settings.* Chicago, ILL: Rand McNally.

Embretson (Whitely), S. (1983). Construct validity: Construal representation versus nomothetic span. *Psychological Bulletin, 93,* 179-197.

Ericsson, K. A., & Simon, H. A. (1984). *Protocol analysis: Verbal reports as data.* Cambridge, MA: Massachusetts Institute of Technology Press.

Fiske, D. W. (1971). *Measuring the concepts of personality.* Chicago, ILL: Aldine.

Fiske, D. W. (1978). *Strategies for personality research: The observation versus interpretation of behavior.* San Francisco: Jossey-Bass.

Fiske, D. W. (1980). When are verbal reports veridical? In R. Shweder (Ed.), *New directions for methodology of social and behavioral science:*

Fallible judgment in behavioral research (Vol. 4, pp. 59-66). San Francisco: Jossey-Bass.

Hess, E.H. (1965). Attitude and pupil size. *Scientific American, 212*(4), 46-54.

Koch, S. (1974). Psychology as science. In S. C. Brown (Ed.), *Philosophy of psychology* (pp. 3-40). London: Macmillan.

Kuhn, T. S. (1977). The function of measurement in modern physical science. In T. S. Kuhn (Ed.), *The essential tension: Selected studies in scientific tradition and chance* (178-224). Chicago, ILL: University of Chicago Press.

Kuncel, R. B. (1973). Response processes and relative location of subject and item. *Educational and Psychological Measurement, 36*, 545-563.

Minor, M. J., & Fiske, D. W. (1976). Response processes during the description of others. *Educational and Psychological Measurement, 36*, 829-833.

Newell, A., & Simon, H. A. (1972). *Human problem solving*. Englewood Cliffs, NJ: Prentice-Hall.

Nisbett, R. E., & Wilson, T. (1977). Telling more than we can know: Verbal reports on mental processes. *Psychological Review, 84*, 231-259.

Rogers, T. B. (1974a). An analysis of the stages underlying the process of responding to personality items. *Acta Psychologica, 38*, 205-213.

Rogers, T. B. (1974b). An analysis of two central stages underlying responding to personality items: The self-referent decision and response solution. *Journal of Research in Personality, 8*, 128-138.

Rosenberg, M. J. (1969). The conditions and consequences of evaluation apprehension. In R. Rosenthal, & R. L. Rosnow (Eds.), *Artifact in behavioral research* (pp.279-349). New York, NY: Academic Press.

Rosenthal, R. (1976). *Experimenter effects in behavioral research* (Rev. ed.). New York: Irvington.

Simon, H. A. (1975). The functional equivalence of problem-solving skills. *Cognitive Psychology, 7*, 268-288.

Sternberg, R. J. (1977). *Intelligence, information processing, and analogical reasoning: The componential analysis of human abilities.* Hillsdale, NJ: Lawrence Erlbaum Associates.

Sternberg, R. J. (1979). The nature of mental abilities. *American Psychologist, 34,* 214-230.

Sternberg, R. J. (1980). Sketch of a componential subtheory of human intelligence. *Behavioral and Brain Sciences, 3,* 573-614.

Sternberg, R. J. (1981). Intelligence and nonentrenchment. *Journal of Educational Psychology, 73,* 1-16.

Sternberg, R. J. (1983). Components of human intelligence. *Cognition, 15,* 1-48.

Sternberg, R. J. (1985). Human intelligence: The model is the message. *Science, 230,* 1111-1118.

Wiggins, J. S. (1984). The "mere" semantics of social perception. In S. E. Hampson (Chair), *The social construction of personality.* Symposium on the Social Construction of Personality held at the Second European Conference on Personality, Bielefeld.

Discussion of "Measuring to Understand and Understanding Measuring"

Susan Whitely Embretson
University of Kansas

In this section, I will discuss Dr. Fiske's chapter primarily from the perspective of interfacing psychometrics with cognitive theory because my own research has been in this area. I also examine some implications of Fiske's ideas for measurement practice.

Fiske has presented a philosophical chapter that outlines a series of issues for measuring social-behavioral constructs. Fiske called attention to the role of the examinee as actively generating data rather than passively responding to the item in the way intended by the test developer. Fiske believes that to understand measurement, the data-generation processes of the examinee must be understood. Further, the contribution of the various underlying components and metacomponents to individual differences must be understood. Then, when the contributing processes are understood, they must be compared to the processes that were intended by the theory that guided the test.

To understand a measure, according to Fiske, we need to consider three areas (a) the elements that are constant throughout the measuring process (e.g., instructional set, psychological conditions of test administration), (b) the behavioral process behind each datum, and (c) transforming the data into scores. Fiske notes that we know a great deal about the first and third conditions, but not the second condition. I agree that we know little about the behavioral process behind test datum, but if we knew more about the underlying processes we also would want to know much more about the constant elements and transforming the data into scores. That is, the constant design of the testing situation, as well as the scoring method, should be geared to maximizing the probability that examinees' scores represent the intended behavioral processes.

Although he does not use the term, Fiske's chapter eloquently elaborates a long-standing problem with the Cronbach and Meehl (1955) construct validity concept. Interestingly, although many "new" types of validity have been proposed, it is only recently that serious examinations of the construct validity concept have appeared. A very important, but little noticed exception, was Bechtoldt's (1959) early critique of construct validity as an ex post facto method of developing measures. That is, according to Bechtoldt, rather than beginning with definitions of the construct and relating the construct to the measuring operation, we learn about what we are measuring only after we have developed the test. Often, it is learned that what was intended to be measured, in fact was not measured. But then, it is too late. We have invested in the test and we cannot afford to abandon it.

Fiske notes that some issues that he raised about the data generation process have appeared in somewhat varying contexts. For example, response styles, such as social desirability and acquiescence have been investigated for their contribution to individual differences. Response styles may be regarded as an undesirable data generation process for the examinee. Fiske's chapter could be regarded as a reaffirmation of the importance of response style research.

I believe, however, that following these guidelines changes both construct validation research and test development practices. Fiske is asking for a basic re-examination of the whole measuring process. He suggests that the aim of studying the data generation process is to compare our data to the best data in accordance with our theory about the construct we are measuring. If measurements are revised so that the best data are obtained, I believe that we approach an a priori method of defining the constructs in tests, such as sought by Bechtoldt. Interestingly, test design--the manipulation and selection of test items to measure specified constructs--becomes a viable possibility with an a priori approach.

To show how data generation may be studied in its own right, Fiske reviews Sternberg's (1977) componential approach to aptitude as a prototype. Particularly significant in Sternberg's work is his unification of issues in componential theory and his innovative application of methods to test the theory. Sternberg's componential theory is really a metatheory because it outlines the various sources of individual differences in performing the task (i.e., component performance, strategies, and knowledge bases). Particularly crucial in the empirical support of Sternberg's theory was his application of methods that permit all aspects of performance to be studied simultaneously so that their relative impact could be assessed. Mathematical modeling of task accuracy and response time from the postulated components has proven to be a very effective general method to study tasks.

I believe that the potential of studying test items as information-processing tasks, as in Sternberg's research, and examinees as data producers, as proposed by Fiske, can be more fully understood by considering two separate goals in construct validation, as I have recently elaborated (Embretson, 1983). The first goal is *construct representation*. Construct representation research seeks to decompose the task into underlying theoretical variables, particularly by mathematical modeling. Using this definition, both Sternberg's componential model and Fiske's data generation model concern construct representation of the test.

The second goal is *nomothetic span*. Nomothetic span concerns the utility of the test as a measure of individual differences. Thus, in nomothetic span research, contributions to the variances and covariances of the tests are studied.

In traditional test research, construct representation and nomothetic span are confounded. Both research goals are presumably accomplished by studying the covariances of test scores. However, we know that many factors contribute to test correlations, so that we can never be assured that measures correlate because they involve the same underlying theoretical constructs or because they involve different, but highly correlated, constructs. However, the experimental methods of cognitive psychology may be applied to study the construct representation of the task independently of the nomothetic span.

A major method from experimental psychology that can be applied to study construct representation is mathematical modeling, as in Sternberg's research on cognitive components. Mathematical modeling provides a unified framework for studying the relative effects of several postulated underlying variables in a task. Mathematical modeling requires data beyond the traditional item response data to identify the postulated constructs. Two types of additional data that may be used are (a) information structure, where the stimulus properties of items are scored with respect to the postulated constructs; and (b) multiple response data, where subtasks are created to identify component outcomes.

Experimental methods, such as mathematical modeling, should have increasing feasibility as we enter the era of high technology. Computer administration of tests may replace paper-and-pencil tests. For example, research is in progress to operationalize computerized adaptive testing in the Armed Services, on a wide-scale basis. Computerized testing is important for construct representation research in at least two ways. First, multiple response data may easily be collected. Second, it is

easy   systematically   to   manipulate   stimulus
characteristics   on   computers   so   that   adapting
laboratory procedures to testing will be quite easy.

Another   implication   of studying   data   generation
processes is for test development.   That is, if we know
the   processes   involved   in the   items and   if   we   have
indices   of   the   difficulty   of   these   processes   in
specific   items,   we can possibly design   the   test   to
represent   only the variables that are specified by   our
theory,   as   suggested by Fiske.   However,   to   design
tests   as a science, rather than as an art, we need   to
embark on very active and unified research programs   to
study   the measuring task.   If we are   successful,   the
item writer becomes an experimenter who manipulates his
or   her   tasks   to   represent   specified   theoretical
constructs.

Perhaps a major change in contemporary   psychology
is   our   concept   of   experimentation.   Within-subject
experiments--in   which   sets of   systematically   varied
tasks   are   presented in   counterbalanced   designs--are
becoming   at   least   as   popular   as   between-subjects
experiments.   Under the information processing paradigm
of   contemporary psychology, our concept of   experiment
is   close   to   that of Cattell (1966)   who   defines   an
experiment   as   systematic observation.   That   is,   an
experiment   records   the behaviors and   the   conditions
under   which the behaviors are obtained.   Notice   that
the   test   situation   is very similar   to   the   within-
subjects   experiment.   An examinee is presented with   a
set   of tasks.   It is the systematic   manipulation   and
counterbalancing of the tasks that has been missing   in
test development.

Also,   of course, we need to develop   psychometric
models   to   link   performance   on   test   items   to   the
underlying   data   generation   processes.   In   my   own
research, I have been developing multicomponent   latent
trait models (Embretson, 1984; Whitely, 1980) both   to
test hypotheses about the processes in the task and   to
estimate the relative role of various processes in each
item.   If   items vary in process   representation,   the

indices can be used to select items to measure specified constructs.

Thus, I believe that viewing the test subjects as data producers, as Fiske proposes, not only changes the way in which we think about measurement, but also changes the type of research and psychometric models that we view as relevant to the test development process.

One last area of Fiske's chapter that I find intriguing is his conceptualization of measurement issues in personality. Particularly illuminating are the examples of the different definitions for the trait "dominance." According to Fiske, dominance can be either (a) disposition to act in a certain way, or (b) an attribution that is made by one person about another person. For the attributional definition of the trait, theory and methods that were used in person perception research (e.g., Anderson, 1965) are relevant to understand the measure. For disposition to act, data generation is somewhat easier to understand if we use direct observation, such as in Fiske's face-to-face interaction research. But, if we measure from self-reports of disposition to act, as in many personality inventories, the data-generation process is crucial. As Fiske noted, the more inference from observation to the construct to be measured, the more questionable the measurement. This same principle also applies to the data generator. Self-report inventories require the examinee to infer and abstract about his behavior. What is the data generator's concept of the trait and the relevancy of his behavior to it? What is his memory of his own behaviors? (It could be quite self-serving.) The Ericsson and Simon (1980) theory of verbal report data and the conditions that lead to inaccuracy could be crucial to understanding self-reports, as Fiske suggested.

I hope that Fiske will continue to develop his ideas along this line. As he noted, the problems of data generation have been considered only in a piecemeal fashion in personality measurement. We need a "metatheory" of the personality measurement task.

Fiske's chapter brings us closer to such a metatheory.

REFERENCES

Anderson, N. H. (1965). Adding versus averaging as a stimulus combination rule in impression formation. *Journal of Experimental Psychology, 70*, 394-400.

Bechtoldt, H. P. (1959). Construct validity: A critique. *American Psychologist, 14*, 619-629.

Cattell, R. B. (1966). The principles of experimental design and analysis in relation to theory. In R. B. Cattell (Ed.), *Handbook of multivariate experimental psychology* (pp. 19-66). Chicago, ILL: Rand-McNally.

Cronbach, L. J., & Meehl, P. E. (1955). Construct validity in psychological tests. *Psychological Bulletin, 52*, 281-302.

Duncan, S., & Fiske, D. W. (1977). *Face to face interaction*. Hillsdale, NJ: Lawrence Erlbaum Associates.

Embretson, S.(1983). Construct validity: Construct representation versus nomothetic span. *Psychological Bulletin, 93*, 179-197.

Embretson, S. (1984). A general component latent trait model for response processes. *Psychometrika, 49*, 175-186.

Ericsson, K.A., & Simon, H.A. (1980). Verbal reports as data. *Psychological Review, 87*, 215-251.

Sternberg, R. J. (1977). *Intelligence, information processing and analogical reasoning*. Hillsdale, NJ: Lawrence Erlbaum Associates.

Whitely, S. E. (1980). Multicomponent latent trait models for ability tests. *Psychometrika, 45*, 479-494.

III MULTIVARIATE AND INTERACTIONIST STUDIES OF PERSONALITY

7 On the Role of Situations in Personality Research: An International Perspective

David Magnusson
University of Stockholm

Before going into my main theme, the title needs some comments. I have deliberately used the term *interactional perspective*. I have done so in order to avoid one of the semantic quarrels that take so much time in psychology and distract us from the real psychological problems. Some people have spent their energy discussing whether what is sometimes designated interactional psychology represents a new personality theory or not, its relation to trait theories, to dynamic personality theories, and so forth. That discussion does not concern us here. To me the interesting and central question is whether, by reformulating our problems, we can promote better research on important matters. Obviously, the paradigm of research in personality has shifted in recent years toward greater interest in two long-neglected directions, namely theorizing and research on the person-situated interaction process, and systematic analysis of the environmental conditions that are effective in that process. If such a shift owes something to that reformulation of old problems which has been called an interactional perspective, then this has made a contribution.

For those who are familiar with what has happened

during the last decades in personality research,   there
is   good reason for choosing the theme on the   role   of
situations   on   this occasion and in this   place.   The
symposium   on "Stimulus Determinants of Behavior"   that
Saul   B.   Sells organized at Texas Christian   University
in the beginning of the 1960s, resulting in a book with
that title (Sells, 1963), was an important contribution
to   the   discussion about the role   of   situations   and
situational   conditions   for theorizing   and   empirical
research   on human   behavior.   Many   of   these   issues
that are central in this discussion were dealt with   at
that symposium.

SETTING THE STAGE

One way of formulating the ultimate goal for theory and
empirical   research in psychology is to say that it   is
to understand and explain why individuals think,   feel,
react, and act as they do in real life situations.

From birth through life an individual is   involved
in a continuous, bidirectional dynamic interaction with
his   or her environment.   When the   process   underlying
current   behavior   is   described in   terms   of   person-
situation   interaction and when individual   development
is discussed in such terms, the problem is not how   the
person   and   the   situation, as two   separate   parts   of
equal importance, interact.   It is, rather, and this is
essential,   how   individuals   by   their   perceptions,
thoughts,   and   feelings function in   relation   to   the
environment.   In   an individual's dealings   with   the
external world, a fundamental role is played by his   or
her   integrated   mediating   system,   of   which   the
main   aspects   are cognitions and   conceptions   of   the
external world (including self-conceptions), particular
ways   of   processing   information,   emotions,   and
physiological   processes.   It is his or   her   mediating
system   that determines which situations an   individual
seeks   or avoids (as far as there are   options),   which
situational   conditions   are attended to,   how   single
stimuli   or   patterns   of   stimuli and   events   are
interpreted,   and   how   the   information   about   the
environment   is   transformed   into   inner   and   outer
actions.

The structure and functioning of an individual's mediating system is formed and changes slowly in a process of maturation and learning that takes place in the continuous interaction between the individual and his or her environment. Understanding the lawfulness of how the subsystems of perceptions, cognitions, emotions, and physiological processes function in interaction with each other and as an integrated total system in current situations, and how they develop during the process of maturation and learning, is a central task for understanding and explaining human behavior (see e.g., Magnusson, 1980). There is a rapidly growing awareness, expressed by many researchers, of the need for models that integrate these various aspects in order to overcome the fragmentation of theorizing and empirical research that is one of the main obstacles for real progress in psychology (see e.g., Hettema, 1979). Among other things, such integrated models are needed as a basis for more precise empirical work that is really scientific in the sense that it yields data that can be accumulated and interpreted within a general frame of reference.

Given this background, I discuss in the rest of this chapter the contribution of the situational context to a better understanding of individual functioning, in terms of mediating processes as well as in terms of molar social behavior. I do so, because the process in which an individual is involved with his or her environment is lawful and understandable, and because the lawfulness of individual functioning can be better investigated and understood if we consider in a more systematic and explicit way than hitherto the situational context in which individuals function and in which behavior takes place. From what I have said, it should be clear that analyses of the roles of situational context for behavior and of situations per se are not goals in themselves. They are of interest only insofar as the results contribute to a better understanding of individual functioning.

Even a layman knows that behavior varies with the character of the situation. Everyone knows that a person does not behave similarly in the kitchen, at church, on a sporting ground, at a committee meeting, or at a party. However, given this fact, it is interesting to note the lack of an everyday language to distinguish between situations or to relate behavior to situations and situational conditions. More important, however, is that we also almost totally lack a scientific language that has the conceptualizations, distinctions, and relevant categories to enable us to communicate systematically about situations and person-situation interactions.

Among researchers in the area of personality it has long been emphasized at the theoretical level that behavior cannot be understood and explained in isolation from the situational conditions under which it occurs. This is true for theorists who hold very different perspectives--for behaviorists (e.g., Kantor, 1924, 1926), for field theorists (e.g., Lewin, 1943), for personologists (Murray, 1938), for trait psychologists (Allport, 1966; Cattell, 1965; Stagner, 1976), for those advocating a psychodynamic position (e.g., Wachtel, 1977), and for those arguing for an interactional approach to the study of human behavior (e.g., Endler, 1975; Magnusson & Endler, 1977; Pervin, 1978). It has sometimes been stated that trait theorists have neglected or at least underestimated the role of situations for understanding and explaining behavior. This makes it especially interesting that one of the best-known trait theorists, Raymond B. Cattell, came out strongly on the importance of considering the situational context in research on personality: "Lack of allowance for the situation is one of the main causes of misjudging personality" (Cattell, 1965, p. 27).

During the 1970s, the role of situations in behavior has been a central issue in the intense debate on personality consistency and in the renewal of what has been designated interactional psychology. The incorporation of situational factors in theorizing on attitudes has led to models that are clearly interactionistic.

In neighboring disciplines, too, the importance of the situational context for understanding behavior has been recognized. For ethologists it has always been natural to refer to situational factors (for example, perceived territories) in explanatory models of animal behavior. From their various perspectives, anthropologists and sociologists have likewise made important contributions--often overlooked and neglected in the theoretical debate in psychology--to the theoretical discussion about the role of situational conditions for human behavior. The long tradition in sociology can be illustrated with the title of an article by Donald W. Ball: "The Definition of Situations: Some Theoretical and Methodological Consequences of Taking W. I. Thomas Seriously" (Ball, 1972, p. 61). The title refers to propositions made by William I. Thomas (1927, 1928), who in the mid-1920s was already discussing many of the problems that are in focus today. Thomas noted the distinction between actual and perceived environments and situations. He discussed the problems connected with defining and demarcating a situation; he stressed the developmental role of the situations that individuals encounter; and he argued that situational conditions must be incorporated into models of actual behavior.

Given this background of decades of theoretical discussion, there is not much new in proposing that we must consider the situational context in models of behavior and theories of personality. It is a fact that situations and situational conditions have not been a neglected or overlooked issue in the theoretical debate in psychology or in neighboring disciplines. On the battlefield of words, where so many wars are waged in psychology, those who argue that situations play an important role in the process underlying behavior have few, if any, enemies.

THE SITUATION IN EMPIRICAL PERSONALITY RESEARCH

Then the interesting question is: What impact have these strong theoretical statements had on actual empirical research? My first point in this chapter is an attempt to answer that question: After that I briefly summarize the theoretical basis for systematic analyses of environments and situations and finally, I give an example of such analyses from my research group in Stockholm.

First, we have to conclude that the theoretical formulations on the role of situational context have not always been very explicit with respect to their implications and consequences for empirical research. Yet they do have important consequences for theoretical models, for research strategies, for models of measurement, for the types of data that are appropriate, and for the choice of methods for data collection and analysis. The consequences are important both for research on current behavior and for research on development. This is true in many fields of research. Most of the theorists who have emphasized the importance of the situational context for individual functioning have done so with molar, social behavior. But the consequences are equally important for research on basic psychological processes, such as perception, cognition, information processing, decision making, and on physiological processes.

When advocating a "representative design" in the 1950s, Brunswick (1956) pointed to an interesting phenomenon in psychological research. Although we carefully adhere to strict rules for sampling individuals--so as to be able to generalize results to the population of individuals from which the sample was drawn--we usually fail to sample the situations in which the individuals are observed in the same strict manner.

Although Brunswick's proposition about representativeness with respect to situational context was expressed forcefully and explicitly, and despite its importance for empirical research, it has certainly not had the influence on empirical research that its importance warrants.

Let me illustrate the neglect of taking the important theoretical statements seriously in empirical research with observations from an important field of research, on stress and anxiety, first by a review, then by three examples, each illustrating a certain aspect of the problem.

In this field, many researchers are well aware of the important role of situational conditions for the phenomena they are studying and have included situational conditions in their discussions.

In order to examine the impact the theoretical formulations have had on empirical research, we went through what was published on stress and anxiety in two leading journals, *Psychosomatic Medicine* and *Psychophysiology*, during the period 1970-1980.

The inspection identified 57 studies on that issue, published during that period. In 31 of these studies the experimental stress factor was physical pain; in 14 it was demand for achievement; in 3 it was threat of separation; in 3, ego threat; and in the remaining 6, stress was induced by social interaction, pregnancy, menstruation, and so forth. In no case was there a systematic variation of situational conditions to investigate or control possible differential effects on stress and anxiety. In only 2 of the 57 studies did the researchers discuss the possible implications, for the interpretation of results, of choosing the specific type of situation for the experiment.

The aim, of course, of all these studies was to arrive at generalizations about individuals and how they react to and act in stress- and anxiety-provoking situations. The result of our inspection of the two journals then raises a series of questions. For instance: Is physical pain a general cause of stress and anxiety? Or is it employed just for its convenience in the laboratory? What happens if there are individual differences with respect to what is experienced as threatening, and with respect to how threatening each specific situation or stimulus is? And so on.

One problem of particular interest in this field during the 1970s has been the question of sex differences in psychological and physiological reactions to stress. It has been concluded, on the basis of much psychophysiological laboratory work, that men display stronger physiological reactions, in the form of adrenalin, than women to stressful psychosocial situations. Typically, the experiments underlying these conclusions have mostly used situations involving demand for achievement. Suppose then, that significant sex differences occur in the interpretation of such situations as threatening, with men interpreting them as more stressful than do women. Empirical results from a study that I briefly present later indicate that this is the case. They also indicate that situations implying separation are reported as threatening more often by girls than boys. Then what would happen if we investigated physiological reactions in situations implying separation instead of demand for achievement? In a recent study at our department, the sex difference in adrenalin excretion found in achievement-demanding situations did not appear in a separation situation (Lundberg, de Chateau, Winberg, & Frankenhaueser, 1981). Actually, the tendency was in the opposite direction.

Another example from the same field illustrates the general point. Funkenstein (1956) suggested that aggression is accompanied by excretion of nor-adrenalin, and anxiety reactions by excretion of adrenalin. Although this assumption has received some support (Cohen & Silverman, 1959; Fine & Sweeney, 1968), the overall picture from empirical studies is not conclusive. One reason for this may be that the situational conditions have not been controlled. Studies in my research group show that a number of crucial situations are described by some individuals as anxiety-provoking and by others as anger-provoking. Obviously, then, an effective test of Funkenstein's hypothesis presupposes that this fact has been taken into account in the empirical study.

My final example is taken from a recently published study performed at our department. Stability in rank orders of individuals with respect to adrenalin and noradrenalin excretion was investigated across two types of situations, namely situations in the laboratory and in everyday situations. One interesting result was that stability in rank orders of individuals was considerably higher across situations in the laboratory than across everyday situations. If these findings are confirmed they indicate that the laboratory situation, as such, is the strong stress provoking factor, and that it takes over the specific factors introduced by the experimenter.

A year ago I had not thought that what I am saying here needed to be said. However, listening to a symposium at Edinburgh convinced me that the resistance to situational analyses is much stronger than I was aware of.

To this experienced audience it is not necessary to draw conclusions from what I have just described. Nevertheless, it leads over to my next main point, analysis of situations and environments.

A NEED FOR SYSTEMATIC RESEARCH ON SITUATIONS

What I have said so far has been to emphasize the necessity of taking the situational context into account when planning, carrying through, and interpreting empirical research on individual functioning.

However, this cannot be done without systematic knowledge of the situations in which individual functioning is investigated. Only with access to such knowledge can the relevant situational features be considered, in a known and predictable way. The need for such knowledge has been emphasized by many researchers for a long time. In his classic article on two disciplines of psychology, Cronbach (1957) made a strong plea for analysis of situations as a prerequisite for further progress in psychology. He said: "The important matter is to discover the organization among the situations, so that we can describe situational differences as systematically as we do individual differences" (p. 677). Saul B. Sells (1963b) concluded: "While work proceeds actively to extend the explorations of individual differences, however, the equally important frontier of situational dimensions is virtually ignored" (p. 700; see also Frederiksen, 1972; Magnusson, 1971; Rotter, Chance, & Phares, 1972; Schneider, 1973). Although much has been written on the issue since then, the state of affairs is still described in much the same way in a recent book on social situations (Argyle, Furnham, & Graham, 1981).

Herbert A. Simon (1969) stated: "A man viewed as a behavioring system is quite simple, the apparent complexity of his behavior over time is largely a reflection of the complexity of the environment in which he finds himself" (p.25). In addition to implying a need for knowledge about the environmental features that are of importance for individuals' functioning, this statement reflects the many problems involved in the search for that knowledge. Although the need for systematic analyses of situations has been formulated for decades, the complexity of the environment that Simon emphasized has led researchers to question the possiblity of arriving at meaningful and useful categorizations of situations. It is interesting to go through the literature and to follow the arguments against the proposition about situational analyses. To a large extent these are the same arguments as were raised against the study of individual differences at the beginning of this century. It would take too long to review the history on this issue. Let me simply conclude, that there is still very strong opposition to the possibility of analyzing situations in a meaningful and systematic way.

Because these critical points exist and in my opinion may prohibit progress, it might be worthwhile to try to summarize the theoretical base for the proposition about systematic analyses of situations and environments.

Let me first emphasize that I certainly agree with those who question a taxonomy of situations, if this is taken to mean that there exists a single static, final solution for the categorization and dimensionalization of situations and situational stimuli and events. But, in a broader sense, a taxonomy of situations and situational conditions is possible, and meaningful, and very important for progress in psychology.

The statement that research on situations and situational conditions is possible, rests on the basic assumption that there is order and regularity in the environment. The environment, as well as the individual, is in process of constant change at various levels. However, there is order and lawfulness both in the structure of the environment and in the process of change and interaction with the individual.

That order and regularity can be perceived in the environment is a necessary prerequisite for individuals' purposive and lawful behavior (cf. Kelly, 1955, and his discussion of "an integrated universe"). Stimuli, patterns of stimuli, and events do not appear to us in anarchical order. Insofar as order and regularity can be observed in the environment, it is possible to arrange patterns of stimuli and events along dimensions, and they can be grouped into homogeneous categories on the basis of common characteristics.

Along the micro-macro dimension of the environment, order and regularity exist on different levels of generalization. Cultures, for instance, can be categorized systematically with respect to the kinds of paths that individuals use to attain their goals (Arsenian & Arsenian, 1948). Situations can be ordered, for example, with respect to the kinds of reward they offer for certain types of behavior (see e.g., Price & Bouffard, 1974), and objects can be ordered, for example, with respect to how fearful they are. At all these levels, the order can be reflected in perceptions and interpretations which people have in common, as well as in individually specific interpretations.

That order and regularity exist in the environment at different levels does not necessarily mean that there is just one single hierarchical system of dimensions and categories that can be established once and for all. The kind of order that can be observed and meaningfully mapped in the total environment space will depend on the level of generality on the micro-macro dimension at which the researcher is working and upon the angle from which it is observed (i.e., on the psychological problem under consideration).

What has just been said leads to the conclusion that one cannot expect a single, definite solution to the problem of categories and dimensions in this area. Depending upon the problem, both the appropriate situation characteristics to investigate and the appropriate kind of data (quantitative or qualitative) will vary, as will the appropriate method of analysis.

For anyone who has approached the field of situational analysis, it is obvious that the road to knowledge here is full of problems. However, the problems are there as a challenge to researchers, not as an excuse for doing nothing. I am convinced that careful research in this field will yield knowledge that will contribute to better understanding of individual functioning in real life situations. The many conceptual and methodological problems connected with situational analysis have been analyzed and discussed by several authors (see e.g., Argyle, et al., 1981; Endler, 1981; Magnusson, 1978, 1981; Pervin, 1978). Here, I end my chapter with an example from empirical work in our own research group in Stockholm. I have chosen this study, because it demonstrates our way of working, besides underlining the main points I have just made. I present the study as an illustration, without having the time to discuss restrictions and reservations.

SITUATION - OUTCOME CONTINGENCIES

The study concerned the question of age and sex differences in the perception and interpretation of anxiety-provoking situations. The problem was investigated in a cross-cultural perspective, using data from five different countries: Hungary, Holland, Sweden, Japan, and Yemen. The data that I report here were collected in Hungary.

Theoretical Foundation

Within our general frame of reference
theoretical starting points.

First, we adopted the generally accepted view that
situation-bound anxiety arises in response to perceived
threat in the environment. This refocuses interest on
the individuals' perceived qualities of the situations,
the meanings assigned by the observer, that are
studied.

Our second theoretical starting point was modern
social learning theory in which it is assumed that
behavior develops in a learning process in which two
types of perceived contingencies are formed, namely
situation-outcome, and behavior-outcome contingencies.
By situation-outcome contingencies, we mean that
certain situational conditions will lead to certain
outcomes; and by behavior-outcome contingencies, we
mean that certain actions on the part of the individual
will have certain predictable consequences. The
formation of such contingencies has a strong
significance for survival: It enables the individual
to make valid predictions about the external world
and to act act effectively in relation to it. This
view implies also that the environment is an
information carrier and not mainly a releaser of
reactions and actions.

Definition of the Population of Anxiety-Provoking Situations

A meaningful investigation of sex and age differences
in the perception of anxiety-provoking situations
presupposes a definition of the population of such
situations.

We approached the problem of the
representativeness of situations by sampling subjects
and using their descriptions of anxiety provoking
situations as a representative sample. The subjects
were 100 boys and 100 girls at each of the age levels
12, 15, and 18. They were instructed to describe as
carefully as possible the anxiety-provoking situations
that first came to their mind. The subjects were

instructed to describe the specific element in the situation that was associated with the experience of anxiety, and then why this specific element was anxiety-provoking.

The instruction was repeated three times, which allowed each subject to present three anxiety-provoking situations.

Classifications of Anxiety-Provoking Situations

The next problem was to construct an adequate structure of the population of anxiety-provoking situations. We started by doing an informal content analysis and used the result to form two classification schemes in accordance with relevant theory about situation-outcome contingencies (Magnusson & Stattin, 1981).

The first of the two schemes is labeled *Situational Characteristics*. Using this subscheme, situations are classified on the basis of the description of the element by which they are associated with experiences of anxiety (see Table 7.1).

The second scale is labeled *Expected Consequences*. The subscheme classifies the situations on the basis of the descriptions of why these situational elements are anxiety-provoking (see Table 7.2).

Table 7.1.
Categories And Their Definitions For The Subscheme
Of Situational Characteristics

Person	*Situation*
1. Self	8. Evaluative Situations
2. Parents	9. Medical Situations
3. Other closely akin adults	10. Accidents
	11. Common Phobia
4. Siblings	12. Animals
5. Authorities outside the family	13. Archaic situations
	14. Supernatural horror
6. Equals	15. Macro-social
7. "Dangerous people"	

Table 7.2.
Categories And Their Definitions For The Subscheme
Of Expected Consequences

| | Personal- | |
Physical-Bodily	Interpersonal	Global
1. Physical pain	5. Personal inadequacy	13. Societal
2. Physical injury	6. Loss of self control	
3. Uneasiness	7. Death	
4. Unrealistic	8. Punishment	
	9. Guilt	
	10. Shame	
	11. Rejection	
	12. Separation	

RESULTS

By way of illustration I present the main trends for boys, and also some age trends in sex differences. All figures stand for the percentage of subjects who reported the various kinds of situations as particularly anxiety-provoking.

Figure 7.1 presents the age trends for the most frequently reported categories of Situational Characteristics for boys.

The most striking difference concerns situations involving demand for achievement, with a strong increase between the ages of 12 and 15. At 15, almost 90% of the boys reported such situations as anxiety-provoking. One can also recognize the continuous decrease in the frequency of parents and the increase in other authority figures (teachers, police, etc.) as reported sources of anxiety.

The review of research on stress and anxiety that I referred to earlier showed that physical pain was used most frequently as a stress factor. Here we can see that very few subjects report physical pain as the most anxiety-provoking.

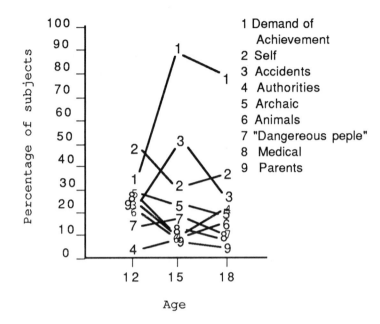

FIG.7.1. Age curves, reflecting the percentages of boys reporting different categories of Activating Conditions.

As an illustration of sex differences in Situational Characteristics, Figure 7.2 reports results for the categories *Accidents* and *Archaic Situations*. The latter category refers to situations that may have a basic biological significance, "Being out in a thunderstorm," "Being alone in the forest at night," "Being home alone at night, when someone knocks at the door."

The sex difference for Archaic Situations is clear across age levels. For the boys the frequency of such situations was about half of that for girls at the age of 18. This sex difference is even more pronounced among Swedish youngsters in our data.

Figure 7.3 presents the age trends for Expected Consequences for boys. The most striking tendency across age levels was the strong increase in expected consequences of Personal Inadequacy or Fear of Failure and the corresponding decrease in expected outcomes in terms of Physical Injury and Punishment.

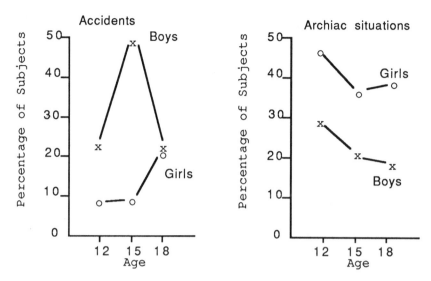

FIG.7.2 Age curves for percentages of boys and girls reporting Accidents and Archaic situations.

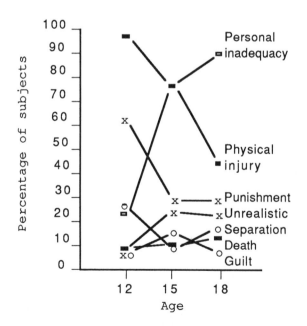

FIG.7.3. Age curves, reflecting the percentages of boys reporting Expected Consequences.

A difference that might be of some significance was found by comparing the patterns we saw earlier in age curves for Situational Characteristics with those for Expected Consequences in Figure 7.3. The age curves for Expected Consequences are much more dramatic than those for Situational Characteristics. This indicates that   the   source   of   anxiety   in   the   situational conditions changes less across these ages than the appraisal of these conditions in terms of expected outcomes.

As an illustration, Figure 7.4 shows the sex differences for two types of Expected Consequences, namely, for Expected Feelings of Personal Inadequacy and for Expectations of Separation.

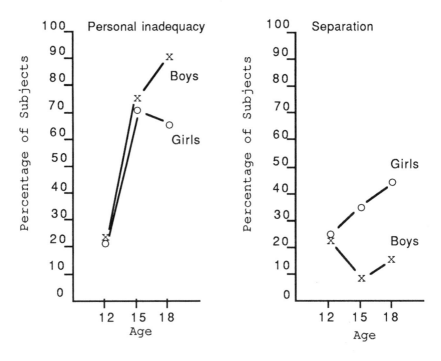

FIG.7.4 Age curves demonstrating sex differences for Personal inadequacy and Separation.

The presentation above shows that the two subschemes can be used separately to investigate sex and age differences with respect to elements in situations that may be associated with anxiety and the expected consequences of encountering such conditions. However, it is most fruitful to use the subschemes in conjunction. The two sets of categories can then be matched in a contingency table with m rows (the number of categories for Situational Characteristics) and n columns (the number of categories for Expected Consequences). Such contingency tables can be used for studying sex and age differences in situation-outcome contingencies, as well as cross-cultural differences in this respect.

COMMENTS

This study and its results raise questions for further research in various directions. Let me here emphasize two points: First, analyses of data from this and other similar studies show that there are significant and conspicuous differences between groups of individuals, sexes, ages, and types of situations with respect to the situational characteristics that are associated with anxiety, and with respect to situation -outcome contingencies. To the extent that behavior is a function of our perceptions and interpretations of the outer world, the conclusions are valid also for manifest behavior. The results firmly demonstrate the necessity of considering the situational conditions when planning and carrying through empirical research on stress and anxiety and I think this conclusion can be generalized to hold for psychological research in general.

My second comment has a bearing on psychological research in general. The fragmentation of psychological theorizing and research obviously has many causes. In my opinion, one of the main causes is that we too often theorize and experiment on important psychological problems, without first undertaking careful and systematic observation and analysis of the persistent phenomena under consideration.

The study that I have just reported demonstrates

how much knowledge can be gained by systematic observation, provided this is performed in a meaningful frame of reference and we observe the right things. Of course, I do not wish to imply any contradiction between theory and observation. My main point is that we need more careful, systematic observation and analysis of the phenomena as a basis for effective theorizing and experimentation. Here we have much to learn from those who have been most influential in psychology: Wundt, Freud, Binet, Gesell, Piaget, Murray and others, as well as from our friends in the natural sciences.

In another study, the same subjects described both anxiety-provoking and anger-provoking situations. This produced the observation that one and the same situation could be described as particularly anxiety-provoking by some subjects and as particularly anger-provoking by others. This gave rise to another study, in which situations were scaled with respect to degree of anxiety versus anger-provocativeness and individuals were scaled with respect to disposition to react with anxiety and anger respectively. As mentioned, for cross-cultural comparisons, data have been collected in Sweden, Hungary, Holland, Japan, and Yemen. Preliminary comparisons show interesting variations and invariances across cultures.

In the introduction to this chapter I assumed that one of the obstacles to progress in psychology is the prevalent fragmentation of theorizing and empirical research. The obvious need, then, is a common frame of reference for planning and for carrying through empirical research and for interpretation of the results. An interactional perspective at a general programmatic level may offer such a frame of reference. Then, in order to arrive at more effective and functional research in such a perspective, one of the things that we have to do is to take the importance of the theoretical formulations about the situational context seriously. It is my conviction that this would yield real contributions to the important subject of why individuals think, feel, act and react as they do in real-life situations; thereby we will also be better equipped for working in the direction of our ultimate goal, to contribute to physical and social environments that are adapted to the needs and potentialities of individuals and groups.

I began my chapter by stating that there is a growing need for theories in psychology that integrate the cognitive, emotional, and physiological subsystems that actually function together, and for models of the integrated mediating system that determine the character of an individual's understanding of him or herself and his or her dealing with his or her external world. Such integrated models are necessary prerequisites, if our strivings in empirical research shall yield results that lead to the accumulation of knowledge and make it possible to interpret the results in a common frame of reference that means real scientific progress. The trends in this direction have become more and explicitly formulated and manifested in different ways during recent years. When we go in the direction of more integrated models it is my belief that they will be more realistic and thereby more efficacious for understanding and explaining why individuals think, feel, react and act as they do in real life situations, if we incorporate the situational context in which individuals develop and live in a more systematic and known way than hitherto.

REFERENCES

Allport, G. W. (1966). Traits revisited. *American Psychologist, 21,* 1-10.

Argyle, M., Furnham, A., Graham, J. A. (1981). *Social situations.* Cambridge, MA: Cambridge University Press.

Arsenian, J. & Arsenian, J. M. (1948). Tough and easy cultures: A conceptual analysis. *Psychiatry, 11,* 377-385.

Ball, D. W. (1972). The definition of situation: Some theoretical and methodological consequences of taking W. J. Thomas seriously. *Journal for Theory of Social Behavior, 2,* 61-68.

Brunswick, E. (1956). *Perception and the representative design of experiments.* Berkeley, CA: University of California Press.

Cattell, R. B. (1965). *The scientific analysis of personality.* Chicago: Aldine.

Cohen, S. I. & Silverman, A. J. (1959). Psychophysiological investigations of vascular response variability. *Journal of Psychosomatic Research, 3,* 185-210.

Cronbach, L. J. (1957). The two disciplines of scientific psychology. *American Psychologist, 12,* 671-684.

Endler, N. S. (1975). A person-situation interaction model for anxiety. In C. D. Spielberger & I. G. Sarason (Eds.), *Stress and anxiety* (Vol. 1, pp.145-164). Washington, DC: Hemisphere.

Endler, N. S. (1981). Sitational aspects of interactional psychology. In D. Magnusson (Ed.), *Toward a psychology of situations* (pp. 361-374). Hillsdale, NJ: Lawrence Erlbaum Associates.

Fine, B.J. & Sweeney, D. R. (1968). Personality traits, and situational factors, and catecholamine excretion. *Journal of Experimental Research in Personality, 3,* 15-27.

Frederiksen, N. (1972). Toward a taxonomy of situations. *American Psychologist, 27,* 114-123.

Funkenstein, D. H. (1956). Nor-epinephrine-like and epinephrine-like substances in relation to human behavior. *Journal of Nervous and Mental Disease, 124,* 58-68.

Hettema, P. J. (1979). *Personality and adaptation.* Amsterdam, Holland: North Holland.

Kantor, J. R. (1924). *Principles of psychology* (Vol. 1). Bloomington: Principia Press.

Kantor, J. R. (1926). *Principles of Psychology* (Vol. 2). Bloomington: Principia Press.

Kelly, G. A. (1955). *The psychology of personal constructs.* New York: Norton.

Lewin, K. (1943). Defining the "field at a given time." *Psychological Review, 50,* 393-310.

Lundberg, U., de Chateau, P., Winberg, J., & Frankenhauser, M. (1981). Catecholamine and cortisol excretion patterns in three-year-old

Lundberg, U., de Chateau, P., Winberg, J., & Frankenhauser, M. (1981). Catecholamine and cortisol excretion patterns in three-year-old children and their parents. *Journal of Human Stress, 21*, 3-11.

Magnusson, D. (1971). An analysis of situational dimensions. *Perceptual and Motor Skills, 22*, 851-876.

Magnusson, D. (1978). On the psychological situation. *Reports from the Department of Psychology, University of Stockholm.* (Report No. 544). Stockholm, Sweden: University of Stockholm.

Magnusson, D. (1980). Personality in an interactional paradigm of research. *Zeitschrift fuer Differentielle und Diagnostiche Psychologie, 1*, 17-34.

Magnusson, D. (1981). Wanted: A psychology of situations. In D. Magnusson (Ed.), *Toward a psychology of situations: an interactional perspective* (pp. 9-36). Hillsdale, NJ: Lawrence Erlbaum Associates.

Magnusson, D. & Endler, N. S. (1977). Interactional psychology: Present status and future prospects. In D. Magnusson & N. S. Endler (Eds.), *Personality at the crossroads: Current issues in interactional psychology* (pp 3-31). Hillsdale, NJ: Lawrence Erlbaum Associates.

Magnusson, D. & Stattin, H. (1981). Situation-outcome contingencies:A conceptual and empirical analysis of threatening situations. *Reports from the Department of Psychology, the University of Stockholm* (Report No. 571). Stockholm, Sweden: University of Stockholm.

Murray, H. A. (1938). *Explorations in personality.* New York: Oxford University Press.

Pervin, L. A. (1978). Definitions, measurements, and classifications of stimuli, situations, and environments. *Human Ecology, 6*, 71-105.

Price, R. H. & Bouffard, D. L. (1974). Behavioral appropriateness and situational constraint as dimensions of social behavior. *Journal of Personality and Social Psychology, 30*, 579-586.

Rotter, J. B., Chance, J. E., & Phares, E. J. (1972). *Applications of a social learning theory of personality.* New York: Holt, Rinehart & Winston.

Schneider, D. J. (1973). Implicit personality theory: A review. *Psychological Bulletin, 79,* 294-309.

Sells, S. B. (Ed.). (1963a) *Stimulus determinants of behavior.* New York: Ronald Press.

Sells, S. B. (1963b). An interactionist looks at the environment. *American Psychologist, 18,* 696-702.

Simon, H. A. (1969). *The science of the artificial,* Cambridge, MA: MIT Press.

Stagner, R. (1976). Traits are relevant: Theoretical analysis and empirical evidence. In N. S. Endler & D. Magnusson (Eds.), *Interaction psychology and personality* (pp 109-124). Washington, DC:Hemisphere.

Thomas, W. I. (1927). The behavior pattern and the situation. *Publications of the American Sociological Society: Papers and Proceedings, 22,* 1-13.

Thomas, W. I. (1928). *The child in America.* New York: Knopf.

Wachtel, P. L. (1977) Interaction cycles, unconscious processes, and the person-situation issue. In D. Magnusson & N. S. Endler (Eds.), *Personality at the crossroads: Current issues in interactional psychology* (pp. 317-332). Hillsdale, NJ.: Lawrence Erlbaum Associates.

Interactionism Revisited: A Discussion of "On the Role of Situations in Personality Research"

Norman S. Endler
York University

The two prime tasks for an interactional psychology of personality are: (a) the description, classification, and systematic analyses of stimuli, situations and environments; and (b) the investigation of how persons and situations interact in evoking behavior, and the reciprocal interaction of persons and behavior, persons and situations, and situations and behavior.

THE RELEVANCE OF SITUATIONS FOR PERSONALITY RESEARCH

Two of the leaders in the investigation of the role of situations in personality research have been Saul Sells, whom we honor with this volume, and David Magnusson, whose chapter I am discussing. Sells (1963) was one of the few among modern interactionists who argued for a description of the objective environment in studies focused on person by situation interactions. In the 1960s, Sells presented a comprehensive outline of characteristics of the environment, which he hoped would serve as a starting point for the development of a taxonomy of situations. For a frame of reference, Sells used four interrelated factors that were originally suggested by Sherif and Sherif (1956) as being relevant to social situations:

(a) factors related to persons; (b) factors related to the problem or task; (c) factors related to the site and facilities; and (d) factors concerned with relations of a person to others, to the site, or to the problem or task. These four sets of factors continue to be relevant.

Magnusson (1971) pointed out that few systematic studies on how individuals perceive situations have been conducted. He then went on to develop an empirical psychophysical method for studying the perception of situations. He suggested that situations should be studied as wholes, and proposed similarity ratings as one method for obtaining raw situation perception data. Magnusson used a multidimensional model of similarity.

Although we have made much progress in dimensionalizing persons, the systematic description, classification, and analysis of situations is still in it's infancy. There are a number of problems involved, including the definitional one. In a very crude and general sense it is possible to distinguish among stimuli, situations, and environments. "The environment is the general and persistent background or context within which behavior occurs; whereas the situation is the momentary or transient background. Stimuli can be constructed as being the elements within a situation" (Endler, 1981, p. 364). It is feasible to compare elements within a situation and determine how they affect behavior. Furthermore, one can make a comparison between situations, evaluating the effects of situations as wholes on behavior.

Pervin (1978) has pointed out that the terms *Stimulus*, *Situations*, and *Environment* have been used interchangeably. He states that "The major distinction appears to have to do with the scale of analysis--ranging from the concern with molecular variables in the case of stimulus to molar variables and behaviors in the case of environments" (p.79). However, in practice, this is not necessarily the case. Environmental psychologists and ecologists have focused on the environment; personality theorists, who have been concerned with person by situation interactions, have focused on stimuli.

One very important issue is whether we can define the situation independently of the perceiver. That is, do we focus on objective or subjective characteristics, of situations? Endler (1981) suggests that the significance or meaning of a situation is an important determinant of behavior. Therefore, we should be concerned with how persons construe the situations they select (or have imposed on them) and with which they interact. Persons react to situations, but they also affect the situations with which they interact. Bowers (1973) has noted that "Situations are as much a function of the person as the person's behavior is a function of the situation" (p. 327). The constant and continuous interaction between persons and situations involves an ongoing process.

Selected Versus Imposed Situations. Frequently we select the situations or stimuli that we encounter. However, at times certain situations are imposed on us. This is a lifelong and continuous process. However, in our research we observe and investigate a cross-sectional slice of situations rather than studying situations longitudinally. We need to examine the ongoing and continuous process of situations. If we live in a city, as opposed to a rural area, we are more likely to experience dense populations, tall buildings, subways, and pollution. We are less likely to experience wide open spaces, farm animals, and unpolluted air. Behavioral consistency, when it exists, may be primarily due to the fact that we experience similar situations, both at work and at play, from day to day. Our daily routines are very similar from one day to the next. We normally shop around and select those situations that are rewarding to us and attempt to avoid those that are painful. Our environment shapes us, but we also shape our environment, including other people.

Differential Psychology of Situations. Magnusson and Ekehammar (1978) have suggested a differential psychology of situations to complement the differential psychology of individual differences. This would involve scaling situations and determining the important dimensions of situations. Situations can be scaled in terms of impact, complexity, relevance, objectiveness, subjectiveness, and representativeness. It is necessary to obtain adequate and representative samplings of situations. A taxonomy of situations should be derived within a theoretical context and should not be developed primarily on empirical grounds. Pervin (1977) sampled situations ecologically on the basis of natural habitats that persons encounter. Endler (1981) has proposed that persons keep daily logs of their behavior and the situations that they encounter. We should study real-life situations and determine how individuals construe their daily life encounters.

Perceptions Versus Reactions to Situations. A number of different strategies have been proposed for studying situations. Two of Ekehammar's (1974) suggested strategies for investigating situations are especially relevant to psychological research: namely, situation perception and situation reaction studies. The psychological importance of the situation can be determined by studying the person's perception of the situation and his or her reaction to a situation. As indicated earlier, Magnusson (1971, 1974) has proposed an empirical psychophysical method for investigating the perception of situations. Using this method, Magnusson and Ekehammar (1973) investigated situations common to university students in their studies, and found two bipolar dimensions (positive vs. negative, and active vs. passive) and one unipolar dimension (social). Many of the reactions to situations studies have used data from inventories originally developed for research purposes (e.g., The S - R Inventory of Anxiousness; Endler, Hunt, & Rosenstein, 1962; The Interactional Reactions Questionnaire; Ekehammar, Magnusson, & Ricklander, 1974). Endler et al. (1962) factor analyzed individuals' reactions to a variety of situations of the S - R Inventory of Anxiousness and found three situational factors: interpersonal threat, inanimate physical danger, and ambiguity. Magnusson and Ekehammar (1975,1978) and Ekehammar, Schalling, and Magnusson (1975) examined the relationship between individuals' perceptions of situations and their reactions to situations, for the same groups of persons, and found a high degree of congruence between perceptions and reactions. In terms of units of analysis it is important to study real-life situations rather to rely only on laboratory studies.

INTERACTIONISM AND PERSONALITY THEORY AND RESEARCH

As indicated earlier, the second major task for an interactional psychology of personality is the investigation of how persons and situations interact in evoking behavior, and the reciprocal interaction of persons and behavior, persons and situations, and situations and behavior. Basically, there are two types of interaction: mechanistic and dynamic.

Mechanistic and Dynamic Interaction. The mechanistic model of interaction focuses on interactions of main factors, such persons, situations, and modes of response within a data matrix. The analysis of variance is used in this measurement model. A clear and precise distinction is made between independent and dependent variables. Here interaction describes the interdependency of determinants (independent variables) of behavior. The mechanistic model is not concerned with the interaction between independent and dependent variables. The interaction is not between cause and effects, but between causes. This model is concerned with the structure of the interaction and not with the process. Both the person-by-treatment research strategy and the variance components research strategy represent the mechanistic model. Because of this, they are inappropriate for studying the dynamic interaction process within the context of the interaction model of personality. The dynamic model of interaction focuses on the reciprocal interaction between behavior and both situational events and person factors. The emphasis is on the relationship between independent and dependent variables, and on reciprocal causation. Dynamic interaction is process oriented and integrates situations, mediating variables, and person-reaction variables. It is also multidirectional.

The interaction model of personality. Endler and Magnusson (1976) proposed four basic assumptions of modern interactionism: (a) there is a continuous dynamic process of interaction; (b) persons are intentional and active agents; (c) cognitive factors are important on the person side; and (d) meaningful situations are important on the environmental side. Endler (1983) has elaborated on and modified these assumptions. Although in theory the assumption that that behavior is a function of a continuous dynamic process of interaction is a laudatory one, in practice most of the studies have examined behavior at one or two fixed points in time and have used the mechanistic rather than the dynamic model of interaction. Future studies should use Markov chains or path analysis. It is important to develop strategies for examining the actual process at a number of points in time, and it is important to study reciprocal causality. The second assumption states that the person is an intentional and active agent within the dynamic process. I do not know of any studies on interactionism that have compared activity versus passivity. Because intentionality involves a motivational construct, it behooves us to examine how motivational factors influence the interaction process. Because behavior is goal-directed, we need to study persons' plans, projects, goals, and strategies and rules of behavior. We also need to study how people interpret situations, how they actively select situations, and how they react to situations imposed on them. In terms of the assumption of the importance of cognitive factors on the person side, we need to understand how the individual processes incoming information (decoding) and how this is integrated with previously stored information. The encoding of information, or execution of behavior, is also important. Originally, this assumption was limited because it did not emphasize emotional and motivational factors. Motivational, emotional, and cognitive factors are interrelated and influence one another. The psychological meaning of the situation as an important determinant of behavior is the fourth assumption of modern interactionism. This assumption, however, ignores the objective characteristic of the situation, which most influences behavior, and it is not clear whether the meaning of the situation is a person variable or a situation variable. In addition, the meaning of the situation is influenced by motivational and emotional variables, by past experience with a situation, and by the objective characteristics of the situation.

Trans-Situational Consistency and Situational Specificity. One of the important issues in personality research and theory of interactional psychology is whether behavior is situation specific or is consistent across situations. Because I have reviewed the relevant research in detail elsewhere (Endler, 1983), I merely present the major conclusions here. The evidence for cross-situational consistency is not very convincing for social and personality variables. For cognitive variables there is evidence for moderate cross-situational consistency. Across similar situations there is evidence for consistency; for dissimilar situations there is little or no consistency. For longitudinal studies there is consistency; for cross-situational studies there is little or no consistency. Mischel and Peake (1982) have convincingly demonstrated little or no cross-situational consistency, but moderate temporal stability (longitudinal consistency).

The Interaction Model of Anxiety. Although it has certain limitations, in that empirically the interactional model of anxiety has used the mechanistic model of interaction, it has made important contributions to our understanding of personality, in general, and in respect to anxiety, in particular. The first basic assumption of the interaction model of anxiety (Endler, 1975, 1980) is that both trait anxiety or A-trait (anxiety proneness, a personality variable) and state anxiety or A-state (a momentary unpleasant emotional reaction) are multidimensional. The second assumption of the interaction model of anxiety is that

in order for a person (facet of A-trait) by situation
(stress condition) interaction to be effective in
producing A-state changes, it is necessary for the
threatening situation to be congruent to the facet of
A-trait being investigated. Elsewhere (Endler, 1983),
I have reviewed 18 field and laboratory studies that
have provided empirical support for the
multidimensional interaction model of anxiety. Here, I
merely summarize some of the highlights. With respect
to classroom exam studies, for both high school and
university students, we found significant interactions
between classroom real-life examination situations and
the congruent facet of A-trait (interpersonal or social
evaluation) in eliciting A-state changes. With respect
to athletics, we found significant interactions between
an athletic event (track meet or karate) and social
evaluation A-trait in eliciting A-state arousal. With
respect to surgery, we found significant interactions
between a medical intervention procedure (D and C) and
ambiguous, physical danger and social evaluation facets
of A-trait with respect to A-state. Analogous results
were found in a psychotherapy study.

SUMMARY AND CONCLUSIONS

We have discussed some of the main issues relevant to
the major task of an interactional psychology of
personality. With respect to the description,
classification, and systematic analyses of stimuli,
situations, and environments, we have discussed the
problems involved in defining stimuli, situations, and
environments; objective versus subjective situations,
selected versus imposed situations; the need for a
differential psychology of situations; perceptions
versus reactions to situations; and some relevant
research. With respect to the second task, namely
interactions of persons and situations and both of them
with behavior, we have discussed mechanistic and
dynamic interaction, the four major assumptions of the
interaction model of personality, trans-situational
consistency versus situational specificity, the
interaction model of anxiety, and relevant research.

In closing, I would like to offer a tentative

definition of *personality*. *Personality* is an individual's coherent manner of interacting with him or herself and with his or her environment. It focuses on how the individual affects and is affected by both situational and behavioral variables. In processing information, cognitive, motivational, and content-mediating variables are implicated. A comprehensive definition of personality should account for abilities, cognitions, emotions, motives, traits, and behavior. An individual's behavior involves a continuous ongoing process--analogous to a movie.

REFERENCES

Bowers, K. S. (1973). Situationism in psychology: An analysis and a critique. *Psychological Review*, *80*, 307-306.

Ekehammar, B. (1974). Interactionism in personality from a historical perspective. *Psychological Bulletin*, *81*, 1026-1048.

Ekehammar, B., Magnusson, D., & Ricklander, L. (1974). An analysis of an S-R Inventory applied to an adolescent sample. *Scandinavian Journal of Psychology*, *15*, 4-14.

Ekehammar, B., Schalling, D., & Magnusson, D. (1975). Dimensions of stressful situations: A comparison between a response analytical and a stimulus analytical approach. *Multivariate Behavioral Research*, *10*, 155-164.

Endler, N.S. (1975). A person-situation interaction model of anxiety. In C.D. Spielberger & I. C. Sarason (Eds.), *Stress and anxiety* (Vol. 1, pp. 145-164). Washington, DC: Hemisphere.

Endler, N. S. (1980). Person-situation interaction and anxiety. In I. L. Kutash & L. B. Schlesinger (Eds.), *Handbook on stress and anxiety: Contemporary knowledge, theory, and knowledge* (pp. 249-266). San Francisco, CA: Jossey-Bass.

Endler, N. S. (1981). Situational aspects of interactional psychology. In D. Magnusson (Ed.), *Toward a psychology of situations: An interactional perspective* (pp. 361-373). Hillsdale, NJ: Lawrence Erlbaum Associates.

Endler, N. S. (1983). Interactionism: A personality model, but not yet a theory. In M. M. Page (Ed.), *Nebraska Symposium on Motivation, 1982: Personality--Current theory and research* (pp. 155-200). Lincoln, NB:University of Nebraska Press.

Endler, N. S., Hunt, J. McV., & Rosenstein, A. J. (1962). An S-R inventory of anxiousness. *Psychological Monographs, 76*(17; Whole No. 536), 1-33.

Endler, N. S. & Magnusson, D. (1976). Toward an interactional psychology of personality. *Psychological Bulletin, 83*, 956-974.

Magnusson, D. (1971). An analysis of situational dimensions. *Perceptual and Motor Skills, 32*, 851-867.

Magnusson, D. (1974). The individual in the situation: Some studies on the individuals' perception of situations. *Studia Psychologica, 16*, 124-132.

Magnusson, D., & Ekehammar, B. (1973). An analysis of situational dimensions: A replication. *Multivariate Behavioral Research, 8*, 331-339.

Magnusson, D., & Ekehammar, B. (1975). Perceptions of and reactions to stressful situations. *Journal of Personality and Social Psychology, 31*, 1147-1154.

Magnusson, D., & Ekehammar, B. (1978). Similar situations-similar behaviors? *Journal of Research in Personality, 12*, 41-48.

Mischel, W. & Peake, P. K. (1982). Beyond déjà vu in the search for cross-situational consistency. *Psychological Review, 89*, 730-755.

Pervin, L. A. (1977). The representative design of person-situation research. In D. Magnusson & N. S. Endler (Eds.), *Personality at the crossroads: Current issues in interactional psychology* (pp. 371-384). Hillsdale, NJ: Lawrence Erlbaum Associates.

Sells, S. B. (1963). Dimensions of stimulus situations which account for behavior variances. In S. B. Sells (Ed.), *Stimulus determinants of behavior* (pp. 3-15). New York: Ronald Press.

Sherif, M., & Sherif, C. W. (1956). *An outline of social psychology*. New York: Harper & Brothers.

8 Handling Prediction from Psychological States and Roles by Modulation Theory

Raymond B. Cattell
Universities of Illinois and Hawaii

THE METHODOLOGY OF DISTINGUISHING STATES AND TRAITS

Every man in the street knows that transient emotional states are as important as traits in deciding action. By 1960 it nevertheless seemed that despite 30 years of progress in factor-analytic structuring and measurement of traits, psychologists were still at sea in regard to the defining and measuring of states.

They had been baffled by two problems. First, how to discover the number and nature of the basic dimensions along which states change, and second, how to assess a person's state level at a given moment, say in a house on fire, when one could not intervene to measure it. I am going to speak of the solutions to those problems that the last 20 years of research, and particular experiments in the last 10, have yielded.

On the first line of research--the location of the unitary dimensions--I spend little time here, for I think most psychologists are aware of what alleged state patterns have and have not been factor-analytically replicated. The methodological solution for reaching the structure of states, uncontaminated by trait patterns, turned out to be factor analyzing difference scores. This has been done in what have now been called *differential R technique* (dR) and in longitudinal factoring over time, by P-technique (Barton, Cattell, & Connor, 1972; Barton, Cattell, & Curran, 1973). In the former one might measure 200 people on, say, 30 variables, first on Monday and then on, say, Wednesday, and factor their difference scores. A *trait* being, by definition, stable and a *state* being a pattern of short-term change, this experimental approach ensures that traits are left out, leaving pure state factors. We now know about a dozen such pure state dimensions.

As to this phase it must suffice, if we are to get our main challenge in the problem of modulation theory, merely to remind the reader that the dR and P-techniques have proved experimentally potent designs and yielded mutually consistent results. At least some eight dimensions of general state response were located in questionnaires, objective batteries, and physiological measures, and others in ergic tensions (drives) in the Motivational Analysis Test (MAT). The former separated out, for example, factors of elation-depression, activation, stress, and genital arousal, additional to the specific ergic tension arousal patterns.

Among other advances, these dR and P-technique researches enabled distinct measures to be made for anxiety as a state and anxiety as a trait. There are now scales and batteries for these, such as the IPAT Eight State Questionnaire, Nesselroade's objective (performance) battery for states, and the seven depression scales in the Clinical Analysis Questionnaire. Any actual psychological state at a given moment in a given person is, of course, a particular combination of these primary states, as all the colors on an artist's palette are combinations of the three primary colors. In both cases the particular combinations can be scored and expressed as a numerical vector measurement.

THE PROBLEM OF PRACTICAL USE
OF STATES AND ROLES IN THE BEHAVIORAL EQUATION

The word "role" appears alongside "state" in the title of this presentation because many roles are adopted temporarily in a particular ambient situation and thus have the same formal property, and call for the same dR and P-techniques for their mapping, as do states. With these advances we have to point out that the analysis or prediction of performance response requires more than psychometrists have commonly put into the behavioral specification equation. One must go beyond traits, to the role in which the person stands at the moment and the emotional state caused in him or her by the situation. Thus, the behavioral equation that psychometrists used 20 years ago had only Ts in it, for trait scores, whereas now we add a class of S scores for states and R scores for roles as follows:

$$a_{hijk} = b_{hjtl} T_{li} \cdots + b_{hjtx} T_{xi} + b_{hjsl} S_{lki} \cdots + \atop b_{hjsy} S_{yki} + b_{hjrl} R_{lki} \cdots + b_{hjrz} R_{zki} \qquad (1).$$

The bs are behavioral indices calculated as loadings, peculiar to each trait, state, or role. The i subscript indicates the score of a particular person. There are x traits, y states, and z roles. (Note a person can act at one time in more than one role; e.g., a teacher might speak to his wife about their son in a way conditioned by his role as a husband, a father, and a teacher.)

In this behavioral equation I have kept to the usual symbolism of a for the act (response); h for the focal stimulus; j for the character of the response; and k for the ambient situation at the moment. The important thing to note is that the *trait* scores of the individual i have no k subscript, because they are timeless over fairly long intervals, but the level of the *states* and the *role actions* are peculiar to the momentary situation k. It is this that seems at first to destroy the psychologist's practical power to predict action, for whereas he can look up the given individual's trait scores from some previous testings on file, the individual cannot know beforehand what the person's state level is at the moment when action is to be predicted. For it must be assumed that it is impractical and disturbing to step in and measure a person's anxiety as he steps into a dentist's chair or his ergic tension level on sex as he kisses his fiancée.

INTRODUCTION TO THE MODULATION MODEL AND STATE LIABILITY CONCEPT

The solution that has been proposed for this practical psychometric impotence is the concept of state liability and the theoretical model of modulation. It supposes first that each person has a measurable proneness or liability to each of the discovered psychological states. The man in the street calls this a "disposition," as in an "amorous disposition" or an "anxious disposition." This personal level of liability to experiencing a particular psychological state, y, we write as L_{yi} in the following equation, wherein we write L instead of T because L covers a special subclass of traits. Modulation theory supposes that each life situation has a particular provocative power for the average person in regard to a particular emotion. We write this as s_{kx} where k is the situation and x is the particular emotion modulated. "Modulator" or "modulation index" is better than "provocation index" for this s_{kx} because k may reduce as well as increase an emotion, as when "music hath power to soothe the savage breast."

At this point, in the interest of clear experiment, we have to take a stand on the choice of a product or a summative (or some other) relation of s and L. I have been persuaded by preliminary observations to try the product form first. Thus our hypothesis is that

$$S_{yki} = s_{ky}L_{yi} \tag{2}.$$

producing S_{yki} in Equation (1). Incidentally, if we substitute Equation (2) in (1), the full state term becomes (switching from symbol b to v for reasons that follow):

$$a_{hijk} = v_{hjsy} \ s_{ky} \ L_{yi} + \text{other terms in (1).} \tag{3}$$

This has the psychological meaning that the state S_y is first raised to the level S_{yki} by the provocative ambient situation k, at value S_{ky}. The psychological state thus reached then exerts its effects on behavior, as measured by the weight of the involvement index, v_{hjsy}. That is to say, at that moment the state is expressing its appropriate power to affect a_{hjk}, just as any trait would. Note, however, that the symbol, b, for *behavioral index*, when applied *as usual* to a trait is simply the empirical *factor loading* as found for the given behavioral act, a_{hijk} in (1). In the case of a state liability this loading, as factor analytically found, actually equals the product vs and needs to be split into v_{hjsy} and s_{ky} by an analysis with which we need not here concern ourselves. However, let us henceforth call v--the measure of how much the state is involved in the act--the involvement index to distinguish it from b.

How is the Modulation Model to be Experimentally Tested?

Now the question that has gone unanswered for most of 20 years since the model appeared (Cattell, 1963, 1971) or at least since clearly factored scales became available (Cattell & Bjersted, 1967; Curran, 1968; Nesselroade, 1960) accurately to test it is "How well do actual state measures in different situations fit the theory."

Theory says that if the modulation formula in Equation (2) holds, the plot of state scores (measured as from a true zero) for any three people measured at any three ambient situations, k_1, k_2, and k_3, of modulation power s_{k1}, s_{k2} and s_{k3}, respectively, should take positions on the state scores that produce straight lines as in Figure 8.1.

The elementary trigonometrical proposition here is that the three L values--the proneness trait scores-- for these three people, a, b and c, appear as the tangents of the lines L_a, L_b and L_c. This supposes that both the base line of ambient situations s_k's, and also the S scores from which the s_k scores derive are

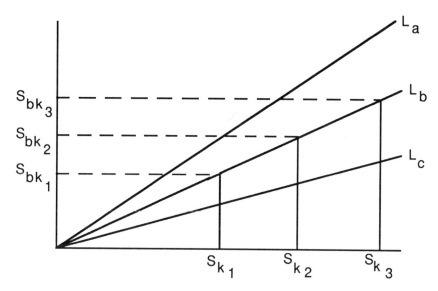

FIG.8.1.   Graphical illustration of the requirements
of the modulation law.

equal interval.   And it supposes that both scales   have
values measured from a true zero.

At   this point, the   psychologist--especially   one
interested   in   the   newly   developing   conceptions
(Cattell,   1979;   Magnusson & Ekehammar,   1975;   Sells,
1963) for assigning meaningful values to   environmental
situations--will ask especially how we get to the scale
values   for the environmental modulator potencies,   for
these   are   obviously important for the   enterprise   of
quantifying   environment.   If   we   take   a   single
individual, say the   person with a   liability L_b in
Figure 8.1, it will be seen from the projections of the
obtained   state scores at S_{bk1}, S_{bk2} and S_{bk3} that   the
assignment   of situational s_k scores derives   from   the
state   scores   with   a   proportionality   as shown   in
Equation   (4),   where L_{yi} (i for an   individual)   stays
constant.   Incidentally, we note that the *size* of   the
units   in   the   state   and   the   situation   scores   is
irrelevant.   If we decide that a door shall be twice as
high as it is broad it is trivial to whether we   decide
to measure it in centimeters or inches.

$$L_{yki} = \frac{S_{yki}}{s_k y} \tag{4}$$

Now if we simply take one person at three positions of stimulation as in Figure 8.1, person (b), and drop perpendiculars from the state level cuts on L to get situational values we have *assumed* the modulation law, not *proven* it. To check it we need more data points that in effect will ask if the s_{k2} value that gives the right S value for the person of proneness (liability) L_b also does so for one of liability L_a, and so on.

Let us omit--because our objective is beyond this point--the algebraic demonstration given by Cattell and Brennan (1987) that in order to check the law we need a minimum of six equations with experimental values. These can be for either two persons at each of three situations or three persons at two situations. In Figure 8.2 let us take the case of two persons measured for state strength in each of the three situations. The equations, with subscripts for persons a and b and situations 1, 2 and 3 (omitting any subscript for the particular state) are:

$$S_{ak1} = s_{k1}L_a \tag{5[a]}$$

$$S_{ak2} = s_{k2}L_a \tag{5[b]}$$

$$S_{ak3} = s_{k3}L_a \tag{5[c]}$$

$$S_{bk1} = s_{k1}L_b \tag{5[d]}$$

$$S_{bk2} = s_{k2}L_b \tag{5[e]}$$

$$S_{bk3} = s_{k3}L_b \tag{5[f]}$$

Let us suppose we choose the first five equations (any five would do) to solve, from the five obtained S experimental values, the value that the modulation law would require for the sixth. The solution for s_{k1}, s_{k2}, s_{k3}, L_a and L_b will, from such equations, be in ratio form, and, as we have seen, the scale units are of no importance so it does not matter what unit sizes we happen to give to our state scales. From these we can calculate what the S value for L_b and s_{k3} would be

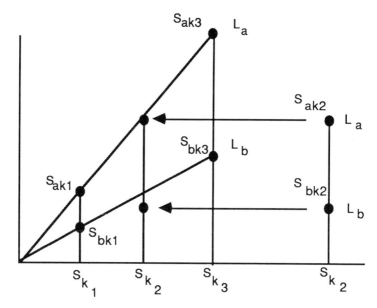

FIG.8.2.   Testing the fit of empirical data to
the model.

expected to be, and see how well it fits the empirical
value.

   In Figure 8.2, in trigonometrical illustration, it
is assumed for greater clarity that S_{bk2} = $s_{k2}L_b$ is
taken as the value to be tested. The test procedure
here has been to plot the scores of persons L_a and L_b
found for situations s_{k1} and s_{k3} with such a ratio of
s_{k1} to s_{k3} that the slopes intersect as the model
requires at the zero of the S scale. We then take the
experimental results at s_{k2} here set out separately at
the right of Figure 8.2 and move it across to the left
until the S score for person b cuts the L_b slope.
Alternatively we could see if an s_{k2} position can be
reached such that both points fit on the slopes.   In
the case illustrated in Figure 8.2, if we fit the upper
point the lower is a little lower than it should be and
the question is whether it is significantly off or
statistically an acceptable fit. Actually, one would
aim to a least squares fit--to an s_{k2} position that
gets the best fit averaged for L_a and L_b. Further, in

a thorough experimental examination, one would take more than 6 points and test the over-all fit.

The Need to Find State Scale True Zeros in Testing the Model

As stated so far, the experimental data needed for testing the hypothesis follow from a simple algebraic or geometric statement of the problem in Equations (1) through (5), and Figures 8.1 and 8.2. But it must be pointed out that this model assumes that the given state scale scores start from the true zero level of the state, and that the scale units have equal interval properties. For the moment, we shall accept the latter experimentally as not too far from the truth, but we certainly cannot assume that zero on the particular items in the scale is zero on the experienced psychological state. An ordinarily constructed scale may miss the true zero of, say, anxiety, by registering zero before the real zero of anxiety excitation is reached, or vice versa. But the modulation law requires that we perform the calculations in terms of a true zero on the state scale in question, and that the zero on the environmental provocation scale coincide with that true zero. That is to say, a situation that is in no sense anxiety-creating should yield a score on an anxiety scale that corresponds to a true zero. In other words, the origin of the plots in Figures 8.2 and 8.3 should be simultaneously the true zero on the anxiety scale and on the scale of modulator values, s_k's, or situations, as it is in the ideal--Figures 8.1 and 8.2.

With the raw numerical values from experiment on any ordinary state scale, therefore, we should not expect Equations (1) through (5) to hold, and we cannot immediately test the modulation theory on such values. There is, however, a means of setting up a checking experiment if we begin with the "contingent zero" of the raw state scale and proceed as is to be described.

In so proceeding it is appropriate to note the significance of this search for a true zero for psychology as a whole.

One of the hitherto inescapable deformities that have kept psychology from marching with the physical sciences has been that almost all of its research has had to be conducted in terms of measurements that are basically of poor scientific worth, consisting at best of equal interval and usually only of rank order validity. Although modulation theory for the moment offers redemption only of state measurements, it could be that this by-product of modulation research--namely a ratio scale--will turn out to be its most valuable contribution.

If we assume, as we reasonably may with equal intervals in the raw scale, that the state reduces regularly with each unit decline in stimulation, then the point at which the declining scores of two persons intersect--the intersection of the higher and lower L slopes in Figure 8.3--must be the ultimate zero. The check on the theory is that three or more persons should all intersect at the same point. We should expect that that point would in most cases define a different zero from that of the literal raw scale. Figures 8.3 and 8.4 illustrate by actual data what happens for two cases. Because a zero on the state is also a zero of environmental stimulation, this intersection point will also give the zero for the situation scale of modulator values-- s_k's. Incidentally, an alternative hypothesis--that with absolutely zero stimulation some remnant of emotional excitement still remains--could be handled by adding a constant to the s_k in Equation (2), as is done in a different case elsewhere (Cattell, 1980).

Of course, the modulation theory will ultimately be tested by other approaches than the present, because it has other consequences, but here we are proceeding on the evidence of this experiment. And in conclusion of the logic of the experiment let us reiterate that the actual numerical values of the units S, s_k, and L are as irrelevant as whether we use Fahrenheit, Celsius, or Réamur units of temperature. The L values being trait scores might be set in standard scores, and the s_k's will then stand in simple ratio to whatever the S score units are. There are, however,

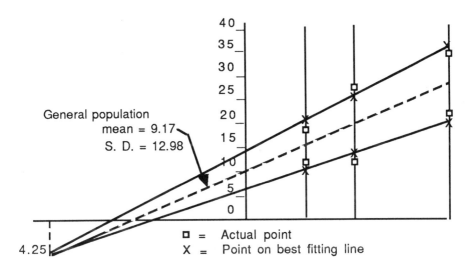

General population
mean = 9.17
S. D. = 12.98

4.25

☐ = Actual point
X = Point on best fitting line

FIG.8.3. Anxiety.

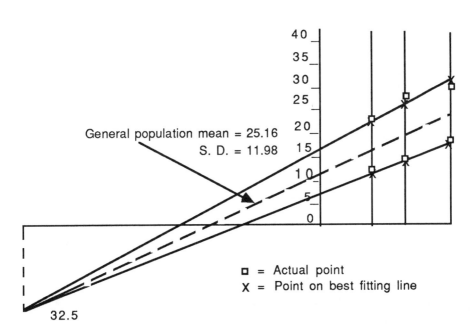

General population mean = 25.16
S. D. = 11.98

32.5

☐ = Actual point
X = Point on best fitting line

FIG.8.4. Depression.

some intricacies in fitting into the behavioral equation alongside other traits, which are discussed elsewhere (Cattell & Brennan, 1987).

A BRIEF ACCOUNT OF THE CATTELL - BRENNAN EXPLORATORY EXPERIMENT

Let us now turn to discuss the outcome of the long-awaited experimental check, which has recently been made by Cattell and Brennan (1987) with respect to two clinically important psychological states--anxiety and depression. Questionnaire scales for these two state dimensions, factor analytically uniquely located, were first constructed (Cattell, 1973) and have been made available in the IPAT Eight State Questionnaire (1975). They consist of eight scales (of which only anxiety and depression were used here) in lengths of 40 items per scale (Curran & Cattell, 1975). Brennan (1978) then chose three 30-minute movies the content of which from the standpoint of anxiety could be characterized as (a) humorous and carefree, (b) moderately anxiety-provoking, and (c) very disturbing (gory automobile accidents); and similarly for depression. It was first checked that on the group of 261 male and female undergraduates the Cattell-Curran IPAT Eight State Scale (1975) was sensitive enough to record significant mean differences in level resulting from the three impacts. The group was then divided, by mean level of individuals across three situations (see Cattell & Brennan, 1987) into two subgroups averaging high and low in mean L values.[1] It is noted that whereas for simplicity we talked of scores of a single high (see Footnote 1) and a single low individual in the above illustration, for simplicity, the experiment was based upon the *mean* of several persons for the usual reason

---

[1]It is seen incidentally from the added broken line in Figures 8.3 and 8.4, based on standardization data for the general adult public, that these undergraduates are above the general population in anxiety and below in depression, which can be interpreted either as an L difference, or as situational, until further investigated.

of reduction of experimental error of measurement relative to the main effects. There is no required change of argument concerning modulation operation in shifting from individuals to groups. The mean scores for the high and for the low were then worked out for each of the three situations and plotted as in Figures 8.3 and 8.4. The abscissa positions for s_{k1} and s_{k2} points were of course initially arbitrary, at convenient lengths along the base since their distance apart is only a matter of scale. The L slope line drawn through the two points for the top group, and through the two points for the bottom group were continued backward until they intersected. Incidentally, it is seen that they will intersect at the same true zero value on the S scale regardless of the arbitrary scale on s_k's, (i.e., of where the k_1 and k_3 modulator values s_{k1} and s_{k2} are initially placed). Only the zero for the modulator scale will change with the distance arbitrarily set out between s_{k1} and s_{k2}. But this is unimportant, for the zero is always such that the distance from 0 to s_{k1} remains the same fixed ratio of that from s_{k1} to s_{k3}.

From Figure 8.3 it is seen that the true zero for anxiety is 4.25 raw score S scale units below the S raw score zero. In the case of Figure 8.4, dealing with depression, the true zero is much below the arbitrary zero given by the raw score scale, being 32.5 units lower. This clinical scale in fact does not touch with its items the levels of freedom from depression that many normal subjects usually experience. This tells the test constructor, incidentally, that it has been fashioned too exclusively for the needs of clinical work.

The next step in testing the modulator model is to take in each case the two group mean points found for the intermediate stimulus situation and slide it along as with a vertical ruler (as in Figure 8.2) to see if an s_k position can be found at which the two S scores will simultaneously fit on the two L lines already drawn for S values at s_{k1} and s_{k3}. It will be seen that in both Figures 8.3 and 8.4 (anxiety and depression) they do so pretty well. The baseline position reached when this is fitted fixes the s_{k2} value of that particular intermediately distressing movie impact. In the detailed account elsewhere (Cattell & Brennan, 1987) it is explained how this is done algebraically (without the looseness of fitting by eye involved in the geometric method just described). Actually the best procedure is to fit the two L slopes, as finally shown here, each for a best fit to *all three* points, before the projection to fix the zero is made, and to check the goodness of the least squares fit of all six points to the two L lines. With the final location of the zero from the best fitting L lines we have ratio scales for both the state and the modulator axes. Then with the new state and situation scores we can move back to the simplified picture of essential relations presented in Figures 8.1 and 8.2, where for the moment we assumed we were operating from true zero.

SOME FURTHER CONSIDERATIONS
IN TESTING THE MODEL

Contemplating Figure 8.1 the psychologist will realize that there are actually two tests of the model available from the data obtained by this experiment: (a) Do the mean points for the third ambient (middle) situation scores fit well to the lines set by the first two L level groups, as previously described, and (b) in each group does the standard deviation of S values retain the same ratio to S, the group mean, over different s_k values? (This test follows from the fixed L in any group, and use of Equation [2].) Our experiment (Cattell & Brennan, 1987) actually showed the second requirement to be only roughly met, for there was a slight systematic tendency for the ratio to decrease with higher mean S values, in both groups and both experiments.

An explanation that would fit both this effect and the tendency for the highest value (L_2 at s_{k3}) in Figures 8.3 and 8.4 to fall slightly below where it should ideally be, is simply that the present raw state scales do not have enough ceiling room for these particular subjects. This is supported by finding that whereas the score distributions at the lower values proved normal, those at the higher S values tended to become quite skewed (downward).

Although the verdict of this pioneer test of the modulator model thus tends to be definitely favorable to the theory, it suggests improvements that would permit more stringent conditions in what we hope will be further experiments. First, let us note that the legitimacy of the model, in requiring straight slopes for the L's, depends on the existence of equal unit intervals in the state scale raw scores, though, as we have seen, there is no need for them to have a true zero. The scales should, therefore, be groomed beforehand toward equal intervals by the *pan-normalization* or *relational simplex* principles (Cattell, 1973, p. 383). Second, the departure of the S/σ_S ratio from the degree of constancy we had hoped for calls for a retest with a raw score scale now reasonably clear of ceiling and floor compression effects. This could be achieved by constructing a much wider range of items, relative to the range in the groups used.

Third, it would be desirable to have in the experiment more than two L level groups and three s_k stimulus levels (i.e. more than the minimum of six points). This would determine the true zero more accurately, as a mean value, while enabling the degree of discrepancy of the estimates to be assessed statistically.

Fourth, there are two oversimplifications in this first presentation of the application of experiment to the theory. They call for some modifications of the data analysis as discussed elsewhere (Cattell & Brennan, 1987). They are (a) that all subjects in a given physicosocial situation will not stand exactly at the same (mean) s_k value, but have significant dispersion, and (b) that all subjects will come to the experimental (movie) situation with different preexisting stimulations from personal environments (e.g., of anxiety). With single individuals the latter would not matter, except as affecting the s_k estimate, for it is merely addition wrapped up in and taken account of in the total considered s_k. But when the ratio test of the *means* and *sigmas* of groups on S is taken, the first point just given indicates an additional contribution to the dispersion.[2] As worked out elsewhere (Cattell & Brennan, 1987), this could account for the observed departure of S/σ_S from strict constancy (see Footnote 2) and in fact calls for a test of the model--by expecting exact constancy, no longer of the original simple expression, but of a more complex one that can be derived (Cattell and Brennan, 1987).

Finally, there is the need to test the model on an extended diversity of states. It is true that anxiety and depression are probably more practically important, but studies of higher order factors show they are positively correlated both over people and over time (within one person). And in any case one is curious whether the law holds universally for such very different states as stress, fatigue, excitement and the

---

[2]To grant that each physicosocial situation, k_x, has a different s_{kx} value for each person seems at first to destroy the main model that L_{xi} is a personal value and s_{ks} is a population value. Actually we are only encountering again the difference between the *R-technique* and the P-technique models. We recognize (Cattell, 1978, p. 350-365; 1979, p. 148) that the behavior indices, b's, which are loadings, are statements for a particular population sample, which later, being reduced in size, eventually becomes the value for a single individual in P-technique. The relation of the average of all individuals' P-technique values in the sample to the R-technique values has never been the subject of theory or experiment, but obviously relates to the relation of over-persons to over-situations variance. We must recognize, as "fact of life," that our test of the modulation law by the sigma/mean ratio--but not by our main test here--is rendered approximate by reason of the psychological reality of the dispersion, from causes (a) and (b), about the central s_k value.

specific ergic tensions (fear, anger, lust, curiosity, etc.).

It is of course conceivable that as these experimental improvements yield their results, the modulation model will be found to operate so that the relation of S with s_k values is not exactly linear, or that long standing of a subject at a high value reduces the usual s_k of another high situation, or that homeostasis calls for prediction of the action of an s_k as a function not only of its nature but of its duration, or that the simultaneous presence of two situations does or does not require a simple addition of their s_k values. Indeed, the opportunities for crucial research on developments of the model are clear cut, numerous, and fascinating subjects for dissertations.

Meanwhile, let us note that this model does not stand in isolation, merely as a means of inquiry into state change, but fits into a broader theoretical horizon, at which we should briefly glance. First, it contributes to and integrates into the last 2 decades of work concerning formulae for the environment--the quantification of the stimulus situation as approached, for example, in the studies of Endler (1975), Cattell (1963, 1971, 1980) Magnusson and Ekehammar (1975), Sells (1963), and others. For if the s_{kyp} values for situation y and state p were extended to states q, r, s, t, and so on we should have a vector of numbers describing many of the properties of the situation.

THE MODULATION MODEL AS A GATEWAY
TO BROADER PERSONALITY AND ECONETIC THEORY

The immediate impact of this chapter is to show that the modulation model is a near enough fit to experimental data to justify more intensive and technically improved further experiment. Granted this confirmation it seems likely that, like the Michelson-Morley experiment in physics, it is going to carry implications for other theories than that directly tested. Let us list these and attempt to explain the relevance, to the extent possible in so brief a space.

The chief theoretical areas are:

1.   The new development in econetics (i. e., the psychological assessment of the environment) discussed further later.

2. In personality the possibility that traits also modulate, and that role traits especially do so, fitting the modulation model.

3.   In psychometrics the possibility of developing true zero, ratio scales for more than state measurements only.

In econetics it has been proposed that each life situation be analyzed into a focal and an ambient situation. Each can then be calculated as a vector quantity, covering a set of scores on all three trait and state modalities, and will be assigned to the two parts of each total situation (Cattell, 1963, 1979, pp. 213-235). The experimental method for thus separating the v_L index (Equation 4), evaluating the focal stimulus (and its response) from the s_L index describing the effect of the ambient situation on mood and motive, has been described elsewhere (Equation 3 above discussed more fully in Cattell, 1979, p. 245).

It happens also that by special factor analytic experimental designs (Cattell, 1979, p. 242) we have an independent way of reaching the v and s_k indexes from b, so that the s_k values reached by the kind of experiment here described could be checked. Future uses in econetics, and in spectrad (attribution theory) of the vectors obtained by these methods for particular situations are considerable. First, there is typal classification of situations by pattern similarity coefficients (Bolz, 1972; Cattell, Coulter, & Tsujioka, 1966; Sells, 1963). Second, there are extensive calculations with econetic matrices (Cattell, 1979, p. 228, 263). Third, there is the new domain of onlooker perception of situations by attribution, using the new spectrad theory (Cattell, 1982) contrasting the true and the biased perception.

In personality theory we are coming to the conclusion, by such experiments as that of Horn (1972) on abilities, that even traits modulate slightly with internal and external situations. The size of the s values relative to the v values may be much smaller but it is now justifiable to consider ordinary traits, T's, and liability traits, L's, as belonging to a single genus, counting perhaps as two different trait species.

Although space has precluded discussing roles, except to say that they can be considered as acquired sentiments uniformly activated by the set of ambient situations peculiar to each, it is evident that they properly belong to a subspecies among L's and are aptly considered here as our title suggests. (They are treated as subspecies because they are not *aroused*, as an L *emotion* is, but *activated* as a *cognitive system*.) Testing for modulation response effects therefore now needs to be done with factors believed, from content, to be roles.

As regards ergs, a slightly more intricate analytical hypothesis of the mode of action of modulators has been given, as follows:

$$S_{EK} = (s_k + c)[C + H + (a - G_a) + (b - G_b)] \qquad (6)$$

(subscript for a particular individual omitted)

The psychologist interested in motivation can read the symbols elsewhere (Cattell, 1980, p.113) and see how this, indeed, links modulation with the whole area of the dynamic calculus.

Last, let us glance at the psychometric implications. The most pleasant surprise after years of having to hang our heads among the sciences through continuing with only counterfeit (rank order) scales is the promise of true zero, ratio scales. Admittedly this also depends on starting with equal interval scales Cattell (1979), but the relational simplex and pan-normalization principles may solve that. And if further research shows that most traits also modulate, the breakthough to ratio scales will be not only for states but also for traits (see the discussion on trait true zero calculations in Cattell, 1972, p. 78).

Because most meaningful psychological calculations

(e.g., the practical ones of criterion estimation and the theoretical ones of conflict and decision, etc.), nowadays deal with unitary (common or unique) traits and states factorially located and measured, the further developments that modulation theory introduces into the behavioral equation will have both practical and theoretical impact. The fact that modulation indices can be calculated as in this article, or alternatively, as previously pointed out, through special factor analytic experiment (giving v and s, or p, e and s) terms (Cattell, 1979, p. 245) will incidentally cause psychometrists to consider seriously shifting from the ordinary factor equation to the real base factor equation (Cattell, 1972, p. 5) model.

A glance down these vistas is at once exciting in the promise of power for our science, and seriously challenging in terms of the amount of sophisticated, hard programmatic research work needing to be done. It often seems that psychologists have too long been content to live in an intellectual slum, the result of a history of theory-less, logically disconnected, one-story, shanty-town research projects. It is surely high time that psychologists turn from so much applied research and give attention to basic concepts and laws that offer promise of potent integration across the areas we occupy.

REFERENCES

Barton, K., Cattell, R. B., & Connor, D. V. (1972). The identification of "state" factors through P-technique factor analysis. *Journal of Clinical Psychology, 28,* 459-463.

Barton, K., Cattell, R.B., & Curran, J.P. (1973). Psychological states: Their definition through P-technique and differential R (dR) technique factor analysis. *Journal of Behavioral Science, 7,* 273-277.

Bolz, C. R. (1972). Types of personality. In R.M. Dreger (Ed.), *Multivariate personality research contributions in honor of Raymond B. Cattell,* (pp. 161-260). Baton Rouge, LA: Claitor.

Brennan, J. (1978). *A test of confactor rotational resolutions on orthogonal and oblique cases.* Unpublished doctoral dissertation, Univ. of Hawaii Library, Honolulu.

Cattell, R. B. (1963). Personality, role, mood, and situation perception: A unifying theory of modulators. *Psychological Review, 70,* 1-18.

Cattell, R. B. (1971). Estimating modular indices and state liabilities. *Multivariate Behavioral Research, 6,* 7-33.

Cattell, R. B. (1972). Real base, true zero factor analysis. *Multivariate Behavioral Research* (Monograph No. 72-1). Fort Worth: Texas Christian University Press.

Cattell, R. B. (1973). *Personality and mood by questionnaire.* San Francisco: Jossey Bass.

Cattell, R. B. (1978). *The scientific use of factor analysis.* New York: Plenum.

Cattell, R. B. (1979). *Personality and learning theory* (Vol. 1). New York: Springer.

Cattell, R. B. (1980). *Personality and learning theory* (Vol. 2). New York: Springer.

Cattell, R. B. (1982). The development of attribution theory into spectrad theory, using the general perceptual model. *Multivariate Behavioral Research, 17,* 169-192.

Cattell, R. B., & Bjersted, A. (1967). The structure of depression, by factoring Q-data in relation to general personality source traits. *Scandinavian Journal of Psychology, 8,* 17-24.

Cattell, R. B., & Brennan, J. (1987). *State measurement: A check on the fit of the modulation theory model to anxiety and depression states.* Submitted for publication.

Cattell, R. B., Coulter, M. A., & Tsujioka, B. (1966). The taxonomic recognition of types and functional emergents. In R. B. Cattell (Ed.), *Handbook of multivariate experimental psychology* (pp. 288-329). Chicago: Rand McNally.

Curran, J. P. (1968). *Dimensions of state change, in Q-data and chain P-technique, on twenty women.* Unpublished masters thesis, University of Illinois, Urbana.

Curran, J. P., & Cattell, R. B. (1975). *The IPAT eight state questionnaire.* Champaign, IL: The Institute for Personality & Ability Testing.

Endler, N. S. (1975). The case for personality-situation interactions. *Canadian Psychological Review, 16,* 12-21.

Horn, J. L. (1972). State trait and change dimensions of intelligence. *British Journal of Educational Psychology, 40,* 159-185.

Magnusson, D., & Ekehammar, B. (1975). Anxiety profiles based on both situation and response factors. *Multivariate Behavioral Research, 10,* 27-44.

Nesselroade, J. R. (1960). *The 7-state objective test battery.* Champaign, IL: Institute of Personality & Ability Testing.

Sells, S. B. (Ed.). (1963). *Stimulus determinants of behavior.* New York: Ronald Press.

Discussion of "Handling Prediction from Psychological States and Roles by Modulation Theory"

Richard L. Gorsuch
Fuller Theological Seminary

The question addressed in Dr. Raymond Cattell's chapter is the basic one of how we evaluate roles and states as they are induced in a variety of situations. But the essential points answering this question are made only by placing them in the context of Cattell's broader theories. I probably understood the essential points best on the second or third reading of the chapter, because--in order to understand them--I found that I had to reduce some negative transfer from my prior assumptions about Cattell. Hence, I begin by sharing with you some points that I found useful to "forget" in going through this chapter, the better to understand its major contribution.

MODULATION THEORY AND CATTELL'S OTHER WRITINGS

The chapter opens with an extensive discussion of how modulation theory is needed and how it fits into the specification equation and other general elements of Cattell's theories. This section is highly useful if that is your need. But the major new points of this chapter can be understood without fitting them into the broader Cattellian framework.

Fitting this contribution into the broader framework may produce negative transfer by reminding the reader that Cattell's main reputation is in trait psychology. Traits, of course, are those enduring characteristics of the individual. But in this particular chapter he is explicitly concerned with roles and states as the foci. Some trait discussion and numerous equations relating roles and states to traits are included but, as I see it, that is only background. It is material from his other writings that helps us to fit his present thinking in this chapter into the rest of his work. That is not relevant for all of us and not relevant to the grasping of the major new points of this chapter. Here instead the major focus, unlike trait psychology, is upon the immediate feelings and reactions of a person in a situation with the explicit acknowledgment--and indeed a crucial defining element--being the fact that the reactions vary from one situation to another, and hence are states rather than traits. Note that unlike other trait based positions, Cattell in this chapter is a strong interactionist, primarily interested in how situations impact particular states. If we fail to grasp this point--that is, if we see him as presented in most introductory personality books as only a "traitist"--the chapter becomes incomprehensible. The Cattell of this chapter is a dynamic, situationally oriented, process psychologist.

The background discussion can also be misleading if, because it integrates this theory into his factor analytic work, we then assume he is always a factor analyst who always uses a linear model. In this chapter, factor analysis provides only a background, and it is mentioned solely in the context of relating this present work to past research and broader theories. Indeed, the major feature of this study is that it is a classical experimental design with experimental tests. It involves multiplicative functions that are nonlinear by definition and so are best examined in an ANOVA. It is a little unusual for me to think of Cattell as an experimental psychologist rather than as a factor analyst, but I felt that I could better grasp this chapter by doing so.

The background discussion also reminds us of Cattell's vital interests in individual differences, but in this chapter individual differences form only the background. The major feature of this chapter is that the group means are important and individual differences are mostly in the error term. He does use individual difference at one point as a blocking variable, but that is as close as the chapter comes to considering individual differences. Cattell does feel that this will ultimately fit back into his individual difference model, but for many points of this chapter, individual differences are part of the error term.

Note that this background is important to connect modulation theory to Cattell's other concepts. A complete psychology has to interrelate its constructs, moving smoothly from one area to another. Such broad perspectives are uncommon in psychology; instead each area of research functions as a domain unto itself with no points of translation across them. What I have termed *background* in this chapter may eventually be crucial to integrating psychology into a cohesive total.

MODULATION THEORY IN PSYCHOLOGY

The basic point of this chapter is how to evaluate states and roles as they are influenced or produced by a variety of situations. I subdivide that point into two different questions that are discussed in the chapter. The first--which is closer to "classical Cattell"--is that of the predisposing characteristics of the person that makes him or her liable to respond with a change in state. The second is how to measure that state.

Predisposition to Response

The question of the states of a person is a function of what Cattell calls the *liability* of the person. I am not sure I like that term, because other uses of the term liability (e.g., liability insurance) have a negative connotation to me. However, Cattell is using it to refer to any predispositional characteristic in the person that makes that person more likely to increase or decrease on a given state in a given situation. (A better term might be *lability*, just as a labile mineral is one that continually changes.)

There is little work on who responds with the greatest amount of state change in a particular situation but there are interesting lines of research to suggest that this is an important topic. One reason for the importance of this topic is the need to have states as an intermediary between traits and the behavior in a specific situation. Fishbein and Ajzen (1974) examined how traits predict behavior and found that traits--being broad and involving general questions such as "How often do you do this or that?"-- related quite well in predicting broad general categories of behavior. Thus a sum across 100 different behaviors correlates highly with traits. But when a particular response in a particular situation was the focus instead of the sum, the correlations were, as has been found in other research, small. And thus we need theory to "go between" the traits and the actual response in the situation, theory that takes into account the situation and the person's reaction.

Suggestive work on the role of states in situations has occurred in the area of anxiety. In three-mode factor analysis of data on anxiety, responses to a variety of situations, the original data of which were collected by people in this audience, some types of people reacted with more anxiety to interpersonal situations than other people. Further identification of the characteristics of this type of person would aid in predicting anxiety in a specific situation.

In Cattell's theories he has suggested that several primary factors, namely C, G, and Q3, (ego strength, superego strength, and self-sentiment) are moderators in anxiety reactions, and hence are predictors of anxiety states. That is, a person who has high ego strength, high superego strength, and strong self-sentiment is the type who is least likely to respond to situations with anxiety. Note that several of these hypothesized precursors of state anxiety are part--but not all--of the scales measuring trait anxiety. Some research (Baker & Gorsuch, 1982; Baker & Gorsuch, 1985) has found differential relationships to components of trait anxiety. Thus we do have some elements already in place that suggest that people will respond with anxiety to particular situations. These are supportive of Cattell's position that the characteristics that predispose some people to have state anxiety in a particular situation can and are beginning to be identified.

Measuring the Impact of Situations

Situational Impact. A second major question of Cattell's chapter focuses on how we can measure the impact of a situation upon roles and states. He introduces his own term for this in his continuing attempts to be more specific and calls this *modulation.* This term is commonly used in electronics to indicate the impact of a particular influence on a wave produced at a particular frequency. For example, the common terms AM and FM are amplitude and frequency modulation to identify two different ways in which a transmitter might impact the carrier wave (thus producing a signal to be decoded by the receiver). By using this term, Cattell is saying that the person has a continuing state or role over time--which could be zero--and the situations modulate the state or role to produce the observed reactions.

A goal of this chapter is to provide a method for identifying how much state each situation produces. This is an essential question if we are to evaluate how situations differ psychologically, for we cannot know how they differ until we know how to compare them. To what extent is one situation more anxiety-producing or more depressive than another situation? Some data do exist, such as the three-mode factor analysis of anxiety data that showed that situations do have a unique impact upon individuals that is independent of the individuals.

The traditional approach to solving this problem is to compute differences. Indeed, that is how we identified state items for the State-Trait Anxiety Index (STAI). The criterion for selecting state items was whether their mean changed radically from what we assumed was a non-anxiety producing situation to an anxiety producing situation. But this of course was only a rank order metric. We only determined if the item means were higher for the high anxiety situation than for the low situation. We did not consider equal interval or ratio scaling, nor do contemporary psychology paradigms generally use more than a rank order metric for this type of problem.

An Improved Metric. Cattell, in his chapter, suggested that we need a zero-based metric, and much of his chapter is oriented toward setting up that zero-based metric and testing modulation theory in that context. This implies that our rank order metrics may be insufficient to test theories of situational impact. "Zero points" and "ratio scales" are somewhat foreign to those of us trained in psychology in the post World War II era, for rank order data are all that we really expect and all that we feel that we need to conduct most types of analysis. For example, Nunnally (1978), in writing about psychometric theory, suggested that our parametric statistics are primarily influenced by rank order (thus the equal intervals assumption can be violated but the results will still be reasonable). Having ratio data would not drastically change, for example, correlations.

But psychology does have problems because it functions with only rank order or interval data. One of the problems is that such data force us to rely on normative based scores to provide meaning. IQ scores are a major example. The normative based IQ does provide more meaning than would raw scores. But it may be time to recognize the limits as well. It is well known that an IQ of 100 on one IQ test is never quite 100 on another IQ test, and we have no principle by which we can decide which one should really be called 100. Nor is the IQ of 100 stable in meaning over time; as we change normalization samples from one decade to another, the actual ability represented by an IQ of 100 shifts, and so the meaning of that IQ has to shift as well. And how accurate are the samples? It is likely that many sociologists would fault even our best tests for poorly sampling the national population of the United States in order to establish our mean of 100. And why should United States people rather than people in Japan, people in South Africa, people in India, or some other group be the defining point for an IQ of 100? And if we norm each culture, the meaning of an IQ of 100 will continually shift. Although normative based scores such as IQ produce equal interval scales that have been useful, we also must remember that there are major limitations to this process, namely, we really do not know what the people of a given score can do, and what those of a given score can do shifts every time we go to a different normalization sample.

Another problem from our lack of ratio measurement is that some statistics become unstable across studies, such as the raw score (or "b") weights in regression analysis. The b weight is a function of the intervals involved and because our scales all have different intervals (and since we have made no attempt to reconcile those intervals to each other), b weights are seldom examined or published because they lack meaning. On the other hand, the major alternative--beta weights--have problems as well. They are primarily, for example, influenced by the variance of a particular scale in the sample; when moving from one sample to another for which the standard deviation is different, the beta weight can shift with the same effect--thus suggesting that the results differ--when in fact the phenomenon is the same. If we actually had a ratio metric, the identical b weight would occur in both studies despite changes in standard deviation, thus showing that we had replicated the effect.

Because our data are basically rank order, instead of ratio, we often fail to see when studies are equivalent and when they are different across research studies. Here are two brief examples. Innumerable studies of anxiety separate people at the median, calling those below the median "low anxiety" and those above the median "high anxiety." When it was originated and up through the mid-1960s, the mean score

on the Taylor Manifest Anxiety Scale was 12 to 13
points. The high anxiety group in that era included
those who scored generally above 13 to 14 points,
running up to 22 to 23. People in mental institutions
normally had means of 24 or so. But all samples need
not have means of 12 to 13; if they had some other
mean, then "high" and "low" groups would include people
at different anxiety levels than those in studies with
means of 12 to 13. At George Peabody College, L.
Wrightsman (personal communication, 1972)
systematically collected anxiety data over the years;
by 1970 the anxiety level of the incoming freshman
class was 22. That means that the low anxiety in that
year by a median split included those who were the high
anxiety group 10 years earlier and that the "high
anxiety" groups were equivalent to those in mental
institutions 10 years previously. Can we expect
results to generalize across such studies? The shift
in who is called low anxiety results from the lack of a
ratio metric and we are forced to rely only upon median
splits. The problems caused by a reliance on median
splits because we have lacked ratio measures also
occurs in studies of "extrinsic religious orientation"
(Allport & Ross, 1967). Classically, such research
divides the sample in half with the higher half labeled
"extrinsics". But the mean on the extrinsic scale is
often low--so low that the average "high extrinsic"
disagrees with most "extrinsic" items (Gorsuch &
Venable, 1983). It so happens that nobody in such
samples was extrinsically religious at all, and yet the
usual mean splitting would label a subset of them
extrinsic. This is inappropriate labeling and any
conclusion could be misleading.

The question of metric raised by Cattell in his
chapter was of greater concern in psychology before
World War II than it has been in the last few decades.
Thurstone, for example, sought equal intervals for
scaling attitudes. Then the postwar period was swept
by the relative success of normative IQs.

But in recent years we have had some research
paradigms that, I believe, have become popular in part
because they have had a ratio metric. Piaget's work

has been of wide interest and a competing alternative to traditional IQ. Piaget's work has an interesting element: Most of the scales are ratio scales. A child conserves or does not. I realize there are some ambiguity and definitional problems for constructs such as "conservation," but basically a child conserves or does not. When we looked at Dr. Hunt's scale (chapter 5), each one of the elements basically was a ratio scale. Dr. Hunt does combine them overall into an ordinal scale--and that is appropriate for his purposes --but we still should not forget that the components are ratio scales. The responses have intrinsic meaning regardless of normative data.

I would like to suggest that one of the bases for the popularity of Piaget's theories, at the same time that IQ theory was losing ground, may be that Piaget used ratio scales while IQ used normative based scales. A child who conserves is a child who conserves regardless of when the research is done, but 10 years later an IQ of 100 is not necessarily an IQ of 100, and thus we do not know what that IQ of 100 means in the same way that we do in saying that a child conserves.

Psychology's lack of ratio scaling may be one reason why leadership in terms of psychological measurement seems to be shifting from psychology to education. They are the ones, for example, involved with the Rasch scale, that is an attempt to give equal intervals to measurement. They are the ones involved in criterion referenced testing, another attempt to give meaning to scores which are not based on norms. (We do have the Skinnerian behaviorist movement, and one of the reasons why it became popular may be because it generally uses ratio scales, e.g., a child wets the bed or does not.) Educational psychology's willingness to take seriously the need for equal intervals and the need for criterion referenced scores that have meaning regardless of any normative group has placed them ahead of the rest of psychology.

In this chapter, Cattell presents an approach that has the possibility of producing a ratio scale for psychology. Modulation theory provides the vehicle by which ratio measurement can be developed for both situational impact and state reactions. The result would be that statements such as "treatment X reduced anxiety by half" or "situation Y is three times more anxiety provoking for this person than situation Z" would have meaning. Norms would be nice for each scale but the true meaning would lie in the phenomena identified by particular scale scores.

CATTELL'S RESEARCH PARADIGM

Cattell's approach begins with approximately equal interval scales, such as his anxiety scale. In his chapter, he mentioned some procedures for establishing equal intervals. Other procedures also could be used. Thurstone's equal appearing interval procedure might, for example, be useful. But once one does have a state scale that approximates equal intervals, the next step is arbitrarily to take high, medium, and low situations, as he shows in his figures, and obtain measures of anxiety for the same people under all three conditions.

Two groups of people who are more or less likely to respond to the situations with anxiety are used to establish the characteristics of the slope of the anxiety reaction for each group. The critical element then is how a third situation fits in. One of the groups of people is used to establish where the third situation is, between the other two situations. Then the mean of the other group on that situation is the test point. If a ratio scale is possible, then that mean should fall in line with the other points. Hence, this gives an empirical test of the model. Its first test at least seems promising and warrants testing by another laboratory.

Cattell also suggests projecting the two lines down to determine if they converge at some point, which then gives a definition of the absolute zero of anxiety. Empirically the two lines need not converge; they could diverge--and although Cattell did not point this out--that becomes another test of the theory.

In the illustration, the zero points were always

outside of the raw score range of the scale. For those who might feel that the lack of ability to measure the true zero point may create problems, let us look to physics. Physics has had an absolute zero for temperature for a long time, and yet it is extremely difficult actually to find in nature or create absolute zero. But absolute zero has been very helpful to physicists in their development of the concept of temperature; indeed advances have been made since true zero has been defined whose occurrence would have been difficult to imagine if only the Fahrenheit scale had been used. The same advantages of knowledge of the true zero point for anxiety might also occur.

At this point it should be noted that we assumed an interval scale earlier. Cattell did not mention it, but it is possible to use a series of studies as previously outlined to produce equal interval scales if modulation theory is assumed to be correct. One would simply adjust the scales back and forth until the situations matched up properly, and that would give an equal interval state scale. Thus, implicit in the modulation theory approach is a procedure for producing and testing an equal interval metric for states as well as a zero point.

CONCLUSION

The major new contribution, then, that I see in this chapter is a fairly simple and easily executable paradigm by which ratio scales can result for the measurement of situations and of states. Secondary points are individual differences affecting responses to situations and relating these ideas to broader Cattellian theory. This may open up a new world of mathematics to psychology. I might also note in concluding that it is fitting for this to be in a symposium honoring Dr. Saul B. Sells. Dr. Sells (1963) is well known for stressing situations and is also well known for his continuing stress upon quality in measurement.

REFERENCES

Allport, G.W. & Ross, J.M. (1967). Personal religious orientation and prejudice. *Journal of Personality and Social Psychology*, 5, 432-443.

Baker, M. & Gorsuch, R. (1982). Trait anxiety and intrinsic-extrinsic religiousness. *Journal for the Scientific Study of Religion*, 21(2), 119-122.

Baker, M. & Gorsuch, R.L. (1985). Anxiety and value: Anxiety as caused by the frustration of a major value: Religion. *The Southern Psychologist*, 2, 35-41.

Fishbein, M. & Ajzen, I. (1974). Attitudes toward objects as predictors of single and multiple behavioral criteria. *Psychological Review*, 81, 59-74.

Gorsuch, R.L. & Venable, G.D. (1983). Development of an "age universal" I-E scale. *Journal for the Scientific Study of Religion*, 22(2), 181-187.

Nunnally, J. (1978). *Psychometric theory*. New York: McGraw-Hill.

Sells, S. B. (Ed.). (1963). *Stimulus determinants of behavior*. New York: Ronald Press.

9 Studies of Personality

Desmond S. Cartwright
University of Colorado

Saul B. Sells' talents have touched and illuminated many facets of psychology as a science, as a body of scholarly knowledge, and as a technology for solving important human problems. In all these enterprises he has also accomplished what so few can do: manage and encourage the work of other scientists through consummate arts of administration. He has co-founded several important scientific journals, and has masterminded numerous compendia of research on personality, delinquency, drug abuse, and other topics.

I have learned in one scientific meeting after another that Saul Sells has encyclopedic memory for the contents of the journals and compendia he has worked with. Do you recall the revered master whom Oliver Goldsmith celebrated in his famous poem The Deserted Village? Everyone was sitting around the master. This is what Goldsmith wrote:

> And still they gazed, and still the wonder grew
> That one small head could carry all he knew.

S. B. SELLS AS FIELD THEORIST

What kind of a scientist is S. B. Sells? In the manner of Kurt Lewin, Sells is a field theorist. He believes that the person can be understood best only in his or her total environmental context. But unlike Lewin, and much more like his mentor Gardner Murphy, Sells has always emphasized the real environment, not just the environment as perceived in the individual's life space. He is interested in the unnoticed effects of changes in barometric pressure as well as the individual's conscious reaction to peer rejection or acceptance. Yet unlike Gardner Murphy and much more like Raymond B. Cattell, Sells has stressed the importance of first establishing the critical variables that must be assessed, both in the person and in the environment.

Sells views even the psychological assessment task with a field perspective. He has written (1952) "that the testing situation may structure the task of the subject in devious and subtle ways. The personality of the examiner, the shift from individual to group administration, the significance of the outcome to subjects, are factors which illustrate this general category [of] the testing field situation" (p. 25). Other categories mentioned by Sells in that paper included the individual's own behavior field, his or her total personality.

In a paper on psychiatric screening of flying personnel, Sells (1955) wrote:

It is assumed that human efficiency in any situation, depends both on the intrinsic personality resources of the total environment...such factors as amount of hazard, quality of leadership, and extent of hardship, deprivation and frustration. Hence not all breakdowns, but primarily those which occur in circumstances under which most fliers can function, can be attributed principally to predisposing personality factors.

The degree of predisposition considered disqualifying is thus not absolute, but dependent on the culture, the population sample involved, and the characteristics of the total situation at any time (p. 36).

Thus Sells calls us to pay attention not only to the total situation at the time of testing (as Lewin would have done), but also to the culture (as Murphy would have done) and to the population sample involved (as Cattell would do).

FIELD THEORY AND INDIVIDUAL BEHAVIOR

In his scholarly review of the state of personality science in the mid 1960s, Professor Sells (1967) said the aim of contemporary personality theory is "to specify principles of self-regulation of individual behavior that achieve consistency of diverse functions in different situations" (p. 935). This definition expresses his field orientation in a new way. The "principles of self-regulation" and the "consistency of diverse functions" refer to the "individual behavior field." The situations in which diverse functions are served constitute the "total field situation." Thus there are two fields in relation to which we must study individual behavior: The situational and the personality fields, as illustrated in Figure 9.1.

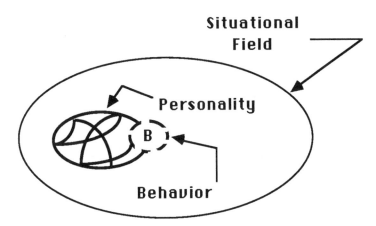

FIG.9.1.   Illustration of the situational and the personality fields.

In that review, Sells (1967) called for increased attention to be paid to the situation, especially through dimensionalization of our descriptions of the environment. Toward that end he had, as usual, already done a great deal of homework, notably in the book he conceived and edited on *Stimulus Determinants of Behavior* (Sells, 1963), in which he provided a systematic classification ranging from natural aspects of the environment (such as gravity and weather), to interpersonal factors such as informal operating patterns and role responsibilities.

FIELD THEORY AND RESEARCH STRATEGY

How does the breadth of vision influence choice of research focus? It seems to allow Dr. Sells to pick the most important topic for concentrated research effort. He surveys the entire field, and then picks out the most salient feature of the panorama.

Let me give an example. In his work with Merrill Roff and Mary Golden on *Social Adjustment and Personality Development in Children* (Roff, Sells, & Golden, 1972), consideration was given to broad determinants in the family background, in parental child-rearing practices and attitudes, and in the current social situation. The investigators then focused upon one factor that was outstanding: peer acceptance or rejection. They wrote:

> A basic assumption of the theoretical formulations in this study was that peer acceptance-rejection is strongly dependent on the stimulus value of the child in his peer society. The variables included measures of child characteristics that were assumed to represent major aspects of the individual to which peers respond. The results give strong support to that expectation. (p. 137).

They also found that in upper and middle socio-economic (SES) levels, delinquent children were rejected by peers; but in lower SES levels, although some delinquents were rejected by peers, others were highly approved. These important results may provide clues for pinpointed delinquency prevention: Change the reaction of nondelinquents peers!

SELLS STUDIES OF PERSONALITY

For many years, Sells surveyed the field of personality assessment systems. Among the many alternatives, he selected those of Cattell and J.P. Guilford. Each claimed to be covering the main dimensions of personality. Yet they were very different. Surely this fact was one of the most salient topics on this particular horizon.

In the late 1960s, Dr. Sells and his colleagues Demaree and Will carried out the most ambitious project ever attempted in personality questionnaire research (Sells, Demaree, & Will, 1968, 1970, 1971) at that time.

Six hundred items in the usual "yes-?-no" format were administered to 2,550 Air Force enlistees. The items were paraphrased marker items for 15 Guilford and 17 Cattell factors. One would expect between 17 and 32 factors to emerge.

The results were quite startling. They actually got 18 factors, only 5 of which were common to the two systems of Cattell and Guilford. Six factors were primarily like related ones in Guilford's system; and 5 were primarily like related ones in Cattell's system. Two factors were quite different from either original system.

A surprising relationship was found between the original marker items and Sells' factors. Did all items loading on a given factor come from one and the same original source factor in either the Cattell or Guilford system? Surely that would be the expected result. But it was not so. Only 3 factors met this expectation. To quote from a recent paper by Sells and Debra Murphy (1984): "although the factors extracted were judged to be item homogeneous in terms of the content of salient and marker items...they were heterogeneous with respect to the source factors from which their salients and markers were drawn" (p. 65). This is illustrated in Figure 9.2.

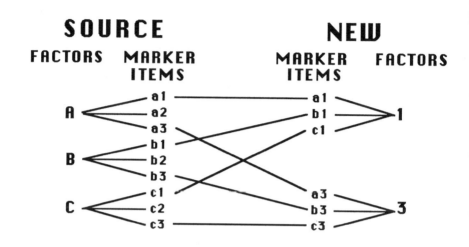

FIG.9.2.   Relationship between source and new factors (Sells & Murphy, 1984).

Some instances were quite extreme. For example, Factor 1 had salient items drawn from 10 different Guilford factors and 12 different Cattell factors; Factor 7 had salient items drawn from 5 different Guilford factors and 9 different Cattell factors.

Critics suggested that at least some of the factors obtained by Sells, Demaree, and Will were second-order factors. This means they would ordinarily have been obtained by intercorrelating several first-order factors from the original systems. Sells and Murphy (1984) pointed out, however, that second-order factors of that kind could not be marked by items having homogeneous content. They believe that there is a good deal of confusion at present as to what exactly is a second-order factor. They pointed out that Comrey's (1970) personality factors are specifically intended to be first-order factors but actually include at least two that are recognized as second-order factors in Cattell's and other systems. These two are Extroversion versus Introversion, and Emotional Stability versus Neuroticism. Later on we refer to these two widely replicated factors in some detail.

Sells and Murphy (1984) recommend that a new concept be substituted for the concept of "order of factor." The new concept is "bandwidth." A factor with very broad bandwidth would be made up of very dissimilar items; one with very narrow bandwidth would be made up of items that essentially are simple rephrasings of the same meaning. They write:

> the bandwidth, reflecting the definition and item content range of a factor, is probably more important than the factor level represented in any particular matrix. Whether or not a particular factor in a particular matrix is a primary or a higher order factor can be an artifact of the composition of the variables in the matrix (p. 60).

They recommend treating the distinction between first- and second-order factors with skepticism. So we are left with simply the number of factors, the particular interpretations of those factors, and their relative degrees of "bandwidth." Such is the "structure of personality" that can be reliably obtained by present methods of factor analysis, according to Sells and Murphy.

THE AIMS OF FACTOR ANALYSIS IN PERSONALITY RESEARCH

What exactly are the goals of modern factor-analytic research on personality structure? Murphy (1947) proposed three levels of complexity that must be addressed in personality study. These are: "(1) a distinguishable individual, definable in terms of qualitative and quantitative differentiation from other such individuals, (2) a structured whole, definable in terms of its own distinctive structural attributes, and (3) a structured organism-environment field, each aspect of which stands in dynamic relation to each other aspect" (p.7; see Figure 9.3).

In agreement with Cattell (1950) and others, Sells and Murphy (1984) say that: "description and measurement of the critical variables implied by

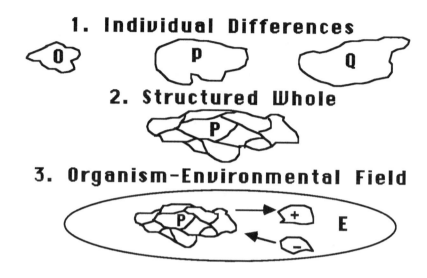

1. Individual Differences

O   P   Q

2. Structured Whole

P

3. Organism-Environmental Field

P → + E
   ← −

FIG.9.3. Murphy's levels.

Murphy's first level are necessary preconditions to the scientific study of personality at the other two levels" (p. 39). It is indeed the aim of factor analysis to discover those critical variables. The work of Cattell provides an example of what can be accomplished in the questionnaire realm. Cattell, Eber, and Tatsuoka (1970), writing about the 16 Personality Factor Questionnaire (16PF), say that we have: "the alternative of describing the structure of personality either in terms of (1) sixteen to twenty-four or so primary factors or of (2) six to nine broader second-stratum factors. In full psychological perspective this is not all, for one can go to five third-stratum factors, and probably two fourth-stratum" (pp. 111).

   This model is shown in Figure 9.4. Here stratum is that layer of actual personality organization which corresponds to a given order of factor. Factors at the first order are coordinated with the first-stratum "source traits."

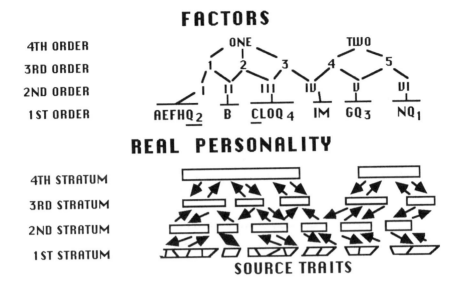

FIG.9.4. The structure of personality.

What about the second-order factors? What is the second stratum? Cattell et al. (1970) state that: "Psychologically, the second-stratum factors may be viewed as broader influences or organizers contributing to the primaries and accounting for their being correlated" (p. 116).

For instance, second-stratum Invia versus Exvia is attributed to

> a complex positive feedback interaction of the primary factors, affectothymia (A+), parmia (H+), surgency (F+), group dependence (Q2-), and dominance (E+). This ...theory views the pattern as one of social inhibition, ...and considers that a higher position on any one of the primaries involved... tends, because of social mechanisms, to generate a higher level on the others. In this way they become correlated (p. 117).

So second-stratum factors are both active and

passive. They are "broader influences" producing correlations among primaries and also they are produced by correlations among primaries due to feedback from social mechanisms.

Third-order factors are likewise coordinated with still broader influences in the real personality; and so on up to the highest order.

Not all factor analysts aim for a hierarchic structure of first- and second-order factors. Many aim for a list of factors at the first order only, ranging from the 2 described by Eysenck and Eysenck (1969), through the 5 factors reported by Jackson (1976), to the 8 factor system of Comrey (1970), and the 18 factors reported by Howarth (1980).

FACTOR RESULTS AND PERSONALITY THEORY

The structure shown in Figure 9.4 actually represents only the results of factoring correlations. It mentions no feedback mechanisms, no social influences. These explanatory concepts are brought to the factor results by the theorist. The correlations between factors could be produced by casual connections, by cooperative utility relations, by third-variable influences, by feedback mechanisms, by part-whole relations, and so on.

Cattell has developed an admirable theory to account for the factor-analytic data. However, it is one among several as yet untested theoretical models, as is made clear by Cattell, et al. (1970). In discussing the second-stratum factor of Adjustment versus Anxiety they again recommend a feedback theoretical model, but they continue: "the factor-analytic connections here would, alternatively, also fit the classical psychoanalytic theory; for anxiety correlates with (i.e., loads on) low ego strength, C-, high guilt proneness, O+, and high ergic tension (Q4+: id pressure) which psychoanalysis has invoked" (p. 118; see Figure 9.5).

We may ask: How would anyone know that "the factor-analytic connections... fit the classical psychoanalytic theory" if that theory had not already

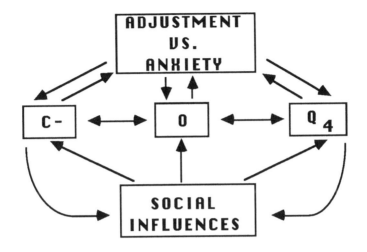

FIG.9.5. Illustration of the factor connections for Adjustment vs. Anxiety.

been formulated? Could we have looked at the factor-analytic data as sketched in Figure 9.5 and, from that alone, could we have arrived at Freud's theory of personality structure? I believe we could not.

Freud postulated three main agencies, id, ego, and superego, organized in varied relationship to three topographical regions of conscious, preconscious, and dynamic unconscious. The ego has adaptive purposes of achieving gratification of needs in reality. Its functions include perception of goals and means, detection of barriers, search for detours, planning, foresight, delay of immediate discharge. The ego also defends itself against anxiety through unconscious mechanisms of repression, projection, and so on (A. Freud, 1936; S. Freud, 1923; Hartmann, 1958).

Ego Strength means the overall adequacy with which the ego does its job of managing anxiety. But as we saw a moment ago, the ego has adaptive functions as well as defensive functions.

If we simply had the factor data in Figure 9.5 and no knowledge of Freud's theory, could we have interpreted Factor C as Ego Strength rather than, say,

Emotional Maturity? Could we have interpreted Factor Q4 as Id Pressure rather than Tension? I think not.

Perhaps factor-analytic methods cannot uncover individual personality structure at all. What they can do is help in structuring our descriptions of individual differences in personality.

Theories of Structure

What is a theory of personality structure? I have elsewhere proposed that most sciences contain theories of structure as well as theories of cause, function, system, and pattern. These are very different kinds of theories, capable of generating quite different models of reality. A theory of structure may be defined as one that

> postulates a finer grain, different component parts, or other forms of deeper reality than appears to our senses or to previous tools of observation. In a theory of structure there are some statements of fact about observed objects. It is hypothesized that some entities exist and are the more basic constituents of the observed objects. Part of the theory may include some proposed laws of composition which deal with how the constituents are supposed to come together to produce the objects which have been observed (Cartwright, 1979, p. 189).

Examples include the cell theory in biology, Dalton's atomic theory, and others. As Rapaport (1959, p. 95) has said, the constructs of id, ego, and superego constitute the essential constituents of Freud's "structural conception."

Individual Personality Structure and Factor Structure

Freud's theory refers to Murphy's Level (2): "a structured whole, definable in terms of its own distinctive structural attributes." Every adult has id, ego, and superego components of personality. But also each individual has distinctive structural attributes shown in the functioning of these components.

For example, Allison, Blatt, and Zimet (1968) describe the ego-functioning of Mrs. T as follows:

One of the outstanding features of Mrs. T is her striking shifts in ego-functioning and ego control. [Her] ... psychotic features ... are variable in nature and at times have a paranoid and depressive quality, and at other times, a hypomanic, grandiose quality. However, there are few disruptions of boundaries between separate Rorschach images and little suggestion therefore of severe issues about ego boundaries... Counterphobic defense is also evident, but it too, like the projection and denial, is unstable, unsuccessful in its attempt to ward off fearfulness and depressive self-loathing (p. 257).

This description of Mrs. T's ego-functioning is depicted in Figure 9.6, and pertains to Murphy's Level (2), a structured whole, with distinctive attributes. Now let us suppose that we have a 16PF profile on Mrs. T. That would be at Murphy's level (1), with Mrs. T being differentiated from other individuals in quantitative terms. As suggested in Figure 9.6, three scores in her profile would show Factor C low, Factor O high, and Factor Q4 high. These would mean low emotional stability, high guilt -proneness, and high tension. All three load Cattell's second-order Anxiety factor, which Sells and Murphy (1984) identify as the highly replicable factor of Emotional Stability.

Using Freud's theory, we could interpret these three scores as ego-weakness, strong critical superego, and erupting id impulses. The three factor scores alone would tell us nothing about ego controls and their shifts, about ego boundaries and their freedom from disruptions, or about counterphobic attempts to shore up an earlier organization of hysterical defenses that has been broken down.

Accepting that Level (2) = Structure, and Level (1) = Performance, what then is the relation between Levels (2) and (1)? I think it is the relation between structural components and output qualities or variables.

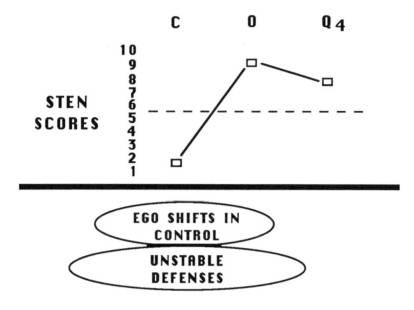

FIG.9.6. 16PF profile: Mrs. T.

Consider an analogy in high-fidelity audio equipment. You are listening to music from two speakers, each in a dark walnut cabinet. You have made eight different measurements of the performance of this system, as follows:

Variable	Score for this individual
Sound quality	Good
Fidelity	Average
Wow	Moderate
Flutter	Low Moderate
Rumble	High
Stereo separation	Good
Bass quality	Fair
Treble quality	Average

We now know a great deal about this system at Level (1). But do we have much idea about Level (2)? How many woofers and tweeters? Are there long-throw woofers? Are there cone tweeters? Is there a 2-inch bass port? Is there quartz lock tuning? Is there a

mute control? Are there subsonic filters? Can we tell
even if the source of sound is a turntable behind the
scenes or a tuner and amplifier tuned to KZFW?

We actually have no idea about these Level (2)
matters.   An expert who knows some Level (2) theory
might offer a guess about the components that possibly
could give rise to the scores of this individual.   But
the scores themselves tell us little about components
in the individual's structure.

It would be easy to develop another analogy from
the performance scores of an automobile. Without other
knowledge most of us cannot tell from such scores
whether we have overhead cams in the engine or even if
it has pistons or a turbine or both.

Personality factors are similarly performance
variables.   We cannot tell much if anything about the
structure of individual personality at Level (2) from
knowledge of those variables at Level (1). We cannot
even tell how many different components the system has.
For example, if Emotional Stability does   reflect
performance of the personality system, and if that
system has components of id, ego, and superego, then
one factor is reflecting joint performance of three
components.

Of course, for all we know, one component may have
two or more uncorrelated functions, even as the ego has
both adaptive and defensive functions.   Such   a
situation seems to arise in Comrey's work (Figure 9.7).

Comrey (1980, p. 38) hypothesizes that his eight
factors correspond to seven of Erik Erikson's (1963)
psychosocial stages of development.   This   is   a
worthwhile and interesting hypothesis. But two of his
factors, Extraversion versus Introversion   and
Masculinity versus Femininity, are both believed to be
coordinated with Erikson's stage of Intimacy versus
Isolation.

Assuming Erikson's theory can be translated into a
theory of structure, how is coordination with Comrey's
factors to be conceived? From Comrey's eight factors
as such there is no indication whatsoever of which one

COMREY	ERIKSON
TRUST	TRUST
ORDERLINESS	AUTONOMY
CONFORMITY	INITIATIVE
ACTIVITY	INDUSTRY
EMOTIONAL STABILITY	IDENTITY
EXTRAVERSION	INTIMACY
MASCULINITY	INTIMACY
EMPATHY	GENERATIVITY

FIG.9.7.   Correspondence between Comrey's factors and Erikson's psycho-social stages.

reflects differences in resolution of conflicts at the first stage, and which at the second stage, which the third, and so on. The factors reveal the structure of individual differences in adult personality. They carry no tags which say this one refers to differences derived from age one year, and that factor refers to differences among individuals created when they were 2 years old. Possible coordinations with developmental stages are the work of the theorist, work indeed which would not be possible if Erikson's theory had not already been there.

Another example of disparity in number of factors and number of coordinated components is given by Gray (1973) who proposed that Eysenck's factor of Extraversion versus Introversion is actually the resultant vector of performances by two independent brain components. As shown in Figure 9.8, one component consists of the medial forebrain bundle and the lateral hypothalamus, which Gray calls the "Go system" because it triggers approach behavior. The other component consists of the medial septal area and the hippocampus, which he calls the "Stop system" because it interrupts any ongoing behavior whenever

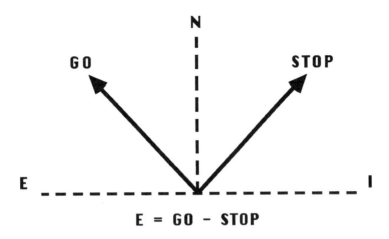

FIG.9.8. Gray's theory of extraversion.

signals of punishment are received. Extraversion, says Gray, is the net output of these two components, being responsiveness of the Go system to signals of reward minus responsiveness of the Stop system to signals of punishment.

SUMMARY AND PROSPECT

Let me sum up. Professor Sells has done yet another great service to the science of psychology. He and his colleagues have shown that only a few well-known personality factors can be replicated, and that whether a factor is first- or second-order is artifactual.

I have argued that factor analysis yields data at Murphy's Level (1) whereby an individual is differentiated from other individuals in qualitative or quantitative terms. Factors do not tell us anything about Level (2), which refers to individual personality structure as a whole. The relation of Level (2) to Level (1) seems to be that of structure to performance, components to output variables.

Sells and Murphy have proposed that factors differ widely in bandwidth, his important new concept. The two factors, Extraversion and Emotional Stability, seem likely to have the largest bandwidth of all.

It seems likely that scientific work on personality must progress simultaneously on Levels (1) and (2). The first does not give insight into the second. Work on performance measures and on structural theory must go forward mainly independently.

At Level (1) our studies of personality can now carry forward Sells' work and calibrate all replicated factors in terms of bandwidth. At Level (2), our theories about individual personality as a structured whole must continue to hypothesize components and laws of composition independently of Level (1). At the same time, it seems that theorists at both levels will have to work harder to spell out rules for coordinating proposed system components (Level 2 theory) with performance characteristics of varying nature and bandwidth. I would hazard a guess that factors of greater bandwidth will prove to reflect the joint performance of larger numbers of components. For example, the factor of Emotional Stability may reflect individual differences in the joint performance of ego, id, and superego components. The Extraversion factor may reflect joint performance of brain components called the Go System and the Stop System.

REFERENCES

Allison, J., Blatt, S. J., & Zimet, C. N. (1968). *The interpretation of psychological tests.* New York: Harper & Row.

Cartwright, D. (1979). *Theories and models of personality.* Dubuque, IA: Wm. C. Brown.

Cattell, R. B. (1950). *Personality.* New York: McGraw-Hill.

Cattell, R. B., Eber, H. W., & Tatsuoka, M. M. (1970). *Handbook for the Sixteen Personality Factor Questionnaire (16PF).* Champaign, IL: Institute for Personality and Ability Testing.

Comrey, A. L. (1970). *Manual for the Comrey Personality Scales.* San Diego: Educational and Industrial Testing Service.

Comrey, A. L. (1980). *Handbook of interpretations for the Comrey Personality Scales.* San Diego: Educational and Industrial Testing Service.

Erikson, E. (1963). *Childhood and society*. New York: Norton.

Eysenck, H. J., & Eysenck, S. B. (1969). *Personality structure and measurement*. San Diego: Knapp.

Freud, A. (1936). *The ego and the mechanisms of defense*. Vienna: International Psychoanalytischer Verlag.

Freud, S. (1962). *The ego and the id*. New York: Norton. (Originally published, 1923).

Gray, J. A. (1973). Causal theories of personality and how to test them. In J. R. Royce (Ed.), *Multivariate analysis and psychological theory* (pp. 409-451). London: Academic Press.

Hartmann, H. H. (1958). *Ego psychology and the problem of adaptation*. New York: International University Press.

Howarth, E. (1980). Major factors of personality. *The Journal of Psychology, 104,* 171-183.

Jackson, D. N. (1976). *Jackson Personality Inventory*. Port Huron, MI: Research Psychologists Press.

Murphy, G. (1947). *Personality: A biosocial approach to origins and structure*. New York: Harper & Row.

Rapaport, D. (1959). The structure of psychoanalytic theory: A systematizing attempt. In S. Koch (Ed.), *Psychology: A study of science,* (Vol. 3, pp.65-183). New York: McGraw-Hill.

Roff, M., Sells, S. B., & Golden, M. M. (1972). *Social adjustment and personality development in children*. Minneapolis, MN: University of Minnesota Press.

Sells, S. B. (1952). Problems of criteria and validity in diagnosis and therapy. *Journal of Clinical Psychology, 8,* 22-28.

Sells, S. B. (1955). Development of a personality test battery for psychiatric screening of flying personnel. *Journal of Aviation Medicine, 26,* 35-45.

Sells, S. B. (1963). Dimensions of stimulus situations which account for behavior variance. In S. B. Sells (Ed.), *Stimulus determinants of behavior* (pp. 3-15). New York: Ronald Press.

Sells, S. B. (1967). Personality. In R. L. Ebel (Ed.), *Encyclopedia of educational research* (pp. 935-946). London: Macmillan.

Sells, S. B., Demaree, R. G., & Will, D. P., Jr. (1968). *A taxonomic investigation of personality. Conjoint factor structure of Guilford and Cattell trait markers.* (Final Report of OE Contract No. 5-010-296). Fort Worth, TX: Texas Christian Univ., Institute of Behavioral Research.

Sells, S. B., Demaree, R. G., & Will, D. P., Jr. (1970). Dimensions of personality: I. Conjoint factor structure of Guilford and Cattell trait markers. *Multivariate Behavioral Research,* 5, 391-422.

Sells, S. B., Demaree, R. G., & Will, D. P., Jr. (1971). Dimensions of personality: II. Separate factor structures in Guilford and Cattell trait markers. *Multivariate Behavioral Research,* 6, 135-185.

Sells, S. B., & Murphy, D. (1984). Factor theories of personality. In J.McV. Hunt & N. S. Endler (Eds.), *Personality and behavior disorders,* (Vol. 1, pp. 39-72), New York: Wiley.

Discussion of "Studies of Personality"

Maurice Lorr
Catholic University

The analysis by Sells and his colleagues of the 600 x 600 matrix of correlations among Cattell and Guilford personality items was unquestionably a remarkable achievement. But an important technical issue remains as to whether a collection of items is better factor analyzed by items or on the basis of homogeneous subtests or clusters of items. In fact, Cattell (1957), Guilford (1975), Comrey (1961), and Cronbach and Gleser (1953) have all recommended the use of what are variously labeled *clusters*, *parcels*, and *homogeneous item dimensions*. Others, like Eysenck and Eysenck (1969) and Howarth and Brown (1971) have emphasized an item-based factor analysis.

That items are unsatisfactory is manifest in several ways. Their repeat reliability is poor, their internal consistency is weak, and the proportion of specific and error variance is large. Clusters of items, on the other hand, reflect much more common factor variance than items (Cronbach & Gleser, 1953). It is worthwhile to remind the researcher that virtually all of the factor studies involving cognitive abilities were based on test scores rather than on items. Thus, there is historical support for summated scores in factor analysis. In current personality inventory construction the so-called rational or construct approach to scale development provides equally cogent evidence of the value of cluster scores. Here the constructs of Jackson (1967), Comrey (1970), and Lorr (1983) come to mind.

One critical objection to item clusters concerns doubts about their internal consistency. If clusters represent arbitrary collections of items with small and/or negative intercorrelations, the clusters cannot be viewed with confidence. What is needed is a measure of internal consistency for each cluster and for the combined set of clusters used to define a factor. Let us assume that the average item intercorrelation within a content area is .18. Application of the Spearman-Brown formula for reliability of a test of length k (say k = 5) yields a coefficient of .52. If four clusters of equal reliability define a single factor then the estimated reliability of the total set will be .81, a fairly respectable value (Gulliksen, 1950, p.65).

Illustrative data for the cluster approach are available from a study (Lorr, O'Connor, & Siefert, 1977) of four rationally devised personality inventories. The inventories compared were the Personality Research Form (PRF; Jackson, 1967), the Interpersonal Style Inventory (ISI; Lorr and Youniss, 1973, 1985), the Comrey Personality Scale (1970), and Edwards Personal Preference Schedule (EPPS; 1954). Except for the latter, with its 9-item scales, all the inventories were composed of 20-item scales. The first step taken sought to minimize possible instrument factors by adopting a uniform true-false answer format. The EPPS forced choice items were replaced by statements to be answered in terms of the subject's likes or dislikes. The PRF and ISI were already in true-false form. Thus, except for the EPPS, all of the scales were defined by 20 items, half of which were keyed true and half keyed false.

In the second step, the purpose of which was to establish homogeneous subtests, the 20-item scales were first divided into the true and false keyed halves, and then each half set was divided into two. The EPPS scales were subdivided only once into subsets of four and five items. The "quarter" scores for each inventory were then intercorrelated and analyzed by the method of principal components. The Cattell scree test was applied to determine the number of components to retain.

Thus the dimensionality of each inventory was determined on the basis of four homogeneous subtest scores representing each scale. Between 11 and 16 factors were isolated in the four inventories in both the high-school and college samples. The critical principal component analyses followed by Varimax rotations were based on 45 cluster scores of the college sample and 48 cluster scores representing the high-school sample. Twelve factors were isolated in both samples. In summary, the factor-analytic task was substantially less formidable than factoring the far larger group of approximately 1,004 items.

Cartwright also considers a number of issues regarding the higher order factors. Certainly the difficulty of controlling for such factors is widely recognized among factor analysts. Especially in regions of attribute space where closely similar subsets of variables are contiguous, the analytic procedure will often fail to separate the embedded dimensions from each other. Thus, when dimensions are represented by a wide range of items that vary greatly in specificity, a higher order factor is likely to emerge at the first-order level.

An alternative model to common factors is Guttman's (1954) facet theory. Facets are defined logically and their elements are the presence or absence of defined facets. The facets can then be used to construct test items. A particular combination of all elements of all facets defines a set of test items. It follows from this that Guttman's simplex and circumplex patterns among item intercorrelations can appear. Guttman distinguishes between the structure of a universe of content and the statistical structure of the empirical observations. Where there is a clear design, facet theory can be used to predict the statistical structure. For instance, the continuity principle in a circumplex leads to an expectation that the closer two variables are semantically, the closer they will be statistically.

Foa (1965) for example, theorized that embedded within the dominance--submission and love--hate dimensions of the Leary (1957) scheme, there are three-underlying facets; these are (a) content (acceptance vs. rejection), (b) object (self vs. other), and (c) mode (emotion vs. social). He suggests that an interpersonal act may be represented by a Cartesian product of the three facets, each of which may take either of the two values. Thus eight (2x2x2) interpersonal profiles emerge. Each facet profile fits a Leary octant in the interpersonal circle. For example, Managerial-Autocratic reflects the Social Acceptance of the Other. Obviously, a facet theory for personality as a whole has not yet been proposed, although limited circumplex orders have been suggested.

There are several other features of Saul Sells' pioneering not mentioned by Cartwright. In 1955 Sells became interested in typology and chaired a *Symposium on Pattern Analysis*. Included in the group were well-known investigators like David Tiedeman, M. B. Danford, Ernest Haggard, Hari Gupta, and Louis McQuitty. The panelists presented a variety of approaches to problems of pattern analysis. Some of the questions panelists were trying to answer were:

How homogeneous are members of group A?
How many discrete subgroups are there in group A?
How similar is group A to group B?

The methods presently used to solve such problems are called *classification, cluster analysis, typology,* and *pattern analysis.* It is of interest to note that by 1970 a Classification Society had been formed. Members represented a wide range of disciplines such as psychology, biology, statistics, education, medicine, and archaeology. Since then hundreds of articles have been published dealing with cluster analytic techniques and the basis for cluster structure. The extent of change in technical knowledge since 1955 has been considerable. The computer revolution, which occurred about the same time, has made it feasible to analyze large blocks of data. The two principal cluster techniques developed were agglomerative hierarchical cluster analysis and nonhierarchical iterative partitioning techniques. The hierarchical methods emerged because of the needs of biologists to determine lines of development. The partitioning methods were developed primarily by statisticians to subdivide data sets into nonhierarchical subgroups. Because the clusters are nonhierarchical they have greater appeal to social scientists. Examples of the application of cluster methods in psychology may be found in studies of alcoholics. In order to identify a distinctive alcoholic type, numerous studies have been conducted with use made of tests such as the MMPI (Minnesota Multiphasic Personality Inventory), the 16PF (16 Personality Factors inventory), and the CPI (California Psychological Inventory). The conclusion reached was that no single alcoholic type exists. Recently the 35 MMPI code types generated by Gilberstadt and Duker (1965) and Marks, Seeman, and Haller (1974) were analyzed (Lorr & Suziedelis, 1982). These authors found that the code types could be reduced to four. The research just described is believed to be important from both a social and scientific vantage point. Thus it is fitting that Sells' early interest and leadership in this field be recognized.

Nowlis and Nowlis (1956) became involved in a series of studies of the personal and social effects of moderate dosages of common drugs. Included here were the amphetamines, antihistamines, and barbituates. To assess the effects of drugs on short-term moods or emotional states they constructed a variety of mood checklists. During the 1960s, Sells also became involved in constructing such lists, and in studying the effects of drugs on mood. Since then, mood study checklists and scales have been constructed by Izard (1972), McNair and Lorr (1964), and Zuckerman and Lubin (1965). The prevailing conception indicates that from

6 to 10 bipolar mood states can be demonstrated. Here again is a psychological field where Sells exhibited leadership.

I agree with Cartwright that factor analysis yields dimensions of individual differences, and that these dimensions do not provide understanding of personality structure. The factors represent the elements in a personality profile. Then, if organized or grouped by higher order factors, the elements of the score profile define the style an individual displays in relating to others and to the world around him or her. The most promising approach for discovering a small number of profiles is probably through cluster analysis (Lorr, 1983).

On the other hand, I do not believe that the order of emergence of higher order factors can be controlled. By using homogeneous clusters as units and factoring their intercorrelations, primary dimensions can be established. Then, analysis of the intercorrelations of the primary-factor scores should yield higher order dimensions. Upon pursuing this route, there is much promise that second-order dimensions can be discovered and replicated systematically.

In comparing second-order factors, such as those established by Eysenck, Guilford, and Cattell, it is important to study the primary dimensions that contribute to the definition of factors. Eysenck's Extraversion (1969) for example, includes Sociability, Impulsiveness, and Surgency. Guilford's (1975) Extraversion-Intraversion, by his own assertion, consists of Restraint and Thoughtfulness. Comrey's Extraversion scale (1970), if inspected for content, will be found to consist only of Sociability items. Cattell's Exvia-Invia (1954) is defined by his factors A (Warmth), F (Impulse), H (Boldness), and Q_2 (Group Dependency). Perhaps confirmatory factor analyses will provide a resolution.

REFERENCES

Cattell, R. B. (1954). *Personality and motivational structure and measurement*. New York: World.

Comrey, A. L. (1970). *Manual for the Comrey Personality Scales*. San Diego: Educational and Industrial Testing Service.

Cronbach, L. J., & Gleser, G. C. (1953). Assessing similarity between profiles. *Psychological Bulletin, 50*, 456-473.

Edwards, A. L. (1954). *Edwards Personal Preference Schedule*. New York: Psychological Corp.

Eysenck, H. J., & Eysenck, S. B. (1969). *Personality structure and measurement*. San Diego: Knapp.

Foa, U. G. (1965). New developments in facet design and analysis. *Psychological Review, 72*, 262-274.

Gilberstadt, A., & Duker, J. (1965). *A handbook for clinical and actuarial MMPI interpretation*. Philadelphia: W. B. Saunders.

Guilford, J. P. (1975). Factors and factors of personality. *Psychological Bulletin, 82*, 802-814.

Gulliksen, H. (1950). *Theory of mental tests*, New York: Wiley.

Guttman, L. (1954). A new approach to factor analysis: The radex. In P. F. Lazarsfeld (Ed.), *Mathematical thinking in the social sciences* (pp. 258-348).

Howarth, E., & Brown, J. A. (1971). An item factor analysis of the 16PF. *Personality, 2*, 117-139.

Izard, C. E. (1972). *Patterns of emotions: A new analysis of anxiety and depression*. New York: Academic Press.

Jackson, D. N. (1967). *Personality research form manual*. Port Huron, MI:Research Psychological Press.

Leary, T. (1957). *Interpersonal diagnosis of personality*. New York: Ronald Press.

Lorr, M. (1983). *Cluster analysis for social scientists*. San Francisco: Jossey-Bass.

Lorr, M., O'Connor, J. P., & Seifert, R. F. (1977). A comparison of four personality inventories. *Journal of Personality Assessment, 41*, 520-526.

Lorr, M., & Suziedelis, A. (1982). A cluster analytic approach to MMPI profile types. *Multivariate Behavioral Research, 17*, 285-299.

Lorr, M., & Youniss, R. L. (1973). An inventory of interpersonal style. *Journal of Personality Assessment, 37*, 165-173.

Lorr, M., & Youniss, R. L. (1985). *The interpersonal style inventory.* Los Angeles: Western Psychological Service.

Marks, P. A., Seeman, W., & Haller, D. L. (1974). *The actuarial use of the MMPI with adolescents and adults.* Baltimore: Williams & Wilkins.

McNair, D.M. & Lorr, M. (1964). An analysis of mood in neurotics. *Journal of Abnormal and Social Psychology, 69,* 620-627.

Nowlis, J., & Nowlis, H. H. (1956). The description and analysis of mood. *Annals of the New York Academy of Sciences 65,* 345-355.

Sells, S. B. (1955). *Symposium on pattern analysis.* USAF School of Aviation Medicine, Randolph Field, TX.

Zuckerman, M., & Lubin, B. (1965). *Manual for the multiple affect adjective check list.* San Diego: Educational and Industrial Testing Service.

IV THE PERSON IN THE WORKPLACE

10 Organizational Climate: Another Look at a Potentially Important Construct

Lawrence R. James
Georgia Institute of Technology

In a recent discussion of measurement models in climate research, James (1982) recommended that a decision of whether to aggregate individual's climate scores should be a function of the magnitude of an intraclass correlation estimate of interrater reliability. This recommendation was based on the following rationale: (a) the basic unit of theory (unit of analysis) for climate is an individual's perception of his or her psychological climate (James & Sells, 1981; Jones & James, 1979; Joyce & Slocum, 1979; Schneider, 1983); (b) a composition theory relating psychological climate scores to aggregate psychological climate scores (e.g., organizational climate scores) may be established if the perceptions of psychological climate are shared among the individuals on whom the aggregate is computed (Roberts, Hulin, & Rousseau, 1978); and (c) the typical design employed in climate studies is a random effects, one-way analysis of variance (ANOVA), from which, given reasonable satisfaction of assumptions, it is possible to estimate interrater reliability (perceptual agreement, degree perceptions are shared) by the intraclass correlation equation for the reliability of a single rating or measurement (referred to here as ICC(1)--cf. Bartko, 1976; Ebel, 1951; Shrout & Fleiss, 1979; Winer, 1971).

The objectives of this chapter represent, in part, a continuation of the previous discussion. It is suggested that the criterion for perceptual agreement and aggregation of psychological climate scores is a reasonably high ICC(1). Based on this criterion, it is shown that traditional indices of interrater reliability render organizational climate a moot issue, where the term *organizational climate* is used to refer to a field of research that involves any type of aggregate psychological climate scores (Jones & James, 1979; Schneider, 1983). It is then demonstrated that estimates of interrater reliability based on an ICC(1) approach may, under specified conditions, furnish serious underestimates of interrater reliability. Finally, a new method for estimating interrater reliability is overviewed, and an empirical illustration is used to show that it is possible to achieve high levels of interrater reliability on climate data. The conclusion reached is that organizational climate is a salvageable construct.

A CRITERION FOR PERCEPTUAL AGREEMENT IN CLIMATE RESEARCH

Climate has been reviewed extensively in recent years, the output focused mainly on restatements of prior positions, reviews of these positions, and reviews of reviews (Campbell, Dunnette, Lawler, & Weick, 1970; Hellreigel & Slocum, 1974; Insel & Moos, 1974; James, Hater, Gent, & Bruni, 1978; James & Jones, 1974; James & Sells, 1981; Jones & James, 1979; Joyce & Slocum, 1979; Naylor, Pritchard, & Ilgen, 1980; Payne, Fineman, & Wall, 1976; Payne & Pugh, 1976; Powell & Butterfield, 1978; Schneider, 1975, 1983; Schneider, Parkington, & Buxton, 1980; Woodman & King, 1978). Represented ubiquitously in these reviews is the logic that perceptual agreement is a prerequisite for aggregation of climate scores. Yet, a criterion for an acceptable level of perceptual agreement--that is, a level that justifies aggregation--remains obscure (James, 1982). Exceptions to this rule include Guion (1973), who recommended that agreement indices should not depart significantly from 1.00, and Roberts et al. (1978) and Schneider (1983), who recommend that within-organization variance in climate perceptions should be small in relation to between-organization variance. The fact that these two recommendations are statistically miles apart is easily demonstrated if we apply their statistical implications to the typical experimental design used in climate research.

Suppose that we have n_k individuals nested in each of K ($k=1, \ldots, K$) organizations. For the present, it is presumed that the assumptions for a one-way random effects ANOVA and computation of an ICC(1) have been reasonably satisfied (e.g., randomly selected organizations and individuals, homogeneity of variance). The ANOVA employs the K organizations as treatments and the n_k scores on a climate variable in each organization as values on the dependent variable. The "empirical criterion" for agreement for Roberts et al. (1978) and Schneider (1983) appears to be a significant F ratio, which connotes significantly greater between-organization variance than within-organization variance. Note that no point estimate of interrater reliability is required. This suggests, for example, that with large samples an ICC(1) of .05 is acceptable as long as the F ratio is significant (cf. Jones & James, 1979, for point estimates of ICC(1) with large samples). The Guion (1973) criterion is much more stringent. It implies, for example, that in each of the K organizations the variance on the climate variable should not depart significantly from zero. This suggests that not only should the F ratio be significant, but also that the ICC(1) should approach 1.00.

The position advocated in this chapter is that a criterion for perceptual agreement requires first a point estimate of interrater reliability. To demonstrate merely that an F ratio is significant is of trivial concern in relation to the magnitude of the interrater reliability estimate, especially when $N(N = \Sigma n_k)$ is large (Cohen, 1960). Thus, the Roberts et al. (1978) and Schneider (1983) criterion is not regarded as sufficient for justifying aggregation of climate scores. The implied necessity for a point estimate of interrater reliability approaching 1.00 (Guion, 1973) is regarded as too stringent. Consider, for example, a criterion for computing an aggregate over items--that is, a composite score for each individual on items designed to assess the same construct. Based on the current literature, it appears that a criterion often employed is an internal consistency reliability, (e.g., coefficient α) of .70 and above (in exploratory studies). Perhaps the same criterion may prove useful for interrater reliability and aggregation of climate scores over individuals. Specifically, given the design in question, an ICC(1) of .70 might be employed as a lower bound criterion for justifying aggregation of climate scores over individuals.

Is Organizational Climate a Moot Issue?

James (1982) summarized estimates of perceptual agreement in climate studies and reported that the range of estimates varied from .00 to .50, with a median of approximately .12. The estimates included in the summary were based on either ICC(1) or on estimates of the proportion of variance in an individual's perceptions associated with variation among environments (eta-squares, omega-squares). For reasons explained in that article, estimates based on aggregates were considered biased and excluded from the summary. Also excluded were estimates of interrater reliability based on correlations among profiles (e.g., a correlation between two raters' scores on a set of climate dimensions) for reasons discussed by numerous authors (cf. Cronbach & Gleser, 1953), and a study by Howe (1977), which confounded stability of perceptions over time with agreement among perceptions at a particular point in time.

Given that legitimate estimates of interrater reliability do not exceed .50, it follows that if we were to adopt a point estimate of interrater reliability equal to or greater than .70 as the operational criterion for perceptual agreement and aggregation, then organizational climate as presently conceived is a moot issue. Or is it?

APPROPRIATENESS OF THE INTRACLASS CORRELATION IN CLIMATE STUDIES

The objective of this section is to suggest that the intraclass correlation, and other statistics that employ a between-groups versus within-group form of design (eta-square, omega-square), may have provided substantial underestimates of interrater reliability in at least some prior climate studies. Discussion focuses on ICC(1), and is based on a statistical paper by James, Wolf, and Demaree (1981b).

Associated with the ICC(1) statistic are a number of assumptions underlying the ANOVA procedure on which it is based. One assumption is that the environments employed in a study compromise a random sample of environments from a heterogeneous population of environments. The somewhat subtle implication of this assumption is that if a mean (aggregate) climate score is computed over the n_k individuals in each environment, then these means will vary among environments, especially in a condition of high interrater reliability. To be specific, between-environments variance in mean climate perceptions is a prerequisite for high interrater reliability. Now, consider the statistical facts that if (a) little variation exists among the K mean climate perceptions for K environments, and if (b) perceivers in each of the K environments agree almost perfectly (i.e., within-environments variance is close to zero), then (c) the ICC(1) estimate of interrater reliability will be low. Note that we have a condition of almost perfect agreement within environments and an estimate of interrater reliability. Restriction of range denotes little or no variation among the mean climate perceptions over environments. (The same logic applies to eta-square and omega-square, although these statistics may themselves differ; cf. Maxwell, Camp, & Arvey, 1981).

These points are easily illustrated statistically. The data presented in Table 10.1 consist of hypothetical scores on a climate item X which has five discrete, approximately equally spaced alternatives (e.g., a Likert scale--cf.   Cooper, 1969; Hsu, 1979). Frequencies of responses are shown for 20 different

Table 10.1
Intraclass Correlation Based on 20 Raters
in Each of Two Environments

Scale for Variable X	Frequencies of Scores in Environment 1	Frequencies of Scores in Environment 2
1	0	0
2	2	2
3	16	15
4	2	3
5	0	0
Mean:	3.00	3.05
Variance:	.211	.261

Analysis of Variance

Source	df	SS	MS	F
Between-Environments	1	.025	.025	.106[NS]
Within-Environments	38	8.959	.025	

Intraclass Correlation

$$\text{ICC}(1) = \frac{.025 - .236}{.025 + (19)(.236)}$$
$$= -.047$$
$$= .00$$

Note: NS = not significant at $p < .05$.

individuals in each of two environments. The frequencies of responses indicate that the individuals in each environment tend to agree, which is reflected by the small within-environment variances (.211 and .261). However, ICC(1) is -.047, which is regarded as .00 (Bartko, 1976). This low ICC is clearly an underestimate of true agreement, and may be attributed directly to the essential absence of variation among the aggregate climate scores (3.00 and 3.05).

Data such as presented in Table 10.1 stimulate the following question: Why should the level of agreement within an environment be contingent on differences among environments? That is, in its most direct form, interrater reliability and agreement address the question of whether people in a particular environment, or people in each one of a set of environments, agree with respect to their perceptions. This question neither assumes nor requires that differences exist among environments. Of course, if environments were sampled randomly from a heterogeneous population of environments in which mean climate perceptions were expected to vary, then we would not anticipate a restriction of range problem such as illustrated in Table 10.1. This point is discussed in the following sections. It is also noteworthy that if the level of agreement varies as a function of environment (i.e., the level of agreement is not the same or similar across environments), then the ANOVA-based ICC(1) approach cannot be used because the homogeneity of variance assumption is violated. Thus, even if one wanted to include between environment differences in an interrater reliability estimate, one could not do so legitimately.

In summary, use of a statistic such as the ICC(1) that relies on between-environment differences will result in an underestimate of interrater reliability (agreement) if the following conditions exist: (a) mean climate scores do not vary appreciably among environments, and (b) individuals within environments tend to agree.

A case can be built that these two conditions

apply to at least some climate studies. The case for low variation among mean climate scores over a set of K environments is predicated on the fact that many climate studies have employed samples of environments from the same basic system or, more typically, subsystem type. It is not uncommon to find the sample in a particular study limited to banks, to classrooms, to dormitories, to hospitals, to life insurance agencies, or to divisions aboard Navy ships. Now consider the possibility that variation among mean climate scores is likely to be restricted if all environments in a sample are of the same or similar basic type, regardless of whether the environments were randomly sampled from within this type. That is, sampling of environments from a homogeneous type of environment, in relation to a more heterogeneous population of environmental types, is likely to lead to restricted variances on situational attributes believed to be causes of climate perceptions, such as technology, structure, norms, and processes (e.g., communication, leadership, and rewards). It follows that if (a) individuals' climate perceptions are a (partial) function of situational attributes, and if (b) sampling from a homogeneous environmental type results in restricted ranges on situational attributes, then (c) the range should also be restricted on individuals' perceptions, and, therefore, on means of individuals' perceptions.

The case for low within-environment variation among individuals' perceptions is based in part on the preceding argument and in part on a recent report by Schneider (1983). Range restriction in regard to the type of environment studied suggests similarity of perceptions because of similarity of situational stimuli. However, similarity of stimuli is not sufficient to guarantee low within-environment variation in perceptions. My colleagues and I have argued on a number of occasions that individuals with different cognitive construction competencies, encoding abilities, self-regulatory systems, beliefs, needs, values, and self-concepts will be predisposed to differ in what they perceive as ambiguous, challenging, fair, friendly, supportive, and so forth (cf. James, et al., 1978; James & Sells, 1981). That is, psychological climates associated with the same or similar actual environments are likely to differ for different types of individuals, and the reasons for these differences are not only psychologically important, but they also can be reliably measured and related to climate perceptions (cf. James, Gent, Hater & Coray, 1979; James, Hater, & Jones, 1981a; James & Jones, 1980).

On the other hand, if, as Schneider (1983) suggests, the environments in question are composed of similar types of individuals, then I agree with his conclusion that the likelihood of variation in perceptions due to individual differences would be reduced. If placement in a particular job, office, position, or role is subject to rigorous selection standards that relate, directly or indirectly, to cognitive information processing competencies and predispositions (e.g., achievement motivation, cognitive complexity, intelligence, perceived competence, and self-esteem), then the resulting relative similarity among individuals suggests a relative similarity among perceptions of climate. Of perhaps equal importance is the degree to which individuals with relative similarities in attributes not necessarily related to formal selection processes (e.g., cosmopolitan vs. local orientation, expectancies, locus of control, need for affiliation) are attracted to (self-select) a particular job, office, position, or role. Here again, relative similarity in individual attributes suggests relative similarity in perceptions. Furthermore, relative similarity among individuals resulting from formal and/or self-selection processes generates forces toward perceptual agreement because (a) environments tend to be shaped to fit the types of individuals who select, and are selected, to work in them, which implies similarity of within-environmental stimuli for similar types of individuals (cf. Endler and Magnusson, 1976; James et al., 1978); and (b) the meaning imputed to an environment by an individual is more likely to be socially influenced by other individuals in that environment if the perceiver views the others as similar to him or herself than if the others are viewed as different (cf. Stotland & Canon, 1972).

In summary, the following two situations appear to be conducive to underestimation of interrater reliability/agreement when estimation is based on an ANOVA design and the ICC(1).

1. Sampling of environments from a single type of environment, which implies restriction of range in the types of situational stimuli (perceived) in each environment and a similarity of stimuli across environments.

2. Similar types of individuals within homogeneous environments, resulting from rigorous formal selection processes and/or self-selection processes. Similarity among individuals implies, in a relative sense, a narrow range of individual differences in cognitive information processing competencies and predispositions. This in turn suggests relative similarities in the psychological meaning and significance imputed to environments (i.e., similar psychological climates). It also suggests similar shaping of environmental stimuli and social influence processes.

These two situations are conducive to the statistical conditions of low within-environment variation resulting from similar types of individuals perceiving similar types of stimuli, and low between-environment variation in mean (aggregate) climate scores. An alternative to the ICC(1) approach is indicated for estimating interrater reliability/agreement if these two statistical conditions are operative, or perhaps even partially operative. Such an alternative was proposed by James et al. (1981b), and is reviewed here.

AN OVERVIEW OF A NEW METHOD
FOR ESTIMATING INTERRATER RELIABILITY
IN CLIMATE STUDIES

The proposed procedure is based on prior work by Finn

(1970) and Cooper (1976), and employs a within-groups design in which interrater reliability is estimated separately for each group (i.e., environment). For each group, interrater reliability is defined as the degree to which raters (perceivers) agree with respect to their ratings (perceptions) of a particular target (e.g., the organization) on a particular rating (climate) scale (e.g., the equity of an organization's pay and benefit system). A within-groups design is used because we desire an estimate of interrater reliability for each group that is not a function of between-groups variation. Thus, the estimate will not be affected by lack of variation in group means. Furthermore, lack of homogeneity of within-groups variation is not a concern inasmuch as a separate estimate of reliability is computed for each group. Consequently, agreement may vary as a function of environment and we may still estimate agreement for each group.

The proposed procedure views interrater reliability (agreement) within a group as a function of two variances, namely (a) the observed variance among the ratings on a climate item X, designated s_X^2 and (b) the expected variance among the ratings on climate item X in a condition of no agreement, designated σ_E^2. An $s_X^2 = 0$ indicates perfect agreement; however, s_X^2 is rarely equal to zero and thus we must ascertain the degree to which raters in a group agreed. This is accomplished by comparing s_X^2 to σ_E^2, where σ_E^2 is the variance on item X that would be expected if raters responded randomly, which implies zero interrater reliability and no agreement (cf. Finn, 1970). Thus, σ_E^2 functions as a statistical benchmark for random responding and absence of agreement. It follows that (a) the value of the proportion indicated by (s_X^2/σ_E^2) reflects the amount of random error variance in the observed ratings, and (b) $1 - (s_X^2/\sigma_E^2)$ is a reliability coefficient because it indicates the proportion of nonerror variance in the observed ratings (Finn, 1970; James et al., 1981b).

It is important to note that σ_E^2 is a statistical abstraction. We use a hypothetical random responding as a statistical benchmark for assessing the extent to which the variance of a set of actual responses, indicated by s_X^2, resembles the expected variance of a set of random responses, indicated by σ_E^2. The assumption of random responding also provides a simple method for computing σ_E^2. Random responding implies that each alternative on the rating scale for item X has an equal likelihood of response. This in turn implies that the distribution of scores over alternatives is rectangular or uniform. Consequently, σ_E^2 may be calculated using the equation for the variance of a discrete, uniform distribution. This equation is: $\sigma_E^2 = (A^2 - 1)/12$, where A corresponds to the number of discrete alternatives on item X. σ_E^2 is a population parameter, and thus sample size does not enter into its calculation.

In summary, building on prior work by Finn (1970) and Cooper (1976), James et al. (1981b) derived the following equation for estimating interrater reliability for a single group of individuals on a single item.

$$r_{WG} = 1 - (s_X^2/\sigma_E^2) \tag{1}$$

where:

r_{WG} = within-group interrater reliability for a single group of raters on a single item X.

s_X^2 = the observed variance on item X in the group. Assumptions associated with s_X^2 (and σ_E^2) are that raters responded independently (this does not preclude prior social influence processes), and that X is a discrete random variable with multiple alternatives arranged on an approximately interval scale (such as a Likert item--cf. Cooper, 1976).

σ_E^2 = the variance on item X that would be expected if the raters responded randomly, which implies zero interrater reliability and no agreement. σ_E^2 is calculated by the equation $(A-1)/12$, where A is the number of alternatives on item X (the scale on X is $1,....,A$).

Equation 1 is easily interpreted. If $s_X^2 = 0$, then $r_{WG} = 1.0$; that is, no variance on X results in perfect interrater reliability (agreement). Conversely, if raters were to respond randomly, then $s_X^2 \approx \sigma_E^2$, and $r_{WG} \approx 0$. The typical situation in research is $0 < s_X^2 < \sigma_E^2$. Equation 1 indicates that as s_X^2 approaches σ_E^2, interrater reliability decreases, and as s_X^2 becomes progressively smaller than σ_E^2, interrater reliability increases.

The use of Equation 1 is illustrated by application to the data in Table 10.1. Item X has five alternatives, or $A = 5$, and thus σ_E^2 is equal to $(5^2 - 1)/12$, or 2.0, in each of five groups. The observed variance (s_X^2) on X in Group 1 is .211, and the estimate of r_{WG} provided by Equation 1 is .89 [i.e., $1 - (.211/2.0)$]. Using similar procedures, the estimate of r_{WG} in Group 2 is $1 - (.261/2.0)$, or .87. Given the similarity of these two estimates (and the observed variances), the estimates were averaged to furnish a value of .88. The value of .88 is obviously different than the ICC(1) of .00, and it is equally obvious that each r_{WG} and the average r_{WG} are more consistent with the data than the ICC(1).

It should be noted that on averaging, the separate r_{WG}s are dissimilar. A homogeneity of variance test on observed variances (i.e., the s_X^2s) assists in ascertaining whether to average r_{WG}s in nonobvious situations.

Interrater Reliability for Composite Scores. Data employed in climate studies often are based on a composite score rather than a single item. For example, each member of a work group rates that group on a set of items designed to measure workgroup cooperativeness. A composite score is then calculated for each rater by computing a sum or a mean over the items, and it is these scores that are entered into the within-group interrater reliability (agreement) analysis. Based on a rationale by Finn (1970), James et al. (1981b) derived an equation for estimating the interrater reliability among raters' composite scores on a set of J ($j = 1,...,J$) items in a single group. The derivation was based on the assumptions that (a) the J items represent a random sample of items from a single, well-defined domain of items (cf. Lord & Novick, 1968); (b) the raters in each group are randomly sampled from a population of raters to which inferences will be made (which allows the population of raters to be homogeneous); and (c) the item variances and interitem covariances are equal, respectively, in the rater population, which implies that the items are "essentially parallel" indicators of the same construct.

An example of the design in question is presented in the data section of Table 10.2. The data represent ratings (i.e., item responses) provided by six raters ($i = 1,...,n_k = 1,...,6$) on four essentially parallel items that measure the same climate dimension. Each of the four items ($J = 4$) employs the same seven discrete, approximately equally-spaced alternatives ($A = 7$).

The generally recommended statistical procedure for estimating interrater reliability for multiple ratings in a within-group design should not be used here. As shown in the within-group ICC section of Table 10.2, the within-group ICC is approximately .00 (equation for ICC, Shrout and Fleiss, 1979). This is due to the fact that the items have essentially identical means, from which it follows that the between-item mean square is close to zero. The within-group ICC can only assume high values when between-item variance is larger than within-item variance. Given essentially parallel items, this is not likely to be the case, and the within-group ICC underestimates interrater reliability.

The procedure described by James et al. (1981b) is designed to estimate interrater reliability among rater composite scores in the form of means, designated $\bar{X}i$. The $\bar{X}i$ are displayed at the bottom of the data matrix in Table 10.2. The estimating equation takes a number of forms; the most direct for computing purposes is as follows:

$$r_{WG(\bar{X}i)} = \frac{J(1 - Ms^2_{Xj}/\sigma_E^2)}{J[1 - (Ms^2_{Xj}/\sigma_E^2)] + (Ms^2_{Xj}/\sigma_E^2)} \quad (2)$$

where:

$r_{WG(\bar{X}i)}$ = within-group interrater reliability for mean rater scores (the $\bar{X}i$) on J essentially parallel items.

Ms^2_{Xj} = the mean observed variance on the J items--it is assumed here that each of the J items employs the same seven alternatives (e.g., the same seven adjectives).

σ_E^2 = same definition as before, namely the expected variance of an item in a condition of zero interrater reliability and no agreement. Technically, the mean σ_E^2, or $M\sigma_E^2$, should be used in Equation 2, but with $A = 7$ for all items, $M\sigma_E^2 = \sigma_E^2$.

The use of Equation 2 is illustrated in the third section of Table 10.2. The estimate of $r_{WG(\bar{X}i)}$ is .98, which contrasts sharply with the within-group ICC of .00. It is also clear that an interrater reliability of .98 is a more accurate reflection of the data than a .00. To be fair here, one could argue that the within-group ICC is low because the items were not sampled randomly from a heterogeneous population of items, thus violating the implicit ANOVA assumption of variation among item means. The within-group ICC was included only to demonstrate its inapplicability.

Equation 2, like Equation 1, may be applied in each of K groups, and the resulting $r_{WG(\bar{X}i)}$ may be averaged over the k groups if the separate $r_{WG(\bar{X}i)}$ are similar. Homogeneity of variance tests on the mean item variances over the K groups might be employed to help to decide whether to average the $r_{WG(\bar{X}i)}$. Finally, it is suggested that if the decision is to average, and the n_k differ, there would be little

Table 10.2

Illustrations of Within-Group ICC and $r_{WG(\overline{X}i)}$ for
a Single Group of Raters

A. Data

			Rater					
Item	1	2	3	4	5	6	Mean	s_{Xj}^2
1	6	6	7	7	7	7	6.67	.27
2	7	6	6	7	6	6	6.33	.27
3	7	7	7	6	6	6	6.50	.30
4	6	7	6	7	6	7	6.50	.30

Mean   6.5   6.5   6.5   6.75   6.25   6.50

B. Within Group ICC

Source	df	SS	MS
Between-Item	3	.41	.137
Within-Item	20	5.70	.285
Between Rater	5	.50	.100
Residual	15	5.20	.347

ICC $\approx$ .00

C. $r_{WG(\overline{X}i)}$

$$Ms_X^2 = (.27 + .27 + .30 + .30)/4 = .285$$

$$\sigma_E^2 = (7^2 - 1)/12 = 4.0$$

$$r_{WG(\overline{X}i)} = \frac{4[1 - (.285/4.0)]}{4[1 - (.285/4.0)] \quad (.285/4.0)} = .98$$

reason to weight the $r_{WG(Xi)}$ by n because the $r_{WG(Xi)}$ should be similar. This applies also to averaging r_{WG}.

In summary, the previous discussions summarize the use of r_{WG} and $r_{WG(\overline{X}_i)}$. Statistical derivations and discussions of potential criticisms of the procedures are presented in James et al. (1981b). It is noted here that very small n (e.g., less than 10 individuals in a group) may lead to unstable results, and that very short (e.g., $A \leq 3$) or very long (e.g., $A > 9$) item scales may produce unrelated results. Additional points developed more fully in the James et al. paper are (a) although the theoretical distribution on an item X may be normal (Hsu, 1979; Selvage, 1976), a rectangular (uniform) distribution should be used to calculate σ_E^2 because the rectangular distribution, and not the normal distribution, models random responses (the normal distribution models partial agreement because of central tendency); (b) the calculation of σ_E^2 may be based on an assumed underlying continuous, rather than discrete, distribution by using $(A - 1)/12$ to calculate σ_E^2 (Selvage, 1976); (c) like ICC(1), the estimates of r_{WG} and $r_{WG(\overline{X}_i)}$ are biased, but the bias is expected to be minimam for small n_k and essentially *negligible* for large n_k; and (d) also like ICC(1), r_{WG} and $r_{WG(\overline{X}_i)}$ can assume values of less than .00, in which case the value is set equal to .00 because all observed distributions on an item X that result in negative values are due to serious degrees of disagreement (the same recommendation was made for ICC(1) by Bartko, 1976).

EMPIRICAL COMPARISON OF BETWEEN-GROUPS AND WITHIN-GROUPS APPROACHES

The data employed in this illustration were collected by David W. Bracken as part of a dissertation project at the Georgia Institute of Technology, and loaned to the present investigator to demonstrate statistical procedures. The data met the two situations and statistical conditions discussed earlier in which an ICC(1) procedure would be expected to provide an underestimate of interrater reliability. Statistical conditions are discussed shortly. Of initial concern is that Situation 1 was satisfied inasmuch as all environments were of the same organization subtype. The environmental sample consisted of field offices of a large business machines company. Each office (a) operated as a self-contained subsystem; (b) performed the same functions, namely marketing, installing, and servicing small business machines; and (c) had the same hierarchical/functional differentiation, where the staff consisted of managerial personnel, marketing personnel, supervisors, technicians (see the following) and clerical personnel. All offices were located in the United States, with the exception of one location in Puerto Rico. The offices varied in size, but size was not related to the data of interest here.

Situation 2 refers to relative homogeneity of within-office variance on individual difference variables that could influence scores on climate variables. This situation was partially satisfied in the following manner. The parent corporation supported a study designed to ascertain if climate moderated relationships between scores on selection tests and performance. The study focused exclusively on the position of technician, which is similarly described for all offices as installing and servicing business machines. For the present study, the relative homogeneity of variance on individual difference variables for technicians was demonstrated by comparing selection test data to published norms in test manuals, where the most heterogeneous norm samples--high school students--were selected for comparison purposes. The test included the Bennett Test of Mechanical Comprehension and the Gordon Personal Inventory and Personal Profile. The personality data were of primary interest here because personality comprises a salient basis for predispositions toward assignment of meaning in higher-order cognitive processing (cf. James & Jones, 1980; James et al., 1978; James et al., 1979; Jones & Gerard, 1967; Kim, 1980; Mischel, 1973; Stotland & Canon, 1972).

Test data were available on approximately 2,800 technicians; all offices ($K = 87$) were represented in this sample. These data were based on test results obtained since 1975, the time at which the parent corporation initiated a formal reporting program. Company personnel reported the opinion that these data were representative of most technicians because the tests had been used in the same fashion for a number of years prior to the initiation of the reporting program. Although it was not possible to confirm or disconfirm this opinion empirically, the results for the interrater reliability on climate perceptions reported shortly suggest that the assumption was valid.

The relative homogeneity of variance on individual difference variables is indicated by the statistics reported in Table 10.3. These results demonstrate that (a) the means on test scores for the technician sample were, with one exception (sociability), far above the averages of the norm samples, as indicated by percentile ranks ranging from 67 to 95; and (b) on the average, the variances of test scores on the technician sample were approximately one-half as large as those on the norm samples. Furthermore, as shown in the third column of Table 10.3, only small portions of the variance in technicians' test scores were associated with differences among offices, which is indicated by the small eta-squares (eta-squares were based on one-way ANOVAs using office as the independent variable). These results suggest that variation on individual difference variables was partially restricted for the technician sample and that technicians did not, on the average, vary substantially across offices. This does not suggest that all technicians reported the same climate perceptions, although it does imply that conditions were operative to preclude obtaining a high ICC.

The sample of technicians employed in the interrater reliability analyses on climate perceptions consisted of 7,180 individuals from 60 offices. The technicians completed a 102 item climate questionnaire, developed specifically for technicians in 1980. Principal components analysis of the climate data furnished 13 components that were interpretable as cognitive representations of the work environment and

Table 10.3
Percentile Ranks, Variance Proportions,
and Between-Group Difference for Technician Sample
on Individual Difference Variables

Variable	Percentile Rank of Technician Sample Mean[a]	Technician Sample Variance/ Norm Sample Variance[b]	n^2 One-Way ANOVA[c]
Gordon Personal Inventory			
Cautiousness	86	.54	.04*
Original Thinking	82	.50	.04
Personal Relations	84	.58	.03*
Vigor	77	.48	.04*
Gordon Personal Profile			
Ascendancy	67	.50	.03
Responsibility	95	.48	.03
Emotional Stability	79	.52	.04
Sociability	48	.45	.04
Bennett Test of Mechanical Comprehension Form BB			
	75	.51	.05*

*$p < .05$ for F-ratio associated with eta-square (n^2).

[a]Total sample size for all offices ($K = 87$) was 3,050 for the Bennett and an average of 2,770 for the personality inventory profile. The norm samples used here for all variables were based on high-school students.

[b]The total-sample variances and mean-square errors from the one-way ANOVA were essentially identical. Proportions are based on total-sample variances. F-max tests on norm sample variance/technician sample variance were significant ($p < .05$) for all variables.

[c]Eta-square for one-way ANOVA to test for mean differences among the 87 offices.

had scale reliabilities of .70 or greater (coefficient alpha). Abbreviated designations of 11 of the climate dimensions for which "office" was a potentially appropriate level of explanation are presented in Table 10.4.

The remaining two climate dimensions (supervisor support, work group cooperativeness) are not included because different levels of explanation were indicated (e.g., different supervisors and work groups within a particular office). Also shown in Table 10.4 are the number of items per climate dimension, dimension internal consistency estimates (coefficient alpha), estimates of interrater reliability furnished by an ICC(1) approach, the variance of the mean climate scores for the 60+ offices, the average within-office variance on each climate dimension, and estimates of interrater reliability supplied by $r_{WG(\bar{X}i)}$, which are reported in terms of the range of estimates for the 60 offices and the percent of offices for which the estimate was .70 or above.

The intraclass correlations were computed by first calculating composite (mean) scores on each of the 11 climate dimensions for each technician. These scores were based on a mean of the scores on the items that loaded on each climate component.[1] For each climate dimension, a random effects, one-way ANOVA was conducted to obtain estimates of the between-office and within-office mean squares. The ICC(1) equation was then employed, as shown in Table 10.1, to estimate interrater reliability, using a harmonic mean of 75.05 for office size (office size ranged from 5 to 215). As shown in the ICC(1) column in Table 10.4, the estimates of interrater reliability were uniformly low, ranging

---

[1]Inasmuch as the $r_{WG(\bar{X}i)}$ procedure does not weight items explicitly, the items were not weighted explicitly (e.g., component scores) in the calculation of means. This provided as comparable a base as possible for contrasting reliability estimates provided by the ICC(1) and $r_{WG(\bar{X}i)}$ approaches.

Table 10.4
Comparison of Between-Office and Within-Office
Estimates of Interrater Reliability on Eleven
Climate Dimensions

	No. Items per Climate Dimension	Coefficient Alpha	ICC(1)	Variance of Office Means[a]	Average Within-Office Variance[b]	$r_{WG(\bar{X}i)}$ Range	$r_{WG(\bar{X}i)}$ % > 70
	(1)	(2)	(3)	(4)	(5)	(6)	(7)
1. Adequacy Of Benefits	7	.84	.08	.04	.42	.87-.96	100%
2. Affirmative-Action Negative Consequences	3	.90	.04	.04	.82	.35-.76	22
3. Involvement	10	.89	.03	.02	.45	.86-.96	100
4. Affirmative-Action Positive Consequences	4	.74	.01	.01	.46	.63-.89	95
5. Habitability	4	.83	.07	.04	.38	.52-.92	95
6. Overload	4	.73	.05	.03	.51	.61-.88	88
7. Resources	4	.79	.03	.03	.56	.69-.93	98
8. Equity of Pay	4	.86	.08	.07	.64	.50-.89	93
9. Fairness-Management	4	.76	.06	.03	.42	.66-.91	98
10. Employment Security	9	.87	.10	.05	.23	.81-.95	100
11. Opportunities For Advancement	3	.75	.03	.05	1.00	.39-.91	65

Note. K = 60 offices, N = 7,180.

[a]Variance of K=60 mean climate scores for offices.

[b]Average within-office variance of technicians' climate composite scores.

from   .01   to   .10.   These   results   are   generally
consistent   with   prior   climate   studies,   albeit   the
ICC(1)s are on the low side.

An explanation for these low ICC(1)s is   furnished
in   columns   4 and 5 of Table 10.4.   A mean   (aggregate)
of   the   technicians'   climate   scores was   computed   for
each climate dimension.   The variances of the means for
the   several   climate   dimensions   in the   sample   of   60
offices   are   reported   in   column   4.   The   range   of
possible mean office scores is 1 to 5. The range of the
11 variances is .01 - .07, which   on   a   5-point   scale
suggests   restriction   of range in   the   mean   climate
scores   for offices.   These results support   the   prior
contention of homogeneity of the environmental   sample.
The   average   within-office variances   of   technicians'
climate composite (mean) scores are presented in column
5.   The   values reflect the variation of   the   climate
composite   scores in an office about the mean for   that
office,   averaged over the 60 offices.   Again using   a
scale of 1 to 5, these variances generally reflect   low
within-office variation of the climate composite scores
(exceptions occurred for dimensions 2 and 11).

The   data shown in columns 4 and 5 of   Table   10.4
are   consistent   with the two   statistical   conditions
(low variation among office means and low within-office
variation of technicians' climate scores) that   suggest
a   low   ICC(1). Low within-office variation   implies
further   that   the interrater   reliabilities   based   on
$r_{WG(\bar{X}_i)}$ should be substantially higher than those based
on   ICC(1).   The   estimates of $r_{WG(\bar{X}_i)}$ were   based   on
applications   of Equation 2 in each of the   60   offices
for   each of the climate dimensions. The $r_{WG(\bar{X}_i)}$s   for
the climate dimensions differed somewhat across the   60
offices,   and thus ranges and the percent of   estimates
greater than or equal to .70 are reported in columns   6
and   7 of Table 10.4.   The estimates furnished by   this
analysis   were substantially higher than the   estimates
provided   by   the ICC(1) procedure.   For   example,   at
least   88% of the 60 offices had $r_{WG(\bar{X}_i)}$s   of   .70   or
greater   on 9 of the 11 climate dimensions.   Moreover,
even for the remaining two dimensions (dimensions 2 and
11),   not   only   did   some   offices   (22%   and   65%,

respectively) have $r_{WG(\overline{X}i)}$s $\geq$ .70, but also the lowest value in the range of $r_{WG(\overline{X}i)}$s exceeded ICC(1). It should also be mentioned that the values of $r_{WG(\overline{X}i)}$ and the percent of $r_{WG(\overline{X}i)}$s $\geq$ .70 tended to be larger for the climate dimensions with the larger number of items (dimensions 1, 3, and 10). This is a result of the fact that $r_{WG(\overline{X}i)}$ is a function of J, the number of items in a composite (see Equation 2). A substantive interpretation of this function is that the mean score per rater (i.e., $\overline{X}i$) will contain less random measurement error as the number of essentially parallel items in a composite increases. Thus, the estimate of interrater reliability among composite scores will be less influenced by random error in the original item measurements as the number of essentially parallel items in the composite increases. On the other hand, inspection of Equation 2 shows that a large J does not guarantee a large $r_{WG(\overline{X}i)}$ (e.g., if $s_{Xj}^2 \approx \sigma_E^2$, the $r_{WG(\overline{X}i)} \approx 0$).

In summary, the results for the $r_{WG(\overline{X}i)}$ analysis, in contrast to the results for the ICC(1) analysis, suggest that the technicians in most offices tended to agree with respect to their climate perceptions on 9 of a possible 11 climate dimensions. Consequently, mean or aggregate climate scores for technicians could be calculated for nine climate dimensions in almost all offices, and used to describe the shared psychological environment (climate) among technicians in particular offices.

CONCLUSIONS

A conclusion that is not warranted by the discussion and illustration is that all prior climate studies that employed between-group designs reported underestimates of interrater reliability (perceptual agreement). For example, given homogeneity of within-group variance and moderate to large between-group differences in group mean climate scores, the ICC(1) can assume high and reasonably accurate estimates of interrater reliability (James et al., 1981b). The primary problem occurs when between-group differences are small and within-group variation is low, which is most likely to occur when groups are sampled from the same environmental type or subtype and the range on individual difference variables is restricted due to formal and self-selection procedures. Inasmuch as many climate studies employ at least samples of environments from the same environmental type, the potential for underestimates of interrater reliability is present.   Unfortunately, published studies do not furnish sufficient data for reanalysis using the methods described here.

It is strongly recommended that climate researchers reexamine their data in light of the substantive and statistical points made in this paper. I believe that it is reasonable to assume that such reexamination will lead to different conclusions for at least some studies. That is, if the empirical illustration reported here is generalizable, then it is quite possible that estimates of interrater reliability will be higher, perhaps much higher, than those reported previously. On the other hand, the empirical illustration may be idiosyncratic and not generalizable. One could argue that the estimates of interrater reliability were higher than would generally be expected because only individuals from the same position (i.e., technician) were included in the analysis. I attempt to counter this argument by suggesting that individuals in different positions in an organization are likely (a) to experience different situational stimuli, which contributes to different perceptions of climate (cf. Newman, 1975), and (b) to vary in regard to individual variables which affect the meaning assigned to situational stimuli. The latter concern is viewed as a function of the formal selection and self-selection processes discussed earlier, and as a function of experience in the organization (e.g., increases in self-esteem resulting from promotions). This suggests that we should consider position, or perhaps families of similar positions, as a key variable on which to base agreement analyses. This, of course, is an empirical question that can be addressed in future research.

In conclusion, it is submitted that estimates of interrater reliability equal to or above .70 should not be all that uncommon in climate research if (a) the data have satisfactory psychometric properties (e.g., high scale reliabilities), (b) attention is given to the appropriate level of explanation of the climate variable, which operationally means that before one computes an interrater reliability, he or she should be reasonably assured that subjects were perceiving the same set of events, and (c) individuals on whom estimates of agreement are based are relatively similar in regard to personalistic variables that relate to cognitive information processing of climate perceptions. It is hypothesized, therefore, that individuals tend to agree at substantially higher levels than reported previously in the climate literature, given the conditions specified. If this hypothesis is confirmed, then the concept of an organizational climate, or perhaps "position climate," is alive and well, although we may wish to adopt a different descriptor than "organizational" to indicate aggregate psychological climate perceptions. Finally, a somewhat obvious but nevertheless important point requires mention. If the environments (positions) in a sample are indeed homogeneous, and if the within-environment variation on a climate variable is low, _ then it follows that the $r_{WG(X_i)}$s can be quite high but the mean climate scores will not relate highly, or perhaps even moderately, to other environmental variables (e.g., structural variables). This, of course, reflects the fact that the restriction of range on interrater reliability estimates such as ICC(1) extends directly to relations between aggregate climate scores and other variables. On the other hand, restriction of range is not as serious for climate data as it may be for other variables inasmuch as climate data often serve an important diagnostic function, such as ascertaining whether individuals in an environment, or sets of environments, perceive their pay and benefit programs as fair and equitable.

ACKNOWLEDGMENTS

Support for this project was provided under Office of Naval Research Contract N00014-80-C-0315, Office of Naval Research Project NR170-904. Opinions expressed are those of the author and are not to be constructed as necessarily reflecting the official view or endorsement of the Department of the Navy. The author wishes to thank David W. Bracken, Robert G. Demaree, Allan P. Jones, Benjamin Schneider, S. B. Sells, and Gerrit Wolf for their helpful suggestions and advice.

REFERENCES

Bartko, J. J. (1976). On various intraclass correlation reliability coefficients. *Psychological Bulletin, 83,* 762-765.

Campbell, J. P., Dunnette, M. D., Lawler, E. E., III, & Weick, K.E., Jr. (1970). *Managerial behavior, performance, and effectiveness.* New York: McGraw-Hill.

Cohen, J. (1960). A coefficient of agreement for nominal scales. *Educational and Psychological Measurement, 20,* 37-46.

Cooper, M. (1976). An exact probability test for use with Likert-type scales. *Educational and Psychological Measurement, 36,* 647-655.

Cronbach, L.J., & Gleser, G.C. (1953). Assessing similarity between profiles. *Psychological Bulletin, 50,* 456-473.

Ebel, R. L. (1951). Estimation of the reliability of ratings. *Psychometrika, 16,* 407-424.

Endler, N. S., & Magnusson, D. (1976). Toward an interactional psychology of personality. *Psychological Bulletin, 83,* 956-874.

Finn, R. H. (1970). A note on estimating the reliability of categorical data. *Educational and Psychological Measurement, 30,* 71-76.

Guion, R. M. (1973). A note on organizational climate. *Organizational Behavior and Human Performance, 9,* 120-125.

Hellreigel, D. , & Slocum, J. W., Jr. (1974). Organizational climate: Measures, research, and contingencies. *Academy of Management Journal, 17,* 255-280.

Howe, J.G. (1977). Group climate: An exploratory analysis of construct validity. *Organizational Behavior & Human Performance, 19,* 106-125.

Hsu, L. (1979). Agreement or disagreement of a set of Likert-type ratings. *Educational and Psychological Measurement, 39,* 291-295.

Insel, P. M., & Moos, R. H. (1974). Psychological environments: Expanding the scope of human ecology. *American Psychologist, 29,* 179-188.

James, L. R. (1982). Aggregation bias in estimates of perceptual agreement. *Journal of Applied Psychology, 67,* 219-229.

James, L. R., Gent, M. J., Hater, J. J., & Coray, K. E. (1979). Correlates of psychological influence: An illustration of the psychological influence: An illustration of the psychological climate approach to work environment perceptions. *Personnel Psychology, 32,* 563-588.

James, L. R., Hater, J. J., Gent, M. J., & Bruni, J. R. (1978). Psychological climate: Implications from cognitive social learning theory and interactional psychology. *Personnel Psychology, 31,* 781-813.

James, L. R., Hater, J. J., & Jones, A. P. (1981a). Perceptions of psychological influence: A cognitive information processing approach for explaining moderated relationships. *Personnel Psychology, 34,* 453-477.

James, L. R., & Jones, A. P. (1974). Organizational climate: A review of theory and research. *Psychological Bulletin, 81,* 1096-1112.

James, L. R., & Jones, A. P. (1980). Perceived job characteristics and job satisfaction: An examination of reciprocal causation. *Personnel Psychology, 33,* 97-135.

James, L. R., & Sells, S. B. (1981). Psychological climate: Theoretical perspectives and empirical research. In D. Magnusson (Ed.), *Toward a psychology of situations: An interactional perspective* (pp. 275-296). Hillsdale, NJ:Lawrence Erlbaum Associates.

James, L. R., Wolf, G., & Demaree, R. G. (1981b). *Estimating interrater reliability in incomplete designs.* Fort Worth, TX: Institute of Behavioral Research, Texas Christian University.

Jones, A. P., & James, L. R. (1979). Psychological climate: Dimensions and relationships of individual and aggregated work environment perceptions. *Organization Behavior and Human Performance, 23,* 201-250.

Jones, E. E., & Gerard, H. B. (1967). *Foundations of social psychology.* New York: Wiley.

Joyce, W. F., & Slocum, J. W., Jr. (1979). Climates in organizations. In S. Kerr (Ed.), *Organizational behavior* (pp. 317-333). Columbus, OH: Grid.

Kim, J. S. (1980). Relationships of personality to perceptual and behavioral responses in stimulating and nonstimulating tasks. *Academy of Management Journal, 23,* 307-319.

Lord, F. M., & Novick, M. R. (1968). *Statistical theories of mental test scores.* Reading, MA: Addison-Wesley.

Maxwell, S. E., Camp, C. J., & Arvey, R. D. (1981). Measures of strength of association: A comparative examination. *Journal of Applied Psychology, 66,* 525-534.

Mischel, W. (1973). Toward a cognitive social learning reconceptualization of personality. *Psychological Review, 80,* 252-283.

Naylor, J. D., Pritchard, R. D., & Ilgen, D. R. 80). *A theory of behavior in organizations.* New York: Academic Press.

Newman, J.E. (1975). Understanding the organizational structure-job attitude relationship through perceptions of the work environment. *Organizational Behavior and Human Performance, 14,* 371-397.

Payne, R. L., Fineman, S., & Wall, T. D. (1976). Organizational climate and job satisfaction: A conceptual synthesis. *Organizational Behavior and Human Performance, 16,* 45-62.

Payne, R. L., & Pugh, D. S. (1976). Organizational structure and climate. In M. D. Dunnette (Ed.), *Handbook of Industrial and organizational psychology* (pp 1125-1173). Chicago: Rand McNally.

Powell, G. N., & Butterfield, D. A. (1978). The case for subsystem climates in organizations. *Academy of Management Review, 3,* 151-157.

Roberts, K. H., Hulin, C. L., & Rousseau, D. M. (1978). *Developing an interdisciplinary science of organizations.* San Francisco: Jossey-Bass.

Schneider, B. (1975). Organizational climate: An essay. *Personnel Psychology, 28*, 447-479.

Schneider, B. (1983). Work climates: An interactionist perspective. In N. W. Feimer & E.S. Geller (Eds.), *Environmental psychology: Directions and perspectives* (pp. 106-128). New York: Praeger.

Schneider, B., Parkington, J. J., & Buxton, V. M. (1980). Employee and customer perceptions of service in banks. *Administrative Science quarterly, 25*, 252-267.

Selvage, R. (1976). Comments on the analysis of variance strategy for computation of intraclass reliability. *Educational and Psychological Measurement, 36*, 605-609.

Shrout, P. E., & Fleiss, J. L. (1979). Intraclass correlations: Uses in assessing rater reliability. *Psychological Bulletin, 86*, 420-428.

Stotland, E., & Canon, L. K. (1972). *Social psychology: A cognitive approach.* Philadelphia: Sanders.

Winer, B. J. (1971). *Statistical principles in experimental design.* New York: McGraw-Hill.

Woodman, R. W., & King, D. C. (1978). Organizational climate: Science or folklore? *Academy of Management Review, 3*, 816-826.

Climate and the Measurement of Consensus: A Discussion of "Organizational Climate"

Allan P. Jones
University of Houston

In the preceding chapter, James proposed an alternative technique for determining the level of interrater agreement among observed psychological climate scores. To evaluate the contribution such a technique makes to climate research, one must first consider the historical and theoretical context that has made the questions of interrater agreement important. James and Jones (1974) suggested that a primary reason for the substantial amount of confusion and debate that permeates the climate literature is the fact that the same term is used to describe different concepts at different levels of analysis. They suggested that terms such as *organizational climate* should be used to describe situationally based consistencies in the organization's treatment of individuals whereas the term *psychological climate* was more appropriate when referring to the individual's perceptually based representation of the work environment. Consistent with these theoretical distinctions, they and other authors argued that one must show similar scores for individual observers before perceptual data could be used as a legitimate index of the situation (see Guion, 1973). Such concerns seemingly provided the impetus for a focus on perceptual measures and the development of increasingly refined techniques for measuring interrater agreement.

In many ways then, James reflects current perspectives about psychological climate. The view that psychological climate is the basic unit of analysis in climate research is becoming more popular as are arguments that perceptual consensus is a prerequisite for measuring situational climate (Field & Abelson, 1982; James, 1982; Joyce & Slocum, 1979; Schneider, 1983). However, James seems to take this perspective a step further when he defines organizational climate as the shared psychological meaning imputed to the work environment by individuals familiar with that environment--that is, the aggregate psychological climate. A similar argument was offered by Joyce and Slocum (1982), who suggested that one should largely neglect formal organizational boundaries and concentrate instead on profile similarities.

It is interesting to note the basic shift in definition that has occurred over the past 10 years. For example, Forehand and Gilmer (1964), Sells, (1968), Tagiuri (1968), and Hellreigel and Slocum (1974) argued that organizational climate represents a set of organizational characteristics that are perceivable and influence member behavior. These earlier definitions stress the establishment of *shared treatment* among members whereas recent definitions stress *shared meaning*. The former can be validated using measures from outside observers; the latter virtually require data from incumbents. Thus, I address my comments to four major issues: (a) the presumed nature of psychological climate, (b) what it means to show agreement on ratings of psychological climate, (c) the degree that the methods espoused in the current perspectives are consistent with theory, and (d) the implications of such viewpoints for future climate research.

PRESUMED NATURE OF PSYCHOLOGICAL CLIMATE

Although a universally agreed upon definition of *psychological climate* is not available, there seems to be general agreement that the term refers to an individual's relatively abstract, cognitively based description of psychologically meaningful influences in the work environment (Jones & James, 1979; Joyce & Slocum, 1979: Naylor, Pritchard, & Ilgen, 1980; Schneider, 1983). Further, psychological climate has been defined as a form of cognitive schema constructed from perceptions of specific actions (Joyce & Slocum, 1979) or cognitive associations among lower order, descriptively oriented perceptions (James & Jones, 1980). These authors agree that psychological climate is subject to the basic principles of perception and cognition.

The traditional justification for using aggregated perceptual measures to describe organizational, subsystem, or other situational attributes is that shared treatments will be reflected in shared perceptions and conversely that the absence of agreement belies common organizational treatment (Guion, 1973). However, the aforementioned ties to schema theory force careful consideration of these assumptions. Current schema theorists argue that an individual's memory for events is guided heavily by a knowledge framework that "selects and actively modifies experience in order to arrive at a coherent, unified, expectation-confirming and knowledge-consistent representation" (Alba & Hasher, 1983, p. 203). These theorists suggest further that only information that is relevant and important to a currently activated schema will be encoded. In the process, the semantic content of the message will be abstracted and the surface form will be lost. The holistic representation described by such a schema does not allow the individual to distinguish externally generated information from internally generated information. Thus, both the interpretation and reporting of such events are liable to extensive distortion.

MEANING OF AGREEMENT

It is this potential for distortion that poses the greatest dilemma for persons who wish to use aggregated psychological climate scores. Perhaps the primary concern is best expressed by the question: "Agreement on what?" It is conceivable that persons may agree on ratings of specific events but interpret them differently (i.e., assign these events to different schemas). Alba and Hasher (1983) for example, concluded that people retain more detailed representations of complex events than schema theory would suggest. Therefore, measurement techniques oriented toward different schemas might elicit differential reporting of events even if all events were stored in memory in similar detail. Further, processes such as cueing and response bias, and task demands alter the retrieval of information so that indices of agreement on items may reflect the common influences of shared methodology more than the presence of shared interpretation.

Alternatively, substantially different events might produce similar schemas. One might not find a sufficiently common base of experience at the event level to obtain agreement but might observe such agreement as ratings are aggregated to higher order levels of abstraction (cf. Jones, Johnson, Butler, & Main, 1983). In fact, concerns such as these led Kaye (1980) to conclude that one should assess interrater agreement only at the levels of measurement that would be used in analysis.

A further point to consider is whether ratings of conditions at different levels of the organization reflect the same conceptual level of abstraction and distortion. Alba and Hasher (1983) argued that ratings on relatively unfamiliar events are more subject to response bias than are ratings on familiar events. Similarly, Jones and Butler (1980) suggested that the dimensions used to organize perceptions of macro-organizational conditions are more strongly influenced by individual characteristics such as cognitive complexity than are the dimensions used to organize perceptions of more directly experienced conditions such as those inherent in the job, workgroup, or leader. Thus, one might argue that interrater agreement on perceptions of immediately experienced or familiar events represents an index of shared or common treatment while agreement on ratings of macro organizational characteristics may tend to reflect more that the members share similar backgrounds, family attitudes, or personality characteristics. To the degree that ratings or perceptions of different levels of analysis are viewed as differentially permeable to individual influences, the meaning of demonstrated agreement may also differ.

CONSISTENCY BETWEEN METHODS AND THEORY

Bowers' (1973) article comparing situationism and trait theory provided an eloquent description of the manner in which a theory and a preferred method can become so codefined that the research in support of that paradigm is not comparable with research addressing alternative paradigms. As one reviews the literature on psychological climate, a similar specter is raised. Not only has this domain of research moved persistently toward the use of questionnaire methods, but there has been growing similarity in items and rating formats. One is forced to ask whether the use of alternative techniques for assessing climate would provide the same conceptual emphasis on shared meaning and the same press for improved methods of assessing interrater agreement.

IMPLICATIONS FOR FUTURE RESEARCH

The answer to the foregoing question largely depends upon the degree to which the theoretical properties of organizational climate require members to possess similar interpretations of the work environment and thus to converge in their psychological climate. In my mind, such a case has not yet been made. To do so seems to require considerable added work in terms of: (a) identifying the properties that make the presence of shared meaning infinitely important for investigating organizational phenomena, (b) specifying what is present when there is disagreement about the psychological meaning of events (namely, what is going on when there is a lack of consensus), and (c) articulating more fully the processes that lead to consensus or lack of consensus. It is not enough to demonstrate agreement if one fails to explain the theoretical importance of such agreement. As noted earlier, if psychological climate is inherently an individually based cognitive construction we run the risk that demonstrating agreement on psychological climate scores might imply that N individuals are similar in other respects, such as personality profiles. Such an observation is useful from a measurement perspective but may contribute little from a theoretical perspective.

In summary, the growing emphasis on psychological climate and the perceived work environment has provided needed clarity about the nature and meaning of the concept, but may have directed attention away from a careful examination of the organizational environment and the nature of the situational information that is perceived and interpreted by members of the respective organization. To date, indices of agreement have tended to suggest that there is little common treatment shared by members of macro organizational units. Yet common sense and experience seem to argue otherwise. Although job or position obviously represents a major influence on the individual's work situation and work perceptions (Jones & James, 1979), we also share many common experiences with coworkers in other positions or in other units of the organization. Such consistencies cannot be discarded cavalierly.

In conclusion, the articulation of a refined measure of consensus seems to provide an important and helpful methodological tool. However, that tool by itself is unlikely to resolve the basic problems inherent in climate research and may even exacerbate some of those problems if it is not accompanied by a clearer conceptual rationale for expecting such consensus, a better articulation of the meaning of consensus, and a direct assessment of the processes whereby environmental information is perceived and interpreted.

REFERENCES

Alba, J.W., & Hasher, L. (1983). Is memory schematic? *Psychological Bulletin, 93*, 203-231.

Bowers, K. S. (1973). Situationism in psychology: An analysis and critique. *Psychological Review*, *80*, 307-336.

Field, R. H. G., & Abelson, M. A. (1982). Climate: A reconceptualization and proposed model. *Human relations*, *35*, 181-201.

Forehand, G. A., & Gilmer, B. V. H. (1964). Environmental variation in studies of organizational behavior. *Psychological Bulletin*, *62*, 361-382.

Guion, R. M. (1973). A note on organizational climate. *Organizational Behavior and Human Performance*, *9*, 120-125.

Hellreigel, D., & Slocum, J.W. (1974). Organizational climate: Measures, research and contingencies. *Academy of Management Journal*, *17*, 255-280.

James, L. R. (1982). Aggregation bias in estimates of perceptual agreement. *Journal of Applied Psychology*, *67*, 219-229.

James, L. R., & Jones. A. P. (1974). Organizational climate: A review of theory and research. *Psychological Bulletin*, *81*, 1096-1112.

James, L. R., & Jones, A. P. (1980). Perceived job characteristics and job satisfaction: An examination of reciprocal causation. *Personnel Psychology*, *32*, 97-135.

Jones, A. P., & Butler, M. C. (1980). Influences of cognitive complexity on the dimensions underlying perceptions of the work environment. *Motivation and Emotion*, *4*, 1-19.

Jones, A. P., & James, L. R. (1979). Psychological climate: Dimensions and relationships of individual and aggregated work environment perceptions. *Organizational Behavior and Human Performance*, *23*, 201-250.

Jones, A.P., Johnson, L.A., Butler, M.C., & Main, D.S. (1983). Apples and oranges: An empirical comparison of commonly used indices of interrater agreement. *Academy of Management Journal*, *26*, 507-519.

Joyce, W.F., & Slocum, J.W., Jr. (1979). Climates in organizations. In S. Kerr (Ed.), *Organizational behavior* (pp. 317-333). Columbus, OH: Grid.

Joyce, W. F., & Slocum, J. W. Jr. (1982). Climate discrepancy: Refining the concepts of psychological and organizational climate. *Human Relations, 35,* 951-972.

Kaye, K. (1980). Estimating false alarms and missed events from interobserver agreement: A rationale. *Psychological Bulletin 88,* 288-295.

Naylor, J.D., Pritchard, R.D., & Ilgen, D.R. (1980). *A theory of behavior in organizations.* New York: Academic Press.

Schneider, B. (1983). Work climates: An interactionist perspective. In N. W. Feimer & E. S. Geller (Eds.), *Environmental psychology: Directions and perspectives* (pp. 106-128). New York: Praeger.

Sells, S. B. (1968). The nature of organizational climate. In R. Tagiuri & G. H. Litwin (Eds.), *Organizational climate: Exploration of a concept.* (pp. 85-103). Boston: Harvard University Press.

Tagiuri, R. (1968). The concept of organizational climate. In R. Tagiuri & G. H. Litwin (Eds.), *Organizational climate: Exploration of concept* (pp. 11-31). Boston: Harvard University Press.

Tagiuri, R., & Litwin, G. H. (Eds.) *Organizational climate: Explorations of a concept.* Boston: Harvard University Press.

11 Pilot Personnel Selection

Robert C. Houston
American Airlines

The specialty of selection has been a major effort of industrial and military psychologists for as long as these disciplines have been in existence. As evidence of success, much of the public reputation of psychologists has been based on contributions in the area of selection. Pilot selection, as a subset of personnel selection, was an early area of investigation with some aspects of selection (or evaluation) going as far back as World War I (McFarland, 1953). Early interest in pilot selection was triggered by the same factor that is of interest today, that is, the high cost of mistakes in selection. This chapter concentrates on more recent pilot selection and a specific example of an airline selection program.

Pilot selection historically took two paths. Initial research primarily concentrated on a battery of perceptual-cognitive tests with some applications using psychomotor devices. The best known example of this approach was the World War II development of the Pilot Stanine battery, developed under the auspices of the Aviation Psychology program of the U. S. Army Air Corps (Flanagan, 1948). The second path, not as well publicized, was Psychiatric Screening, which evolved into personality measurement.

Perceptual-Cognitive Tests

The Army Air Corps/U. S. Air Force studies of perceptual-cognitive tests were based upon an extensive body of research made possible by the active duty status of a large number of psychologists highly competent in selection research (DuBois, 1947; Guilford & Lacy, 1947). Research continues in the Air Force as well as other military services (Brown, Dohme, & Saunders, 1982; Hunter & Thompson, 1978). Initial validation was based on a pass-fail criterion, primarily in the early stages of training. The criterion was subject to more than the usual limitations in that the percentage of failures varied from training base to training base as well as from month to month. Part of the variation was the result of difficulty in defining the pass-fail criterion and part a result of varying needs of the service. When pilots were in short supply, the failure rate dropped; when supply caught up to demand, the failure rate increased. On occasion, there were massive "washouts." Although there have been subsequent efforts to develop validation methods based on operational criteria, the vagaries of the pass-fail criteria continue to haunt pilot selection research as reported in a 1982 study by Koonce. Psychomotor tasks have periodically been included in Air Force pilot selection programs, but these had the limits of administrative complications in test administration as well as variability in operation of the devices. Electronic methods of perceptual-motor testing have opened up a new medium (Kennedy, Bittner, Harbeson, & Jones, 1982) along with greater dependability and scoring precision.

Initial airline pilot selection research was conducted just after World War II (Gordon, 1947). The civilian counterpart to the Air Force pilot stanine for pilot selection is the American Institute for Research Pilot Selection Battery. It is also a battery of perceptual-cognitive tests, initially validated on performance in training. It has been used by major world airlines for approximately 30 years.

Psychiatric Screening

In an attempt to add variance to the work done by the pilot stanine, the U. S. Air Force School of Aviation medicine initiated a program of psychiatric screening of flying personnel. A report by S. B. Sells (1950) to the Lovelace Panel on Aviation Medicine in 1948, constituted the first in a series. This program resulted in a series of studies conducted, supervised, or contributed to by Sells through 1959 (Holtzman & Sells, 1954; Sells, 1951, 1955, 1956; Sells & Barry, 1953; Sells, Trites, & Parish, 1957; Sells, Trites, Templeton, & Seaquist, 1958). As a result of these studies, Sells was the recipient of the Longacre award in 1955 by the Aerospace Medical Association and the Air Force Commendation Medal for meritorious civilian service. In the process of conducting the research, *psychiatric screening* was redefined as *personality measurement*. It was demonstrated that many personality tests that were fashionable at the time had no validity. Therefore half of the resulting test battery were tests originated by the staff and the other half were from the conventional testing literature. Serious efforts were made to validate test batteries against other criteria in addition to pass-fail. In 1951 and again in 1953, USAF research teams collected data in the Far Eastern Theatre of Operations to determine, among other things, whether combat criteria were predictable by precombat measures of performance and adjustment. Trites and Sells (1957) reported that ratings of combat performance and adjustment by peers, superiors, and psychologists were related to each other and to objective data collected at the same time. It was shown that combat criterion measures could be predicted by precombat measures. Other criteria examined were schools attended, military assignments, and accident data. In a study of aircraft accidents versus characteristics of pilots, Trites, Kubala, and Sells (1955) reported that pilots who had a greater number of aircraft accidents had a higher exposure risk and tended to be younger, better adjusted to their jobs and status, and more skillful than pilots who had fewer accidents. This was contrary to common sense expectation, but nevertheless increased understanding both of the wisdom of the assignment process and the role of hazard exposure in the causation of aircraft accidents.

The natural extension of military pilot selection was to selection of personnel for space flight. Beyer and Sells (1957) concluded that space flight is not drastically different from most aspects of aviation with which everyone was familiar at that time, but they did conclude that one of the greatest problems involved the seemingly complete break from earth. The moon landings years later confirmed this conclusion.

Airline Pilot Selection

It was quite natural for Sells to move on to the field of airline selection when he left the school and moved to TCU in 1958. The first project involved selection for ground positions in 1958 when he consulted with American Airlines (AA). A few years later he consulted with Eastern Airlines on pilot selection. His work with American Airlines on pilot selection started in 1974.

Since development of the initial pilot stanine test battery for airline pilots, the pilot's job has changed significantly and the qualifications of the job candidates have been markedly different from those of post-World War II applicants. By 1974, all major aircraft carrier flying was in turbo powered, high-performance aircraft with sophisticated instrumentation and navigation systems. It was also recognized that even greater levels of sophistication of operation were under development. Not only were aircraft becoming more technologically advanced, but the pilot was becoming more a manager of aircraft systems than a manipulator of flight controls.

Selection of new airline pilot crewmembers in the United States is currently a matter of selecting from among highly experienced candidates. This means, of course, that those applying are already a highly select group from every point of view--technical skills, education, motivation, and medical attributes. The successful pilot applicants have, on the average, 2,000 to 3,000 total hours of pilot experience, with much of it in multiengine reciprocating engine aircraft or high performance jet aircraft. Those with military experience have college degrees as a requirement of Air Force, Navy, or Marine service. Those with civil experience most frequently have obtained college degrees while obtaining their pilot experience. Motivation of the civil pilot is self-evident, in that he or she paid a high price for his or her training and may have worked for very low pay to gain experience. The military pilot would have to be motivated to complete a vigorous flying training program and 4 to 6 years of demanding flying in preparation for a flying career. Medical fitness is indicated by the selectiveness of military screening or civil exams meeting Federal Aviation Administration (FAA) standards over the years of training and experience.

AMERICAN AIRLINES PILOT SELECTION STUDY AND SELECTION PROGRAM

The 1974 American Airlines contract with S. B. Sells and the Institute of Behavioral Research (IBR) was to develop a new pilot selection battery. The study, including the development of the test battery, was a critical part of the selection process through 1980, when selection of new pilots was discontinued.

The initial step in the study was to define the characteristics desired in a newly hired crewmember. Physical attributes had previously been established in terms of height, weight, vision and minimum education (see Table 11.1). Minimum medical requirements and licenses are specified by FAA regulations.

Within these very broad requirements, no specific standards had ever been set to guide employers in selecting one candidate over another. Because there were literally thousands of applicants that met the minimum requirements, but only hundreds to be hired, it was essential for an effective program to define the pilot characteristics desired. The first step in the IBR study was to develop this definition and to submit it to management for confirmation that it was, in fact,

Table 11.1
Pilot Applicant Minimum Qualifications

Age: 21
Height: 5'6" to 6'4"
Weight: In proportion to height
Vision: 20/20 without glasses
Education: College degree or its equivalent preferred
Citizenship: No restrictions
            Speak, read, and write English fluently

---

the proper goal of the selection program. The definition was developed by IBR staff members after interviewing members of Flight Department management, pilot union officers and committee members, and line pilots of varied seniority levels. These were open-ended interviews that allowed complete freedom for the individual interviewed to express him or herself. The interview responses were categorized and there was found rather surprising unanimity among those interviewed. Management, union representatives and line pilots expressed reassuringly uniform views. Simply stated, all wanted pilots with captain potential --technically skilled pilots, highly motivated to fly, able to withstand stress, and with all the characteristics common to good employees. More specifically, the ideal captain must be able to process information from a variety of sources and simultaneously be able to integrate that information to solve problems logically, demonstrate emotional stability and sensitivity to the needs of others, be able to anticipate problems in flight situations and plan ahead for their solution, demonstrate an understanding of mechanical/electronic systems, and be able to divide attention among many sources of information while under stress. There was not agreement that a college education was required other than that a degree indicated a level of intelligence and motivation to complete a systematic course of advanced study (see Table 11.2).

Table 11.2
Ideal Captain

Strong career motivation in aviation
Able to share attention
Able to solve problems through logical processes
Mature, free from neurotic symptoms
Sensitive to needs of others
Able to plan ahead
Interest, knowledge, and skill in technical areas
Able to work well under stress
Motivation and intelligence to complete college

Although the aforementioned factors were identified as being critical for the ideal captain, they were in effect hypotheses to be examined for validity. The task, then, was to measure these factors and to determine their relationship to successful performance as a line pilot. For the purposes of the selection program they were, however, endorsed by management as highly desirable goals. Those flight supervisors who had been involved in pilot selection previously welcomed this guidance enthusiastically.

Design of Selection Program

Before looking at the details of the program, an overview will be helpful. It consisted of four phases as follows:

Phase I: Personnel/Mini-Medical. Because of the large number of applicants who met the minimum requirements, experience cut-offs were set to insure that the highest qualified candidates were given full consideration. Basically, that minimum was set at 1,000 hours jet or multiengine pilot time, with consideration of less hours for an interceptor pilot whose entire time was "in command" versus a multi-engine pilot with a high proportion of co-pilot time. The Personnel Resources Department reviewed the applications and invited for interview the applicants that met the experience

minimums in addition to meeting the physical and
licensing requirements.

Each applicant was given a personal interview by the
manager of pilot recruitment or his designee. This was
a standardized, structured interview to insure that he
or she did, in fact, meet the minimum requirements
(including a review of pilot records). In addition,
the first estimate was made of the applicant's
motivation, appearance, and attitude. Some applicants
were rejected, but only after a review by a Flight
Department representative.

As a part of Phase I, a mini-medical was
administered to determine that height, weight, and
vision met selection standards, that blood pressure was
within appropriate limits, and that the applicant's
medical history was acceptable. Approximately 25% were
eliminated in this preliminary medical and interview
phase.

Phase II: Major Medical, Psychological Test Battery.
Applicants who successfully met the requirements of
Phase I were given a thorough medical examination that
was used as the basis for a risk profile (Lederer,
1976).

Such profiles were developed from the wide variety
of medical factors and laboratory analyses for each
applicant. The medical examination included the
administration of the MMPI. A group of three flight
surgeons reviewed the records of each individual and
rated the applicants in terms of known-medical
limitations or the projected risk of developing a
disabling defect prior to normal retirement age. If
the applicant had no detectable defects, he or she was
rated an M-5. If there was a minor defect that would
not affect longevity, the applicant was rated an M-4.
The surplus of applicants made it feasible to be highly
selective and process only those candidates rated in
these two categories. Candidates with more medical
defects were rated M-3 or M-2 and were deferred as
greater risks, but not formally rejected. M-1s were
pilots judged not to be likely to maintain flying
status to age 60. These were advised that they did not

meet AA medical standards. If they needed specific medical attention, they were called and personally advised.

The medical evaluation plays a very critical role in the pilot selection process for two reasons. The first is that an airline pilot represents a large investment by the company. During his or her tenure initial, transition, and recurrent training will cost the company over $500,000. This is a sizeable investment for which the company wants as much return in years of service as possible. The second is that a pilot disabled prior to age 60 is entitled to sizeable disability benefits that can add up to hundreds of thousands of dollars per pilot, for which the company receives no productivity (Anderson & Gullett, 1982). The company, then, must take all feasible steps to reduce its exposure to these costs.

The pilot selection test battery was administered during this phase. It was given by trained Texas Christian University graduate students in groups of up to 20 applicants under carefully controlled conditions.

Phase III: Flight Department Management Interview, Practical Sumulator Test. Those applicants who met medical standards (evaluated as M-4 or M-5) were processed in Phase III.

Each applicant was interviewed by a team of three flight department directors or managers, at least two of whom were from field or area offices. The interviewers were specifically trained in interviewing techniques, and each completed standard observation forms designed to evaluate the critical factors previously defined for new pilot personnel. Each interview lasted approximately 45 minutes during which the interviewers recorded observations. They wrote up their observations and made independent evaluations immediately upon the conclusion of the interview. Each interviewer also wrote a short descriptive paragraph on the applicant's strengths and weaknesses as a potential crewmember, with his recommendations for hiring.

After these evaluations were complete, the

interviewers then discussed their evaluations with each other. If there were significant differences between the interviewer ratings they were discussed and, if possible, resolved. Each then assigned an overall evaluation on a scale of 1-5. The three evaluations were added to give a total interview score for the applicant. Interviewers were not aware of the pilot selection test battery results or of performance on the practical simulator evaluation.

For the practical simulator test, candidates were scheduled to fly a flight simulator through a series of approach and traffic pattern maneuvers designed to evaluate pilot aptitude, not proficiency, to fly the simulator. Each applicant was carefully briefed on the maneuvers to be flown, procedures to be used, and characteristics of the 707 simulator. The applicant was given an opportunity to adjust to the simulator, then required to fly the maneuver pattern specified. Factors such as technical aptitude, learning ability, functioning under stress, and division of attention were observed and evaluated by flight instructors trained and standardized on this aptitude test procedure. In addition to the aptitude test, each applicant was tested for strength in holding rudder pressure in an engine-out situation, and control yoke pressure in a runaway-stabilizer situation.

Phase IV: Pilot Selection Board. The results of the pilot selection procedures for each individual were summarized and presented at periodic meetings of the Pilot Selection Board. This board was chaired by the vice president-flight, with members representing Flight Training, Line Flying, Personnel, and Medical. The board considered each applicant's evaluation on medical, pilot selection test battery, pilot aptitude, and team interview; and selected those individuals that showed the most promise as effective American Airlines crewmembers. For the most part, selections were made of those individuals who were evaluated highest in the four areas, but the selection board was not bound by rigid cutoff points or evaluation scores. Rather, the Board carefully reviewed each file, considered the merits of each applicant, and made judgments based on these merits. Those selected included women and members of minority groups.

Training Evaluation

Applicants selected were scheduled for initial training as AA flight officers and qualified as flight engineers on the B727 aircraft. Because all of these new pilots were highly experienced, had passed the FAA Flight Engineers written examination before employment (many were already certified as flight engineers and/or air transport pilots), initial training was limited to qualification on American Airlines operating procedures and company policies, and training on the B727 aircraft systems. This training was to proficiency, and was approximately 5 weeks in length. During this training, new crewmembers were continually evaluated in ground training, cockpit procedures training, and simulator. A special form was developed to evaluate trainees on those dimensions defined as being critical for the ideal captain. Each instructor completed a form for each student and added whatever comments he considered appropriate to the new pilot's potential. The forms were included in the new crewmember's file when assigned to his operating base.

Probationary Evaluation

Each new crewmember is on probation for 1 year after completion of training. During that period, additional evaluations were conducted, beginning with his or her line qualification, by a check airman. In addition to the normal worksheet for flight engineer proficiency, evaluation forms comparable to those used in training were used for the check airman to rate the new crewmember on the critical dimensions. Each was also rated by all the captains with whom he or she flew, again on the same dimensions. During the 5th month, a line check was given by a check airman, and prior to the 11th month, a check airman instructor gave a proficiency check in a flight simulator. All of these evaluations were reviewed during the 6th month of probation and again during the 11th month by a management board of flight supervisors. Satisfactory review by the 11th month board and completion of 12 months of duty completed the probationary period.

Because of the high experience level of the new crewmembers and the careful selection process, deficiencies observed during probation were rare. The evaluation process brought any deficiencies observed to the attention of management, and appropriate steps were taken to correct them, with the result that eliminations were rare.

Scope of the Program

Of the 3,400 applicants who were processed, 898 were hired. Management reaction to the selection program was excellent, with the conclusion that the new crewmembers were the best yet.

DEVELOPMENT OF PILOT SELECTION BATTERY

The development of the pilot selection battery was keyed to the definition of the ideal captain, which was the first step in the study. Although that definition was really a hypothesis to be evaluated, it was looked upon by management as the goal for which predictive tests should be developed. The objective of the test battery, then, became the development of tests to measure those characteristics. That was a large order, for many of the dimensions were very difficult to measure.

A fundamental assumption in developing test material was that it must meet the Equal Employment Opportunity standards and not discriminate against women or minorities--another large order.

Materials assembled for the battery were in part standard tests and in part developed specifically for this application. Because of the necessity for security of the test items, tests can be discussed only in generalities.

Tests of general aviation, scientific, and technical knowledge were included for face validity (obvious applicability to a pilot's job), as an indication of mechanical aptitude and as an indirect index of flying motivation. Anyone who was well informed in the field of aviation had to have some interest in the field. Flying experience and personal history could also give some indications of motivation for a career in aviation and ability to plan ahead for a career. The personality profile was aimed at measuring emotional stability, sensitivity to others, and planning ahead (Sells, Demaree, & Will, 1968). Other tests were devised to measure multiple-channel information processing and wide attention under stress. A real-life traffic control tape recording was used as an attention-sharing device and, because of the nature of the tape, as a means of inducing stress. It becomes apparent in looking at the characteristics of the ideal pilot that the paper-and-pencil battery can best measure some of those characteristics; the simulator practical test and the team interview, others. Many more items were developed than would be expected to be used operationally. The initial administration time was over 5 hours, but was later reduced by approximately 1 hour. The pilot selection test battery was administered under carefully controlled conditions, not only to ensure standard administration, but to ensure the security of the test.

There were two special administrations of the pilot selection battery. One of those was to minority pilots, in an attempt to determine the extent of cultural bias in the tests. The assistance of the Organization of Black Airline Pilots was requested in obtaining volunteers to take the test battery. The leaders of the organization were most cooperative and offered an opportunity for the Institute of Behavioral Research to administer the tests during their annual convention. Thirty-five Black pilots, most of whom were currently employed as pilots by U. S. airlines, completed the tests.

The second special administration was to currently employed American Airlines pilots who volunteered. The intent was to give the test to qualified captains who could be considered "successful" airline pilots, thus obtaining a measure of validity as well as reference norms. Because of a requirement for anonymity, it was not possible to relate test performance directly to any measures of job performance. Although 627 pilots volunteered to take the tests, conflicts between pilots' work schedules, testing schedules at the nine domiciles involved, and a major snow storm at the scheduled testing time at two large bases, only 255 completed the battery.

Results of Test Administration

The pilot selection test battery was first administered to 250 crewmen who had been recalled from furlough. From 1976 to 1981, approximately 3,400 applicants were processed. Preliminary data analysis was performed on two large applicant groups. The "AAL 77 Sample" consisted of 746 individuals tested between October 1977 and July 1978, of which 325 were hired and completed their probationary year in late summer of 1979. Complete probationary evaluation data were available on this sample. The second sample (AAL78) consisted of 1,665 applicants tested between August 1978 and August 1979. Of this sample, 586 were hired. Evaluation data were available only through the completion of training on this sample. In each case, sample size of pilots hired was reduced by 5% to 10% because of incomplete evaluation data on some individuals.

No applicants were specifically eliminated because of performance on the selection test battery in 1976 and the 1977 sample. For the 1978 sample, a cutoff score was established that eliminated only the poorest performers (approximately 10%). The test score, in both cases, was one of the factors considered by the pilot selection board in its final decision.

Problems of Evaluation

The criterion problem that has been plaguing pilot selection from the very beginning is still a serious problem. As previously stated, the American Airlines' selection program is directed toward hiring pilots with captain potential, but it may be as much as 15 to 20 years before the new employee will fly as captain.

Validation of the selection battery on performance as captain would be proper, but is obviously impossible. To make matters more difficult, the new pilot does not even fly as a pilot, but rather as a flight engineer, for a period of up to 5 to 8 years. Of necessity, then, validation data has to be based on the individual's performance as a flight engineer even if he or she is being hired as a pilot and, ultimately, as a captain.

The pilot's association shares management's interest in developing a valid pilot selection battery, but there is a limit to what the membership will accept. Any number of evaluations during a crewmember's probationary year are readily accepted, but after the first year, the only evaluations are routine line checks and recurrent training and checking. These evaluations assure that the crewmembers meet qualitative standards of performance but do not permit quantitative differentiation. Recurrent training is to proficiency, with some variation in time to reach proficiency. There are, however, other factors that affect training time, thus making it an unreliable index.

The pilot's association did agree that AA could obtain detailed evaluations on flight engineers upgrading to first officer. Unfortunately, shortly after that agreement, flying time was reduced and upgrades to first officer ceased. The bottom line, then, is that in the studies reported here evaluations were essentially limited to the probationary year while the new pilot was flying as flight engineer.

Types of Evaluation

Because of the just mentioned limitations, every effort was made to obtain extensive validation information from early in training to completion of the probationary year. Written examinations are of very questionable validity for evaluation of complex flight crew tasks. Therefore, proficiency in training at American Airlines is determined by evaluation of the individual actually performing the task for which he or she is being trained. Evaluation forms oriented specifically to training situations as well as to line operating situations were developed. Content of the evaluation forms was directed toward the ideal captain characteristics against which new crewmembers were hired. The number of items was determined by the training or operational situation and the feasibility of evaluating each dimension. The number of items observed varied from a total of 17 in the ground training situation to a minimum of 9 for the line captain's evaluation. Each item was scaled over 5 points, with 5 the best performance. Short operational descriptions were used to define the low, midpoint, and high end of the scale. Each form provided for an overall evaluation (again on a 5-point scale) phrased in terms of the evaluator's estimate of the type of captain the new crewmember would be. Space was provided for additional comments on areas needing improvement, areas of excellence, or other remarks. Dimensions evaluated included technical competence, motivation, and personality characteristics.

During initial ground training, each instructor who had contact with a new pilot completed an evaluation form. The instructor observed the student's performance throughout ground training, including that in a cockpit procedures trainer. Each simulator instructor and check airman prepared a similar evaluation. In addition, each line captain completed an evaluation of each new crewmember who flew with him. The evaluation forms were scored by using the average rating for all items except the captain potential item, or by using the captain potential rating alone which was, in effect, the evaluator's overall rating.

Because of the large number of instructors, check airmen, and captains involved, it was not possible to train or brief the raters individually. Rather, it was necessary to rely on instructions printed on each form.

As might be expected, compliance was considerably less than 100%, but a large amount of data was generated on each new pilot. All of the evaluation forms were retained in the individual's file until the time of his or her probationary board. After passing his or her board hearing, all forms were sent to the IBR for use as criterion data. The ratings were skewed toward the high end of the scale, thus severely restricting the range of the criterion data. When these results were discussed with instructors, check airmen and captains, their response was that the performance of the new crewmembers were almost all outstanding and they could only evaluate them that way.

Initial Validation and Development of Operational Selection Scores

Initial analyses of the 118 pilots hired in 1976 involved determining the correlations between individual components of the selection battery (cognitive tests, personality scales, flying experience items) and 5 performance criteria (initial simulator ratings, ground school ratings, 5th month check ratings, spot check ratings, captain ratings). A subset of the original predictors was then selected for further consideration in multiple regression analyses with each of the five criterion measures. Table 11.3 shows the validity coefficients for seven of the predictors with the captain's rating criterion. (Because of missing data on some individuals, the analysis was based on 107 pilots.)

Table 11.3
Criterion: Captain's Ratings

Predictors		
Description	Zero Order Validity	N
Hours flown last 12 months	.19**	107
Jet: Multi-Eng.-1st pilot	.19**	107
Verbal test (#97)	.20**	107
Personality--emotional stability	.22***	107
Personality--trust vs. skepticism	.33***	107
Perceptual test (#108)	.17**	107
Non-verbal reasoning (#114)	.15*	107

*p<.2
**p<.1
***p<.05

Eighteen of the predictors were finally selected for provisional operational use based on an evaluation of their correlations with the criterion measures, their lack of redundancy with other predictors, and their logical interpretability. These 18 predictors were combined with equal weights to yield an overall predictor composite.

Because other parts of the company's pilot selection process utilized 5-point scales to evaluate applicant qualifications, the composite predictor score distribution was converted to an approximately normal distribution of five score categories on a 5-point scale where "1" represents the lowest scoring group and "5" represents the highest scoring group. This rescaling was done to make the predictor composite more useful to flight management in making selection decisions.

In order to provide some assessment of the expected utility of using the predictor composite for selection decisions, cumulative expectancy tables were developed to show the percentage of pilots expected to perform above the mean on the various criterion measures corresponding to different score levels on the five-category predictor scale. Figure 11.1 shows the cumulative percentage of new pilots that would be expected to have above mean captain's ratings for each

PREDICTED   NUMBER   CULULATIVE PERCENT IN UPPER
 SCORES   INCLUDED   PERFORMANCE GROUP (ABOVE MEAN)

10 20 30 40 50 60 70 80 90 100

Predicted Scores	Number Included	Cumulative Percent
5	07	86
4	24	83
3	48	65
2	61	56
1	72	53

FIG.11.1.   Criterion: Captain's ratings.

of the five score categories. For example, 53% of all new hires would be above this mean, but 83% of those who scored 4 or 5 would be above mean captain's ratings for the whole group.

The final correlation between the overall predictor composite and a unit-weighted composite of the five criterion measures was .48. Refinement in test scoring continued, and the final predictor composite contained eight cognitive tests, four personality scales, and six flying experience items. After some operational use, the total predictor composite was further broken down to yield two additional score composites; one based on the 12 cognitive-personality predictors and the other based on the 6 flying experience items. Table 11.4 shows the predictor composite versus the mean of all items on

Table 11.4
Predictor Composites versus Mean of All Items Criterion
(AAL 77 Sample)

	TRAIN	PRO	11th			INIT	5th	11th
	GS	SIM	SIM	SIM	CAPT	LCK**	LCK**	LCK**
Total Composite	10*	06	08	11*	11*	12*	-02	-03
Cognitive-Personality Composite	18*	08	13*	10*	11*	16*	-01	-07
Experience Composite	-03	05	-04	05	05	09	-05	-10
Predictor Simulator	08	14*	04	08	13*	07	04	-10

*Significant at .05 level
**Line Check

each of the eight criterion measures used for the AAL 77 sample. You will note that the pilot experience composite had no relationship to any of the criteria. The cognitive-personality composite showed significant correlations (.05 level) with five of the eight criteria. The predictor simulator showed a correlation significant at the .05 level with two of the criteria. Table 11.5 shows predictor composites versus ground school and training simulator criteria. Again, the cognitive-personality composite showed the most correlations significant at the .05 level.

For the purposes of this chapter, only a very small part of the large amount of validation data can be discussed. The initial study of 107 applicants showed a strong positive relationship between predicted score and the five criterion scores (Arno & Sells, 1978). The relationship to captain's ratings is one example, shown in Table 11.3 Table 11.4 shows the relationship between the predictor composite and the mean of all items of each of the various criteria for the 1977 sample of 312 new hires. The composite score based on previous pilot experience failed to yield any significant validities. The composite score of cognitive and personality tests yielded correlation significant at the .05 level with five of the eight criteria. Cross validation validity coefficients were positive but low, significant in most instances at the .05 level (Greener, 1980).

Table 11.5 shows the relationship between predictor composites and early training criteria for a 1978 sample of 586 hires. Again, the experience composite failed to yield any significant validities. The cognitive-personality tended to give the best validities.

Results of Special Test Administration

The administration of the selection test to currently qualified line pilots attracted 46 check airmen (captains), 107 line captains, 87 line first officers, and 15 pilots flying as flight engineers. These were compared with 325 new pilots hired during 1977-1978 and for whom complete data were available at that time

Table 11.5
Predictor Composites versus Early Training Criteria
(AAL 78 Sample)

	Ground School		Training Simulator	
	Type Capt	All Items	Type Capt	All Items
Total Composite	07*	10*	10*	09*
Cognitive-Personality Composite	09*	11*	11*	11*
Experience Composite	03	03	07	04
Predictor Simulator	10*	08*	05	03

*Significant at .05 level

(Arno, 1981). To make this comparison, all scores had to be adjusted for age. Differences between scores of check airmen, captains, first officers, and new hires were quite small. Check airmen ranked slightly higher than line captains, and captains slightly higher than first officers. The new hires scored the best (a mean 2.83 vs. 2.70 for check airmen). This could be interpreted as reflecting the high quality of new pilots. The unsolicited comments of many check airmen and line captains would confirm that interpretation. Table 11.6 compares composite score distributions for captains and new hires.

The testing of 35 Black pilots showed that their performance on the selection battery was comparable to the AA line pilots. In fact, their mean composite cognitive-personality score were identical. The sample of Black pilots was quite small and they were a highly select group. In any event, there was no evidence of a

Table 11.6
Normative Distribution of Composite Scores Based
on the American Airlines Pilot Selection Test Battery

Composite Score	Captains (N=153)	New Hires (N-325)
5	7.8%	7.4%
4	17.6%	20.9%
3	30.7%	34.2%
2	17.6%	22.2%
1	26.1%	15.4%

bias against minorities in this test sample of new hires.

PILOT SELECTION BOARD

The pilot selection board met on an approximately biweekly schedule, depending on the demands of training quotas. The manager-flight recruitment prepared a list of all candidates to be considered by the board, showing scores on the predictors available: Pilot Selection Test Battery, Simulator Aptitude, Medical Rating, and Supervisory Interview. Attached were summary sheets showing each applicant's pilot experience (hours by type of aircraft), college degree and major courses of study, supervisory interviewers' comments and recommendations, and simulator aptitude comments. The board members studied the records for each applicant prior to the meeting and independently ranked the candidates in their order of priority for hiring. The Vice President-Flight started the meeting by reviewing his top candidate and invited discussion. Generally, there was unanimous agreement on the top 25% and their selection was easy. As the board moved down the list, there was more discussion to resolve differences of opinion. If agreement could not be reached on a candidate, he or she could be deferred for consideration at the next board meeting. When there was agreement that a candidate should not be given further consideration, the individual was so advised by the Personnel Department.

This method of operation of the selection board provided needed flexibility for board members to exercise their judgment in weighing the information available on each candidate. It took more time than would have been the case had cutoff scores been rigidly set, but made it possible to select the very best of a group of well-qualified applicants. Deferral of a candidate over one or more board meetings insured that no one was rejected just because he or she happened to be considered with an exceptional group.

SUMMARY AND CONCLUSIONS

The American Airlines selection program primarily selected from among a very highly qualified group of both civil and military trained applicants. The procedures of psychological testing, medical examination, team selection interview, pilot aptitude testing in a simulator, and a final selection board are designed, however, to evaluate less experienced applicants as well. The psychological selection test battery is designed to measure those dimensions considered to be critical for airline captains. All other facets of the selection and probationary evaluation process were also designed to be consistent with those dimensions. The selection test battery was subjected to a validation process that emphasized operational criteria in a manner possibly more extensive than ever before attempted. Evaluation indicates that at least portions of the test battery are valid predictors of training and operating criteria.

Statistical validation findings for the selection battery were limited by the exceptionally high caliber of those pilots selected, thus severely restricting the range of scores in the data collected. The success of the program in selecting highly qualified pilots thus adversely affected the statistical analysis because validities were substantially lower than if the selection process had not restricted the range of new hire performance. Performance of new cremembers on line operations as flight engineers has been excellent. Although it will be years before their performance as captains will be known, there is every confidence that it will be of highest quality.

ACKNOWLEDGMENT

The assistance of Dr. J.M. Greener in reviewing the text of this chapter is gratefully acknowledged.

REFERENCES

Anderson, R., and Gullett, C. C. (1982). Airline pilot disability: economic impact of an airline preventive medicine program. *Aviation, Space, and Environmental Medicine*, April, 398-402.

Arno, D. H. (1981). *Performance of American Airlines line captains in the American Airlines version of the IBR pilot selection test battery* (Rep. No.81-4). Fort Worth, TX:Institute of Behavioral Research, Texas Christian University.

Arno, D. H., & Sells, S. B. (1978). *American Airlines pilot selection studies* (progress report). Fort Worth, TX:Institute of Behavioral Research, Texas Christian University.

Beyer, D. H., & Sells, S. B. (1957). Selection and training of personnel for space flight. *Journal of Aviation Medicine, 28*, 1-6.

Brown, W. R., Dohme, J. A., and Saunders, M. G. (1982). Changes in the U.S. Army selection and training program, *Aviation, Space and Environmental Medicine*, December, 1173-1176.

DuBois, P. H.(Ed). (1947). *The classification program.* (Rep. No. 2). Washington, DC: Army Air Forces Aviation Psychology Program.

Flanagan, J. C. (Ed). (1948). *The aviation psychology program in the Army Air Forces.* (Rep. No.1). Washington, DC:Army Air Forces Aviation Psychology Program Research Reports.

Greener, J.M. (1980). *American Airlines pilot selection studies: New hire validation (1979-1980).* (Rep. No. 80-14). Fort Worth, TX: Institute of Behavioral Research, Texas Christian University.

Gordon, T. (1947). *The Airline Pilot - A Survey of the critical requirements of his job and of pilot evaluation and selection procedures.* (Rep. No.73). Washington, DC: CAA Division of Research.

Guilford, J. P., & Lacy, J. I., Eds. (1947). *Printed classification tests*, (Rep. No. 5). Washington, DC: Army Air Forces Aviation Psychology Program.

Holtzman, W. H., & Sells, S. B. (1954). Prediction of flying success by clinical analysis of test protocols. *Journal of Abnormal and Social Psychology, 49*, 485-490.

Hunter, D.R., & Thompson, N.A. (1978). *Pilot selection system development.* Washington, DC: Air Force Human Resources Laboratory.

Kennedy, R. S., Bittner, A. C , Jr., Harbeson, M., & Jones B. (1982). Television computer games: A 'new look' in performance testing. *Aviation, Space, and Environmental Medicine, 53*, January, 49-53.

Koonce, J. M. (1982). Validation of a proposed pilot trainee selection system. *Aviation, Space, and Environmental Medicine*, December, 1166-1169.

Lederer, L. G. (1976, November). *A risk profile system for the medical selection of pilot personnel.* Paper presented at the International Air Transport Association Fourth General Flight Crew Meeting, Lucerne, Switzerland.

McFarland, R. A. (1953). *Human factors in air transportation.* New York: McGraw-Hill.

Sells, S. B. (1950, October). *Development of psychiatric screening for flying personnel.* Presented at the Lovelace Panel on Aviation Medicine Conference, Randolph Air Force Base, TX.

Sells, S. B. (1951). *A research program on the psychiatric selection of flying personnel*, (Rep. No.1) *Methodological introduction and experimental design.* Randolph Air Force Base, TX: School of Aviation Medicine, USAF Project No.21-37-002.

Sells, S. B. (1955). Development of a personality test battery for psychiatric screening of flying personnel. *Journal of Aviation Medicine, 26*, 35-45.

Sells, S. B. (1956). Further development on adaptability screening of flying personnel. *Journal of Aviation Medicine, 27*, 440-451.

Sells, S. B., & Barry, J. R. (1953). A research program to develop psychiatric selection of flying personnel. I. Theoretical approach and research design. *Journal of Aviation Medicine, 24,* 29-47.

Sells, S. B., Demaree, R. G., & Will, D. P., Jr. (1968). *A taxonomic investigation of personality. Conjoint factor structure of Guilford and Cattell trait markers* (Project No. OE-0772, Contract No. OE5-10-296). Washington, DC: U. S. Department of Health, Education and Welfare.

Sells, S. B., Trites, D. K., & Parish, H. S. (1957). Correlates of manifest anxiety in beginning pilot trainees. *Journal of Aviation Medicine, 28,* 583-588.

Sells, S. B., Trites, D. K., Templeton, R. C., & Seaquist, M.R. (1958). Adaptability screening of flying personnel. Cross-validation of the personal history blank under field conditions. *Journal of Aviation Medicine, 29,* 683-689.

Trites, D. K., & Sells, S. B. (1957). Combat performance: Measurement and prediction. *Journal of Applied Psychology, 41,* 121-130.

Trites, D. K., Kubala, A. L., & Sells, S. B. (1955). Accidents versus characteristics of pilots. *Journal of Aviation Medicine, 26,* 486-494.

Discussion of
"Pilot Personnel Selection"

Jack M. Greener
Institute of Behavioral Research

Dr. Houston has provided an overview of the history of pilot selection and an excellent illustration of the development, implementation, and initial validation of a pilot selection program at American Airlines. Because I really do not take issue with any of the points made by Dr. Houston, I make a few general observations about personnel selection research and then highlight what I see as some of the strengths and limitations of the American Airlines program. Finally, I present some additional validity data from two other pilot selection programs similar to that of American Airlines.

Any time there are more applicants than available job openings, selection surely takes place. The question is how will the decision be made and what, if anything, can the field of psychology contribute to the decision making process? If we can make the reasonable assumption that not all applicants will be able to perform a particular job equally well and that better job performance is related to personal attributes (aptitude, skill, knowledge, interest, personality characteristics, education) of applicants, then we have the basis for applying the psychological principles of measurement and individual differences to help decision makers in the organization make more informed decisions

regarding whom to select to increase the overall level
of expected job performance. The same principles are
also applicable to the problem of evaluating actual job
performance of current employees to support various
other personnel decisions.

Most frequently, the objective of personnel
selection research is to apply existing principles and
methods in psychology to the specific problem at hand
rather than establish new theoretical constructs,
although at times the latter is undertaken if the
existing knowledge base does not appear to offer a
reasonable solution. The basic principles and
technology of selection research have been long
established, with relatively minor changes in the last
20 years. These long standing principles need to be
applied again and again to develop selection programs
for specific purposes and specific jobs within specific
organizations.

STRENGTHS OF THE AMERICAN AIRLINES PROGRAM

The American Airlines program is an extremely
comprehensive one that includes medical assessment,
multiple structured interviews, psychological ability
and personality assessment, extensive previous
experience requirements, and a demonstration of at
least some basic piloting skills in a simulator. This
program also represents a tremendous commitment of
financial and personnel resources by American Airlines
to pilot selection.

The initial stages of the program included
analyses of the pilot's actual duties and
responsibilities, which were used in the development of
the selection and performance measures. Thus, the test
battery includes test instruments tailored to some of
the more unique demands of the pilot's job as well as
measures of more basic cognitive abilities and
personality characteristics widely used in conventional
selection programs.

The program is based on an actuarial approach of
statistical verification in that the test battery is
actually related to performance in training and on the

job. This is in marked contrast to other programs
which use clinical assessments or professional
judgments of pilot suitability without formally
relating assessment results either to training or to
job performance.

LIMITATIONS OF THE AMERICAN AIRLINES PROGRAM

As is typical in most selection programs, the primary
limitations lie in establishing good performance
evaluation data for criterion purposes.

The most obvious is the fact the initial
validation of the test battery is against performance
in training as flight engineer when the primary
objective of the program is to select good captains and
it may be 10 or 15 years (or longer) before the pilots
in the selection program will assume the duties and
responsibilities of captain.

The realities of the bargaining contract with the
pilots union restrict the opportunity to collect
quantitative performance evaluations beyond the first
probationary year of employment.

The training and performance assurance orientation
of the company is "training to criterion", which tends
further to reduce individual differences in job
performance among the pilots.

The criterion measures are all performance ratings
provided by instructors and supervisors on 5-point
scales. In spite of considerable efforts by American
Airlines flight management, the ratings are still
subject to the usual problems of unreliability and lack
of standardization.

I have heard several flight managers in the
airline industry argue that written tests are not
adequate indicators of pilot proficiency and I would
not dispute this argument; however, I do believe that
written examinations and standardized performance tests
can provide more accurate and reliable assessments of
some aspects of pilot performance, such as "technical
knowledge," than can be obtained by instructor ratings.
In my view, the two methods should not be treated as

mutually exclusive choices, but rather should be treated as complementary methods which, when properly combined, can yield better overall performance assessments than either method used alone. The FAA (Sells, Pickrel, & Dailey, 1983), in dealing with similar problems with the evaluation of air traffic controller performance, has developed some fairly elaborate systems of combining tests of technical knowledge, tests of the application of technical knowledge, and "over-the-shoulder" instructor evaluations of controller skills.

The pilots have already been so preselected that with few exceptions the prediction task is to differentiate between good and outstanding pilots. Under these circumstances it is remarkable that the validation efforts yield any incremental validity and yet, even with the considerable shrinkage from the initial validation study, the two follow-up cross-validations studies continued to show significant incremental validity for the American Airlines test battery.

SOME ADDITIONAL RESULTS

The Institute of Behavioral Research has recently developed and validated similar pilot selection test batteries at two other airlines with results that suggest generalizability of the findings.

One study utilized a sample of 185 newly hired flight engineers selected from a sample of 888 applicants, where the criterion utilized consisted of performance in ground school measured by written examinations over relevant technical information topics. An equally weighted predictor composite composed of cognitive tests and previous flying experience yielded a correlation of approximately .50 with the ground school grades in two cohorts of approximately 90 each. This study used a predictive validity paradigm in which the test scores were not used in the initial selection decision.

The other study, with another airline, used a concurrent validity paradigm with a volunteer sample of

75 airline pilots, most of whom were actually operational pilots, functioning as captains or copilots. This study yielded equally weighted cognitive - personality predictor composite validities in the .40 range with a criterion composite consisting of the most recent ground school grade and ratings of technical proficiency by the assistant chief pilot.

Dr. Houston reported that the number of actual failures in the American Airlines program was quite small; 7 out of 900 hires. Similar rates of failure or documented marginal performance occurred in the other two studies that I mentioned; 7 out of 185 in one and 7 out of 75 in the other. Most of the failures were attributed to technical knowledge and skill deficiencies.

In the American Airlines study, 71% (5 out of 7) of the failures were in the lower 34% of the applicant predictor distribution; in one of the other studies, 71% (5 out of 7) of marginal performers were in the lower 40% of the applicant distribution and in the other, 100% (7 out of 7) of the failures were in the lower 42% of the applicant distribution.

Thus, even though the base rates of actual failures are quite low, it appears that a considerable proportion could be further eliminated by rejecting the lower 40% of the applicant distribution.

CONCLUDING REMARKS

Although it often seems that the primary concern in evaluating a selection program is to determine whether the program has demonstrable validity, the major concern should be with the utility of the program, in terms of the question: Is the organization better off with the program and would the gains of implementing the selection program be sufficient to offset the cost of administration? In pilot selection, given the very high cost of training and maintaining pilot proficiency as well as the responsibilities that pilots have for a large number of lives and very expensive aircraft, the answer would usually be yes, even for programs with very small validities. Even in situations where it

would not be feasible to demonstrate the validity of a
selection   program   in   terms   of   statistical
relationships, personnel selection procedures based on
the application of the principles of psychological
measurement   could   still   be   expected   to   have
considerable   utility   by   virtue   of   reducing   the
influences of irrelevant factors,   individual   biases,
and arbitrary judgements in the selection process.

REFERENCE

Sells,   S. B.,   Pickrel, E. V., & Dailey, J.T.   (Eds.).
   (1983).   *Selection   of   air   traffic   controllers*.
   Fort   Worth,   TX: Texas   Christian   University,
   Institute of Behavioral Research.

V EFFECTIVENESS OF DRUG ABUSE TREATMENT

12

Treatment Evaluation Research Based on the Drug Abuse Reporting Program (DARP)

D. Dwayne Simpson
Texas A&M University

As is evident from chapters in this volume, Dr. Sells has dedicated much of his career to dealing with problems in the real world. This philosophy and its execution through the Institute of Behavioral Research (IBR), which he founded in 1962, has had a significant impact in several professional areas as already discussed in this book. Under his direction, the IBR has carried the reputation of representing the applied research interests in the Department of Psychology, and his research activities have been accompanied by notable benefits to the university and local community. This has been particularly true with regard to the support and research training opportunities for graduate students. For example, about 40% of the 123 Ph.D. graduates in Psychology from TCU received some or all of their financial support and research training through funded projects in the IBR during the last 20 years.

One of the largest and most comprehensive research activities led by Dr. Sells has been in the field of drug abuse and evaluation of treatment. This work has not only included innovative research of his own but also efforts to create an international archival resource for all major research conducted on drug abuse. For instance, Dr. Sells developed a system called the Drug Abuse Epidemiology Data Center (DAEDAC) for storing hard copies of monographs, technical reports, and journal reprints of drug abuse research publications, as well as for collecting and maintaining computer tapes of raw data from major drug abuse studies. Prior to its recent discontinuation due to federal funding cuts, this archive has served as an invaluable literature resource for many investigators and as an inexpensive data source for conducting secondary data analysis. In recognition for his contributions to drug abuse research and treatment evaluation, the National Institute on Drug Abuse honored him in 1978 with the Pacesetter Award.

Some of his most widely recognized and influential work has centered around the Drug Abuse Reporting Program (DARP). This project has received continuous federal funding since 1968--totaling about $7 million, and it represents an unusual effort to address governmental administrative demands for short-term management needs while simultaneously maintaining the scientific integrity necessary for achieving long-range research goals. Like many of his other research activities, of course, the record for this project is marked by Dr. Sells' ever-present vision of a "grand plan" as well as his tenacity for pursuing the funds for linking together successive stages of this research enterprise over the span of the last 15 years. Probably the most significant aspects of this work include the innovations in treatment evaluation methodologies and the demonstration of posttreatment follow-up research with "street addicts."

From their positions as federal administrators in the funding agency that has supported and relied on data from the DARP, Dr. Barry Brown (chapter 13) and Dr. Lois Chatham (chapter 3) both address policymaking ramifications of the DARP program. The major treatment evaluation findings of this program are summarized in the remainder of this chapter.

DEVELOPMENT OF THE DARP DATA SYSTEM

First, it may be helpful to review the data-reporting process that was used in developing the DARP. Conceptually, the project grew out of a need for an information system that would address management and evaluation goals in conjunction with the federal funding in early 1968 of new drug abuse treatment services in six community mental health centers scattered across the United States. These six original programs were located in Albuquerque, Chicago, Manhattan, New Haven, Philadelphia, and St. Louis. Prior to 1968 (and the passage of the Narcotic Addiction Rehabilitation Act in 1967 that allowed civil commitment for treatment of addicts), the only government-supported treatment for addicts was in the Public Health Service hospitals located at Lexington and Fort Worth. Dr. Sells had carried out some research at the Fort Worth Hospital, and as an outgrowth of this work he became interested in the challenges associated with the new treatment system that was beginning to emerge.

Pursuant to that interest, Dr. Sells submitted an unsolicited research proposal that was funded in 1968 by the National Institute of Mental Health (NIMH). This first proposal represented a pilot study for the development of a data collecting system, beginning with a meeting of program participants to identify and define the data elements to be used. In June 1969, the program was formally implemented when client-level admission and bimonthly status evaluation reporting began. It was referred to then as the Narcotic Addiction Reporting Program and was funded through the Narcotic Addict Rehabilitation Branch (NARB) of the Division of Narcotic Addiction and Drug Abuse, NIMH. Dr. Chatham served as Chief of NARB and it was primarily through her persistence and influence that the limited federal funds continued to include an allocation for treatment evaluation during these early years.

In 1970 and 1971, there was a substantial growth in federal funds for community-based drug abuse

327

treatment and the Narcotic Addiction Reporting Program was changed in name to the Drug Abuse Reporting Program to reflect the broadening emphasis in treatment to include other, non-narcotic drugs. This growth is indicated by the increase from the initial set of six agencies reporting in the DARP in June 1969, to 12 in mid-1970, to 23 in mid-1971, to 36 in mid-1972, and to 52 in mid-1973; the numbers of client admission records over these 4 years were 3,114, 8,269, 15,831, and 16,729, respectively, for a total of 43,943 persons.

The participating agencies were generally multi-modality treatment programs and operated autonomously with regard to treatment assignments and service delivery to clients. Even within these field constraints, however, Dr. Sells continued to emphasize the importance of research and evaluation to complement the sole interest of many programs in the counseling and treatment delivery. The agencies reported client data to the DARP as a stipulation of their federal funding, although not all federally funded programs were assigned by NIMH to participate in the DARP. Nevertheless, the DARP included over half of all federally supported treatment agencies up to the last year of DARP data collection when the number of these agencies increased to over 200.

Treatment strategies for community-based programs in the DARP were relatively new to the field of drug abuse at that time, but they have continued over the years to serve as the major modalities of drug abuse treatment. Four major modalities have been the focus of the DARP treatment evaluation research: (a) methadone maintenance--the substitution of prescribed methadone for illicit opioid use for periods of time exceeding 21 days, and usually combined with group or individual therapeutic counseling; (b) therapeutic community--a residential facility in which the therapy process involves highly structured and demanding social relationships and in which clients frequently function as therapeutic change agents; (c) outpatient drug-free treatment--outpatient services that rely on counseling and social skills training but with an emphasis on abstinence from both licit and illicit drugs; and

(d) detoxification--short-term use of licit drugs (such as methadone for 21 days or less) that focus on withdrawal from illicit drugs and usually provide no subsequent therapeutic services.

Reporting of new admissions in the DARP agencies was discontinued in March 1973 (although the during-program progress records for clients in treatment continued until March 1974, in order to allow a full year of performance data). Its discontinuation occurred in conjunction with a decision to create the Client Oriented Data Acquisition Process (CODAP) for use by all federally funded drug abuse treatment agencies. The CODAP was adopted primarily as means of monitoring the treatment population in these agencies at the sacrifice of the treatment evaluation research system represented by the DARP. Arguments were made at that time for retaining the DARP as an on-going research component in the federal treatment system, but they were unsuccessful. (Interestingly, however, this same type of research component was later resurrected, in 1977, as the Treatment Outcome Prospective Study, or TOPS.)

PURPOSE OF THE DARP DATA SYSTEM

The DARP was created to meet management as well as treatment evaluation needs in a new federal service delivery system for drug abuse. The management applications were prominent in the early years of the DARP, and they included summary feedback reports to federal administrators as well as to each participating treatment agency on client flow (intake and terminations) and sociodemographic characteristics. This feedback became more detailed and sophisticated in 1972 with the Management-by-Exception reports designed to identify significant deviations in program operations.

The research applications of the DARP, of course, were most interesting to Dr. Sells even though his enthusiasm was not universally shared among federal and treatment agency administrators in the early years of the system. This research officially began in April 1972, with the funding by NIMH of a separate research component when the DARP data base had matured to contain adequate numbers of client admission and during-program status evaluation records. Procedurally, the DARP research on during-treatment performance in the following years was organized using a multiple-year cohort design to replicate and refine research findings on the three successive admission cohorts (i.e., 1969-1971, 1971-72, and 1972-1973). This research included studies on classification of treatment types and client types, development of outcome criterion scores, during-treatment retention and performance evaluations, death rates and other areas as detailed in a five-volume series of books (Sells, 1974; Sells & Simpson, 1976).

In 1974, funds were approved by the newly created National Institute on Drug Abuse (NIDA) for beginning the DARP follow-up research phase to assess posttreatment outcomes. This work serves as the basis for most of the results I present here and it was carried out using a replicated research design with samples from each of the three DARP admission cohorts. The fieldwork for the 6-year follow-up studies was completed from 1975 to 1979 with the National Opinion Research Center as the primary subcontractor. Collectively, 6,402 former clients from 32 agencies in the DARP were selected to be located and interviewed in the follow-up research. Of these, 5,340 (or 83%) were found; 73% were interviewed after granting informed consent, 5% were deceased, 1% were out of the country (mainly due to military service), and 4% exercised their right of refusal to be interviewed. Within the time and resources allocated, the remaining 17% (N = 1,062) could not be located. About 50 studies have been conducted on various aspects of these data and reported in professional journals, books, and monographs.

Finally, it should be noted that a long-term DARP follow-up study of addict careers (covering about 12 years after DARP admission) is currently in progress. It was funded by NIDA in late 1981 and data collection by the National Opinion Research Center for the target sample of about 700 former heroin addicts admitted to the DARP from 1969 to 1972 was scheduled for completion in 1983.

HIGHLIGHTS OF THE DARP FINDINGS

The major focus of the DARP research during recent years has been on the posttreatment follow-up studies (Sells & Simpson, 1980; Simpson & Sells, 1982a, 1982b). Treatment effects have been evaluated using a variety of multivariate analytic approaches on independent research samples and the results have been highly consistent. The major issues involved the comparative behavioral outcomes of clients in different types of treatment and the search for factors that were associated with more favorable outcomes. For this research, outcome measures were usually defined on the basis of the first 1 to 3 years immediately after termination of DARP treatment, although a general interest in the long-range outcome status of individuals at the time of the follow-up interview has led to work in this area as well.

Treatment Comparisons

The DARP follow-up research has included methadone maintenance (MM), therapeutic community (TC), outpatient drug free (DF), and outpatient detoxification (DT) as the major drug abuse treatment modalities under study; in addition, a sample of "intake only" (IO) clients who were admitted but never returned to the DARP agency for treatment services was included as a comparison group. Because the treatment assignments of clients in the DARP system were not randomized, however, treatment groups often included systematic client differences that had to be taken into account in the analysis. Different methodological strategies (such as applying post hoc statistical controls to select client variables as well as limiting comparisons to more homogenous subgroups) have been explored and generally have led to very similar conclusions from the data. A large part of the DARP treatment evaluation research has been devoted to daily users of heroin or other opioid drugs, and therefore the results I summarize are based primarily on the

sample of Black and White male addicts (N = 2,099,   for
all three cohorts combined).

First,   I illustrate the changes that occurred   in
daily opioid use from the 2 months pretreatment to   the
1-year period immediately following client   termination
in   the DARP treatment groups.   Figure 12.1 shows   that
the 100% rate of daily pretreatment use of opioid drugs
dropped to a low of 36% in the MM and a high of 64%   in
the DT treatment groups during 1 or more months of   the
first   year posttreatment follow-up period.   Note   that
the   rates   for the MM, TC, and DF   groups   were   below
those   for the DT and IO groups, and   this   exemplifies
the   overall   pattern   of results found   throughout   the
DARP studies.

For   instance,   Figure 12.2 shows   that   the   same
pattern of results prevails   for   combined   measures   of
posttreatment   drug   use   and   criminality.   In   this
figure, two different outcome standards are depicted in
recognition of the fact that there unfortunately is   no
consensus   on   the definition of   "treatment   success."
Treatment   modalities frequently differ in   significant
ways   with   respect to their outcome   expectations   for
clients,   and there are further differences even   among
similar treatment programs within each modality.   Thus,
the DARP research has systematically addressed problems
of   criterion development and has explored   empirically
determined outcome scores as well as logically   defined
behavioral profiles.   In Figure 12.2, the two different
outcome   standards   are defined according to   level   of
involvement   in   drug use and criminal   activity   in   a
manner   that   allows   some   degree   of   flexibility   in
outcome   interpretations.   The highly   favorable   level
signifies   no   use of illicit drugs (except   for   less-
than-daily   use   of   marijuana)   and   no   arrests   or
incarcerations   in   jail or prison during the   1-year
posttreatment   period; the moderately   favorable   level
denotes no daily use of any type of illicit drug and no
major   criminality (i.e., no more than 30 days in   jail
or prison, and no arrests for crimes against persons or
crimes of profit).

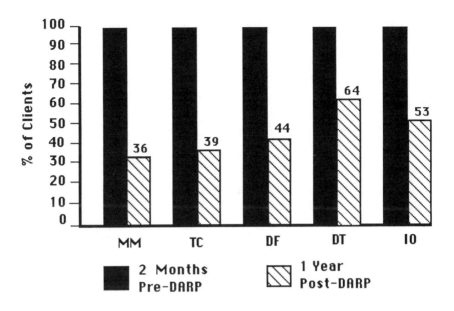

FIG.12.1. Daily opiod use.

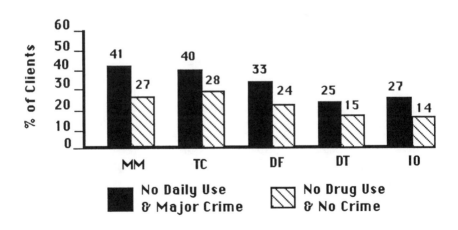

FIG.12.2. Drug use and crime in Year 1
Post DARP.

With regard to DARP treatment comparisons, it is noteworthy that most outcome differences in drug use, criminality, and productive activities (such as employment) between the major modalities of MM, TC, and DF have been statistically insignificant. Thus, these treatments appear to be roughly equal in their effects on client outcomes--and all three are more favorable than for clients in the DT and IO groups. Furthermore, client outcomes associated with specific treatment types within each modality (as well as with individual treatment agencies within each modality) have not been significantly different. These results, along with the related DARP findings showing that types of treatment do not appear to be differentially related to outcomes for various types of clients, have unfortunately offered little guidance so far in trying to identify discriminating treatment process dimensions.

Prediction of Individual Client Outcomes

Beyond the group effects of different drug abuse treatments, the DARP research has examined factors associated with individual client outcomes. In these studies, client background and treatment characteristics have been analyzed in relation to posttreatment outcome measures using stepwise regression procedures within each separate DARP treatment group. The results have identified several factors as significant predictors of outcomes, particularly the criminal history of the individual prior to treatment and the individual's performance during treatment in the DARP.

The length of time in treatment has proven to be one of the most notable and consistent predictors of favorable outcomes. Longer DARP treatment tenure is related to more favorable posttreatment outcomes as shown in Figure 12.3 for the MM, TC, and DF treatment groups. In this figure, the same highly favorable outcome standard of no drug use and no criminality referred to earlier (see Figure 12.2) is presented in relation to time in DARP treatment. A similar positive statistical relationship between treatment tenure and

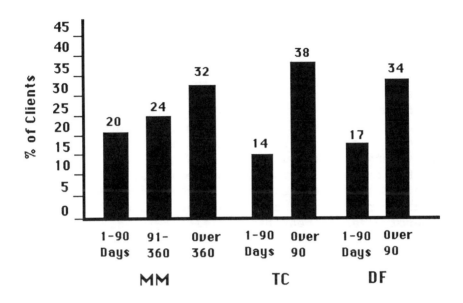

FIG.12.3. Outcomes by time in treatment
(no drug use and no crime in Year 1 post-DARP)

favorable outcomes has also been documented in
conjunction with other treatment experiences that
occurred during the post-DARP follow-up period.

An important aspect of the DARP studies on
treatment tenure is that outcomes of short-term clients
(i.e., those who remain in treatment for less than
about 3 months) were the same regardless of their
treatment assignment. Thus, short-term MM, TC, and DF
clients had comparable (and relatively unfavorable)
posttreatment outcomes; furthermore, their outcomes
were not significantly different from the poor outcomes
for DT and IO clients. These results suggest that
treatment effects accrue to measurable levels only
after a minimal period of about 3 months.

The conceptual focus of DARP studies on the
prediction of individual client outcomes, of course,
differs from the focus of studies involving group
comparisons of treatment outcomes--one set addresses
within-group variations in outcomes whereas the other

gives emphasis to between-group variations that are presumed to reflect treatment effects. Nevertheless, the results are complementary in the sense that treatment was consistently related to follow-up outcomes. That is, some treatments were shown to be more effective than others, and more time in those treatments was associated with better outcomes. As already noted, however, the important features of the treatment process have not been identified, and the preliminary work in the DARP on treatment type classifications needs to be extended and refined. Because the findings of the individual client outcome prediction studies could be used to suggest that a general client "treatability" factor may also exist (in terms of certain client traits or background factors), future work in this area should jointly address treatment and client characteristics. James (chapter 10, this volume) suggests some of the potential methodological strategies that can be applied to these problems, and indeed he and Dr. Sells have carried out some pilot work in recent years that helped to identify the complex issues involved.

Long-Term Outcomes of Addicts

In addition to the study of treatment effects based on immediate post-DARP follow-up data, the status of individuals at the time of follow-up has also been examined. Roughly 6 years transpired between the time of admission to DARP treatment and the follow-up interview, including an average of over 4 years after termination of DARP treatment. Each person's behavioral status at the time of follow-up therefore represented a collage of assorted influences from over the years. Measures of outcome status at follow-up have been analyzed in relation to original DARP treatment groups and the results have indicated that the early posttreatment differences are diminished over the period of the follow-up years to generally insignificant levels. Thus, it appears (as one might expect) that other post-DARP treatments--reported by about 60% of all DARP clients followed up--as well as other life events exert an attenuating influence on the DARP treatment outcomes effects over the years.

Table 12.1 describes the behavioral status of addicts (combined from all DARP treatment groups) during the last year of the 6-year follow-up period. Again, outcomes are presented in terms of the highly favorable and moderately favorable standards presented earlier. More information is reported in this table, however, including a set of "other relevant measures" (i.e., drug treatment, alcohol use, and employment). For each behavioral measure listed, outcomes were tabulated independently of one another (shown under the column labeled "% of Total") as well as in a joint sequential fashion (shown under the column labeled "Cumulative %"). In the latter tabulation, the percentages represent persons meeting each given criterion as well as all preceding criteria. For instance, under the highly favorable standard it is shown that 60% of the sample reported no use of opioid drugs during the last year before follow-up, but the percentage dropped to 37% when no nonopioid use (other than occasional marijuana use) and no criminality (no arrests or jail/prison) were added as behavioral criteria. Under the moderately favorable standard, 78% reported no daily drug use in the last year and 49% also met the standard of no major criminal involvement (defined previously). It is also interesting that the "% of Total" column indicates that the majority of persons had favorable status as defined on each behavioral measure when considered independently, but the "Cumulative %" column shows that only 15% and 24%, respectively, met the collective set of all six criteria as stated for the two standards.

In an effort to identify some of the major events that occurred during the follow-up period leading to these long-range outcomes, records for a sample of 990 addicts were closely inspected and classified as shown in Table 12.2. Results for the total sample are presented at the far right, where it can be seen that 18% of the sample terminated opioid use (without further relapse) during DARP treatment and had no additional drug abuse treatment during the follow-up period (and 1% quit opioid use in conjunction with continuous treatment throughout the follow-up period).

TABLE 12.1
Six Year Follow-up Status for the Combined
Samples from all DARP Treatment Groups

Behavioral Measures	% of Total	Cumulative %
Highly Favorable Status		
Primary Measures:		
1. No opioid use	60	60
2. No nonopioid use[a]	55	43
3. No criminality[b]	68	37
Other relevant measures:		
4. No drug treatment	63	28
5. Low alcohol use[c]	64	19
6. High employment[d]	64	15
Moderately Favorable Status		
Primary measures:		
1. No daily opioid use	78	78
2. No daily nonopioid use	71	60
3. No major criminality	70	49
Other relevant measures:		
4. No drug treatment	63	31
5. No heavy alcohol use[e]	78	28
6. Some employment[f]	76	24

[a]Excludes occasional (less-than-daily) use of marijuana.
[b]No arrests or jail/prison.
[c]Under 4 oz. 80-proof per day.
[d]Six months or more.
[e]Under 8 oz. 80-proof per day.
[f]One month or more.

TABLE 12.2

Classification of 6-year Follow-up Outcomes of Opioid Addicts
by DARP Treatment Groups Based on DARP Cohort 3

Outcome Patterns	% of MM	% of TC	% of DF	% of DT	% of IO	Total No.	Total %
Immediate opioid abstinence:							
a. Without further treatment	19	18	21	12	19	180	18
b. With continuous treatment	1	0	0	0	0	5	1
Delayed opioid abstinence:							
c. After further treatment	11	16	11	21	14	134	14
d. After jail/prison	7	5	4	7	3	54	5
e. After treatment and jail/prison	3	5	3	2	4	35	3
f. With continuous treatment	14	10	9	10	18	119	12
g. Without treatment or jail/prison	7	9	10	11	4	81	8
Heavy and sustained opioid use:							
h. Without treatment or jail/prison	3	2	6	5	4	36	4
i. With long-term treatment	7	3	3	4	4	47	5
j. With short-term treatment or jail/prison	10	16	11	13	6	115	12
Special problems:							
k. Heavy alcohol use	5	5	6	2	4	45	5
l. Heavy nonopioid use	2	3	5	4	5	33	3
m. Continuous jail/prison	6	2	6	5	5	51	5
n. Periodic opioid use	4	4	2	2	7	35	3
o. Abstinence to relapse	1	2	3	2	3	20	2
TOTAL NUMBER OF PERSONS	374	630	685	124	77	990	100

Another 42% quit opioid use later during the follow-up period (and remained "clean" throughout the last year or longer before follow-up), usually in conjunction with some type of treatment; only 5% reported quitting opioid use during jail or prison incarceration (i.e., without treatment), and only 8% reported quitting without a simultaneous jail/prison or treatment experience. Finally, 21% continued heavy opioid use (either with or without treatment) and 18% experienced other special problems (such as drinking or having extended prison sentences). Overall, these data show that 35% of the sample eventually quit using opioid drugs during contact with drug abuse treatment.

The permanence of these changes in drug use behaviors is one of the issues of interest in the 12-year DARP follow-up study currently in progress. Preliminary tabulations based on the first 355 completed interviews indicated that 75% of the sample terminated daily opioid use a year or longer prior to the follow-up interview, and of those, 63% reported being in a treatment program when they quit. In addition, 72% of all persons who had quit daily opioid use judged drug abuse treatment as "very important." Even in these new and most recent data, therefore, treatment continues to have a convincing presence with favorable follow-up outcomes and I look forward to this next phase of the DARP research with Dr. Sells.

ACKNOWLEDGMENTS

I want to express appreciation to Karst Besteman and Lois Chatham for their contributions to the DARP in its early years (and for their memory of events from that period), and to Barry Brown and Frank Tims for their contributions to the follow-up research in more recent years. Numerous IBR faculty and staff members have served as part of the DARP research team, led by S. B. Sells and joined by Robert Demaree and George Joe in key leadership roles throughout the project. I gratefully acknowledge these colleagues and friends as primary contributors to the work reported in this paper. Finally, I wish to express my personal appreciation to Dr. Sells for his patient attention, tutelage, and friendship over the past 17 years.

REFERENCES

Sells, S. B. (1974). *The effectiveness of drug abuse treatment* (Vols. 1-2). Cambridge, MA: Ballinger.

Sells, S. B., & Simpson, D. D. (1976). *The effectiveness of drug abuse treatment* (Vols. 3-5). Cambridge, MA: Ballinger.

Sells, S. B., & Simpson, D.D. (1980). The case for drug abuse treatment effectiveness based on the DARP research program. *British Journal of Addiction, 75,* 117-131.

Simpson, D.D., & Sells, S.B. (1982a). *Evaluation of drug abuse treatment effectiveness: Summary of the DARP follow-up research.* (National Institute of Drug Abuse ADM 82-1209). Washington, DC: U.S. Government Printing Office.

Simpson, D.D., & Sells, S.B. (1982b). Effectiveness of treatment for drug abuse: An overview of the DARP research program. *Advances in Alcohol and Substance Abuse, 2,* 7-29.

13

Contribution of the DARP to Treatment Research Methods and Policy

Barry S. Brown
National Institute on Drug Abuse

As Simpson has noted, the Drug Abuse Reporting Program (DARP) is founded on the vision of two people. Dr. Saul Sells' creativity and capacity for merging practical considerations with research integrity constituted a sine qua non for the development of this major research project. At the same time, Dr. Lois Chatham's foresight in appreciating the need for just such research, as well as her ability to negotiate often near-intransigent systems, permitted this important effort to be implemented and maintained. Fortunately for me, I arrived in time to bask in the somewhat reflected, but still extraordinarily bright, glory of their efforts. However, I would be remiss, and worse yet Saul would be displeased, if I did not also cite the important contribution of Dwayne Simpson who has provided both significant guidance to the DARP and the benefit of his own original thinking, albeit shaped perhaps a tad by his years as a student of Dr. Sells. In addition, I want to acknowledge Bob Demaree's contribution to the structuring of the methodology of the DARP; Krishna Singh's ability to look beyond treatment to clarify the role of community in treatment outcome; and George Joe's ability to manipulate the resulting data in ways that quickly and completely surpassed my poor efforts at understanding. Finally, let me also mention the considerable contributions of Jim Savage and Mike Lloyd and apologize to those others I have not cited and not yet had the good fortune of meeting. It should be clear that a part of Saul's considerable skills has involved the development of a strong research staff whose members are then given ample opportunity to make their contributions to the research effort.

It is, however, the several and varied contributions of the DARP to which I wish to address the remainder of this chapter. First, I discuss the contributions of the DARP to research and methodology in the area of drug abuse. Only because of space, I restrict myself to two important issues.

A first priority in any area of evaluative research is the establishment of meaningful and appropriate outcome criteria. This would seem patently obvious and eminently achievable. However, anyone who feels that such criteria are simply lying about waiting to be picked up and used, might consider the situation in the field of mental health. In spite of its far lengthier history as a field of research, there are no uniform, widely accepted behavioral criteria of treatment outcome that can be generally applied to mental health programming. It is likely not a coincidence that there are no large-scale investigations of the efficacy of mental health programming comparable to those that exist for drug abuse programming. Dr. Sells established as basic outcome criteria the three measures alluded to by Simpson (this volume): drug use, criminality, and productive activity. Today, all treatment programs agree on the appropriateness of those measures although, as Simpson indicated, there may be somewhat differing emphases within and among these criteria for different programs. In a field that has seen treatment programs dramatically at odds over appropriate strategies of service delivery, that constitutes no small achievement. As is obvious, with agreement on outcome criteria, and by implication on treatment goals, comparative study becomes possible such that we can explore the efficacy of differing treatment processes. Indeed, exactly such studies are a happy commonplace in drug abuse.

However, the establishment of acceptable outcome criteria has a further, and perhaps even more significant, impact on the treatment field. It is, of course, important that researchers can speak together (i.e., that researchers share common understandings in terms of evaluative study) and it is certainly important that researchers in the area of evaluation are enabled to measure events in terms that service providers view as meaningful. However, it is also important that service providers themselves are given the means to critically assess their own functioning and effectiveness. The development of agreed upon outcome criteria is central to the development of a routinized assessment procedure within clinics.

And there is evidence that just such programmatic assessment is conducted in treatment settings. In a recent survey of drug abuse treatment programs, it was found that of 341 randomly sampled programs, 44% reportedly conducted in-house assessments involving at least a definition of outcome criteria, data gathering and analysis, and the reporting of findings. Almost all used in-house personnel and all used the DARP outcome criteria to measure program performance. Speaking as someone who has made efforts to serve the gods of both clinical practice and research--however haltingly--I feel it is vital to provide those tools that permit not only a consistency in research efforts, but that also allow the responsible clinician the means to make that careful assessment of his or her own treatment efforts, which never appears in the research literature, but which permits of the reworking of the treatment process to serve clients more effectively. In the accomplishment of those ends, the DARP has been more than helpful, it has been essential. I should note parenthetically that well over half of the programs conducting assessments reported changes in their treatment processes consequent to the making of those assessments (Tims, 1982).

However, it is in a second area that I feel the DARP has made even larger, if somewhat more controversial, impact and contribution. Within the drug abuse field there is a body of thinking that holds that if one cannot manipulate relevant variables there is no point in measuring the impact of those variables. For some proponents of clinical trials, the random assignment of subjects to an experimental and control condition is not simply the means to an end, it very nearly becomes an end in itself. Now, there is no denying that all manner of important research problems lend themselves to just such a design. Indeed, at the National Institute on Drug Abuse, and in my own division, we support many such investigations and I would argue that we do so appropriately. However, those involve clinical problems that lend themselves to classical research design. Many of the most urgent clinical issues do not. This not-so-simple truth was recognized by Dr. Sells, and he set about developing a rigorous and credible research design that allowed for the intrusion of real world considerations without doing harm to scientific integrity. As many know, not all of those who have followed have been that wise or that capable. In a word, Dr. Sells has lent a dignity as well as an expertise to field research that it lacked before his arrival on the scene. As a consequence, he has paved the way for others to undertake like research and to make their own contributions to evaluative study. And although there remain some who would try to make the world conform to their own images of a proper research design, there is a growing number of investigators who are willing to adapt research to the dimensions of the real world-- again with no sacrifice in scientific rigor. And for that singular contribution, I think the field is very genuinely indebted to Dr. Sells.

Parenthetically, let me say that the wish to adapt the world to our own limitations is not peculiar to the research community. In clinical settings one hears time and again about unmotivated clients (i.e., clients who do not fit the therapeutic regimens we have available). One hears too rarely about clinicians willing to modify their accustomed and comfortable clinical practices to the needs of the client.

The rest of this chapter dwells on another area to which a contribution has been made by Dr. Sells and the DARP--the area of policy. Perhaps understandably, concern about a study's contribution to policy is directly correlated with dollars expended. I think it is safe to say that a Federal grant under $50,000 is seen as being under little or no obligation to make a contribution to policy. However, thereafter the demand for contribution to policy increases in accord with dollars spent. Follow-up studies like the DARP are expensive, and consequently, the terms *policy* and DARP have been frequently linked. I would like to deal with the issue of drug research and policy in two parts. But first, I should explain that policy, in the context of the DARP and of other studies of the treatment process, has come to mean policy as related to clinical practice and/or activity allied in some way to clinical practice. Consequently, policy can embrace efforts to influence the budget process on behalf of treatment activities, the recasting of regulations affecting treatment, and so on, as well as direct suggestions regarding the refinement of treatment.

In that context, I first acknowledge the considerable role played by the DARP in relation to treatment policy and then discuss the larger issue of the relationship of research, and especially applied research, to systems change. As Simpson has suggested, the basic thrust of the DARP research has been to explore the relationship between treatment outcome and the typical modalities, or types of drug treatment, considered in conjunction with clients' demographic and background characteristics. As such, the DARP was able to establish incontrovertibly a major truth. Consequent to their entry into three of the four usual modalities of drug abuse treatment, and assuming that individuals stayed in treatment for periods of 4 months or more, drug abuse clients showed dramatic change in targeted behaviors. The significance of that finding has not been lost on Congress or on state legislatures. Money spent on drug abuse treatment could be expected to achieve generally favorable results. These findings have been of obvious importance to budget planners and to those who vote on budget appropriations. Consequently, these findings have been of major significance to the service providers and to the clients dependent on tax dollars for the development and maintenance of programs.

At the same time, the DARP has highlighted areas in which further innovation in treatment is warranted and those efforts have also been implemented. Findings from the DARP indicated a relatively high rate of return to treatment by drug abuse clients generally, and by drug abuse clients attending methadone maintenance and outpatient drug-free programs specifically. As a result, studies have been initiated to examine the impact of innovative strategies for the delivery of aftercare or relapse prevention services. In turn, those strategies have been evaluated and a successful model in this area has been shared with the service delivery community.

Similarly, the DARP highlighted the problems experienced by traditional programs in permitting clients to obtain employment, as well as the relationship between employment and the capacity of clients to remain drug and arrest free. Again, a body of studies was initiated to develop and test innovative strategies for delivering vocational rehabilitation and employment-related services. And again, through the ingenuity of those investigators, we have been enabled to share models of service delivery that can enhance traditional drug abuse treatment.

These, then, are some of the contributions of the DARP to policy and to real progress in the drug abuse field, but the very contributions of the DARP beg an important issue in the area of applied research. How do we guarantee that the contributions of the research community are made available to the service delivery community in a form and manner that permit their application on behalf of clients?

In the field of drug abuse--and I would add alcoholism and mental health--there appears to be a gap between service delivery personnel and research personnel, and, if anything, that gap would seem to be widening. For the most part, the two groups do not speak to each other effectively and, to a large degree, lack mechanisms that would permit any meaningful communication. The researcher communicates through the medium chiefly available to him or to her, the research journal. It can be argued that the researcher's findings are thereby made available to the service delivery community or, at least, to the professional service delivery community. As a practical matter, it is highly questionable whether that is, in fact, the case. There seems little reason to believe that service providers or treatment planners in mental health, alcoholism, or drug abuse become much immersed in the research literature.

Although initial communalities may exist in terms of some aspects of the education and training of both service and research groups, these are nearly rendered moot by later experience. The researcher and service provider rarely share the same setting for their work, and that physical separation soon has profound consequences for behavior. The separation not only reduces the incentive for research staff to describe and clarify their findings to the service delivery community, it denies to the service delivery community the ability to explain to research staff its information (i.e., its research) needs. Moreover, research staff do not simply lack incentives for sharing information with service delivery personnel, there are clear and powerful incentives for relating to one's research peers instead. Publication in those journals more clearly wedded to academic than to practical concerns are, not surprisingly, more likely to win rewards in the academic community. The most practical journals (i.e., those that make greatest effort to speak directly to the service provider) are rarely valued as highly as those that speak to one's research peers.

To further complicate this problem, and further widen the gulf, service delivery people often are poorly trained in, and little enthused about, research

technology, whereas research people often are similarly
without investment in tasks of service delivery.   Each
group has available a language that denies easy access
to the other.   Each has the capacity to attend to his
or her own professional sessions and, as implied
earlier, to read publications geared to his or her own
background of interests.

The special character of service delivery in the
field of drug abuse heightens some parts of this
dilemma.   The field of drug abuse treatment had been
constructed, in no small part, through the labor and
accomplishment of the paraprofessional worker.   That
staff member is not only estranged from the world of
research by virtue of different educational
experiences; that estrangement has been widely
encouraged and supported by both professional and
paraprofessional workers.   The drug abuse
paraprofessional worker has been valued--and told he
or she is valued--by virtue of experience acquired
rather than education achieved. Although it is thought
to be the responsibility of the treatment professional
to complement that experience in the structuring and
implementing of service programs, there is a clear
message in the drug abuse field that personal
experience is a fitting and adequate preparation for
service delivery.

In addition to these problems specific to drug
abuse research and service delivery, a number of more
general factors have been cited as capable of
inhibiting the transfer of technologies and information
from the research to the service community.   For those
interested, an excellent review of this literature has
been reported recently by Leviton and Hughes (1981).
However, I would again like to point to the
contributions of Dr. Sells and of the DARP in creating
a model for establishing communication between the
research and service communities.   It was early
recognized by Sells and by NIDA that the DARP had
important things to say to the service planner and
provider about the efficacy of traditional or normative
drug abuse treatment.   Saul and his staff felt an
obligation to make their findings known to the service

delivery community, and to the research community as well. As was usual with Sells and his staff, an extraordinarily ambitious communications strategy was developed. On the one hand, DARP staff undertook to prepare materials for presentation to the research community in terms of journal articles, conference papers, and books. As Simpson (chapter 12) mentioned, to date at least 50 such publications have been produced. On the other hand, Sells and his staff have endeavored to work with NIDA such that the findings they obtained could be made available to service providers through a use of mechanisms that NIDA was to develop in conjunction with DARP staff. It rightly became the role and responsibility of the funding agency to work with staff at Texas Christian University in, if you will, packaging DARP findings in a format and language that made those findings most largely accessible to planning and service delivery communities. As noted earlier, in the battle to garner funds to provide assistance to drug abuse clients, it became extremely important for non-researchers to speak knowledgeably about DARP findings. In order to achieve those ends, it was vital that NIDA have the support and assistance of Dr. Sells and his staff, and we always did.

This latter work with the DARP, which resulted in the publication of more than 15 reports directed to service providers, points the way to a new sharing of responsibilities between the research community, the service community and the funding agency. In this paradigm, the funding agency must first assume responsibility for learning from the service delivery community the issues around which the service community needs information, i.e., the issues around which the funding agency should seek research. The funding agency is in a unique position to assess the concerns of the service provider and to make good on those concerns through the formulation and implementation of a research agenda. In short, the funding agency can, and must, act as an advocate for research on behalf of the service provider, and, through the service provider, as an advocatae for research on behalf of the client.

Once having encouraged and initiated research relevant to the service provider's needs, it becomes the responsibility of the funding agency to work with the researchers to structure reports and materials that can answer the service provider's questions. In so doing, fairness as well as common sense dictate that the research community produce reports in a language and style appropriate to their backgrounds and practices. It becomes the function of the funding agency to have available those persons who can work with research staff in recasting materials received to fit the needs and the experiences of the service community. At the same time, research staff can act to guarantee that resulting clinical interpretation continues to bear an appropriate resemblance to research findings. It is, of course, incumbent on the funding agency to have developed mechanisms that permit the effective sharing of the resulting materials with the service delivery community. In this regard it becomes important to explore the potential of mechanisms beyond the print medium (e.g., the use of audio and/or video cassettes, of workshops, of interactive computer technology, etc). Inasmuch as we are engaged in efforts to achieve systems change through the sharing of new information, it also behooves us to make study of the capacity of different strategies of systems change to achieve the desired ends.

It is perhaps most fitting to stop here with that suggestion of a research agenda for the future. Dr. Simpson ended his chapter with a comment about looking ahead to work with Dr. Sells toward the resolution of problems. I can think of no more agreeable way to either end my chapter or to look ahead to the future.

REFERENCES

Leviton, L.C., & Hughes, E.F.X. (1981). Research on the utilization of evaluations: Review and synthesis. *Evaluation on Review 5*, 525-548.

Tims, F.M. (1982). *Assessing treatment: The conduct of evaluations within drug abuse treatment programs* DHHS Publication ADM-84-1218. Rockville, MD.

Author Index

Subject Index